JEWELRY

CONTEMPORARY DESIGN AND TECHNIQUE

JEWELRY

CONTEMPORARY DESIGN
AND TECHNIQUE

by Chuck Evans

Professor of Jewelry and Metalsmithing
Iowa State University

Davis Publications, Inc. • *Worcester, Massachusetts*

Copyright 1983
Davis Publications, Inc.
Worcester, Massachusetts U.S.A.

Every effort has been made to ensure that the information in this
book, which is based on the author's experience, is accurate.
However, the author and publisher take no responsibility for any
harm which may be caused by the use or misuse of any materials or
processes mentioned herein; nor is any condition or warranty
implied.

Printed in the United States of America
Library of Congress Catalog Card Number: 82-74005
ISBN: 0-87192-141-3

All jewelry work and photos by the author unless otherwise noted.

Cover photos:

Front cover, top left: Lisa D'Agostino. Pin of sterling and nickel
silver, brass and copper. Married metals and constructed.
Photograph by Peter Krumhardt.

Center: Harold O'Connor. *Boiler Unit.* Pendant of 750 gold with
lapis lazuli and ruby. Constructed. Courtesy of the artist.

Right: David Freda. *Quadratic Form No. 6" × 2".*
Pendant/neckpiece of silver, copper, brass, acrylic, ivory, garnet and
bird beak. Forged and constructed. Courtesy of the artist.

Bottom: Chuck Evans. Neckpiece and pendant of sterling and nickel
silver, brass and mokume with moonstones. Forged, torch textured,
laminated, constructed and gold plated. Collection of Teri Knuth.

Back cover: Marcia Lewis. *Clone Brooch #1.* Silver with 24 karat
gold plate, jadite, ebony and ivory. Repousséed and constructed.
Courtesy of the artist. Photograph by Lewis-Hunter.

Designer: Janis Capone

10   9   8   7   6   5

Dedicated to
all those busy being born.

Acknowledgments

The creation of this book has been, in the truest sense, a collaborative venture. My part was eased considerably by the generosity and talent of many friends, colleagues, and fellow jewelers. Aside from their support, I had only to gather and add the compilations of my studio and classroom technical practices. Thanks to Iowa State University and our students, this was possible. My students provided patient assistance throughout and, while perhaps not realizing it at the time, became major contributors.

I wish to express my sincere gratitude to the jewelers who responded to my requests for photographic examples of current jewelry work. They all gave considerable time and effort to share the wonderful examples pictured. To those who responded with photographs, but whose work, for one reason or another is not pictured, I also give my thanks.

I am especially indebted to William Fiorini, Al Gilmore, Kerr Manufacturing Company, David Luck, Lee and Naomi Peck, David Pimentel, Kate Wagle, and Jan Yager for photographs, their technical expertise, and their overall help in putting this together. I also give my thanks to Mary Lee Hu, Curtis LaFollette, Tim McCreight, and Heikki Seppä for their critical but very constructive reading and evaluation of the manuscript. A special acknowledgement must be given to Tim McCreight for the many hours he spent evaluating the illustrations.

Phyllis Behrens of Iowa State University is congratulated and given thanks for the many hours she gave in the manuscript's preparation, the smoothing of details, proofing and typing what to most would be illegible.

My appreciation also goes to the staff at Davis Publications and editor Wyatt Wade who demonstrated great diplomacy, patience, and hard work in tying all this together.

Finally, and most special, my gratitude to Sherrill and Eric, my daughter and son, for their patience and love through this and many other projects.

CONTENTS

Preface

The inspiration behind this book is the desire to offer fellow jewelers, students, and all interested in the subject a body of information on contemporary approaches to the creation of handcrafted jewelry. The approaches outlined in the technical sections are compilations of techniques I have employed in practice and in teaching. In the discussions of topics where my experience is limited, I have asked professionals working in these areas to share their expertise. All of the processes covered have been refined and proven workable, and most can be accomplished in the average studio with routine success. A broad range of topics is provided in order to challenge jewelers of all levels. Those having made jewelry for years may be inspired simply by the presentation of a different view or fresh approach. Each technical section is illustrated with photographs and line drawings to complement and clarify the text.

One of the most productive ways to learn design principles is through visual exposure and analysis. To that end, the book is profusely illustrated with contemporary jewelry encompassing a myriad of forms and personal styles of expression. In many instances, the illustration captions point out particular design approaches, materials uses, and technical applications.

A brief historical perspective of jewelry making's rich heritage and the various roles jewelry has played opens the book. This section emphasizes the importance of adornment from three viewpoints: the maker's, the wearer's, and the onlooker's. Jewelers through the ages have been linked to their cultures, some significantly, others less so. This brief perspective touches on these links and discusses both how and why our forerunners made jewelry.

Like many other fields, the craft of jewelry making is not without health hazards. Many of the materials and processes used are potentially dangerous, either immediately or accumulatively. Every effort has been made

to note potential danger areas and point out proper procedures to safely avoid the hazards. **Bold face type is used throughout the book to draw attention to safety information. In order to become familiar with proper procedures, the reader is encouraged to read carefully and completely through each chapter before beginning work. After a complete familiarization with a chapter, check the work space to ensure it is properly equipped and that needed safety devices are at hand. Additional safety precautions are pointed out in Appendix 5; these should also be examined before any work is begun.**

The reader's desire, patience, and creative vision will determine the results of the application of the information offered in these pages. To become proficient, practice each step until you develop the most comfortable and expedient means of achieving a task.

Finally, do not assume the approaches presented here are the only ones possible. While I have attempted to present information that will provide routinely successful results, I realize there is more than one way to skin a cat. Feel free to question and experiment along the way.

Perspective

Contemporary jewelry making is grounded in forms and techniques that have evolved over thousands of years. Today's jeweler is closely linked to past jewelers by many of the same symbols, materials, tools, and processes. At the same time, jewelry making is ever evolving in new ways dictated by changes in the physical environment and especially the social climate. Most of the major changes in the evolution of jewelry making, in fact, have been impelled by people's changing ideals, values, and attitudes.

As cultures were born, grew, and passed away, changes occurred in adornment, some subtle, others dramatic. Throughout history, variations appeared in aesthetics, forms, function, and materials. Unfortunately, we will never have a complete picture of the history of jewelry making. The destruction of artifacts by natural phenomena, war, and vandals leaves many voids.

The earliest form of personal adornment was body painting, tattooing, scarring, and disfigurement. In the earliest applications, these marks related to religious symbolism or social status. For example, the tribal leader might be heavily adorned to indicate authority, or certain members of the tribe would be adorned with specific symbols asking the gods for plentiful food or victory in battle. Needless to say, adornment was extremely important to our earliest relatives.

A gradual evolution in visual perception and appreciation for these crude images led people to apply paint and tattooing for decorative purposes. Still, these direct applications carried symbolic implications: magic, birth rights, marital status, social rank, tributes to nature, fertility, bravery, and so on. The art of tattooing spread throughout the world, crossing cultures as trade and commerce grew. Primitive societies still practice scarring, painting, and disfigurement. Americans have recently witnessed a revival in tattooing. Today tattoos

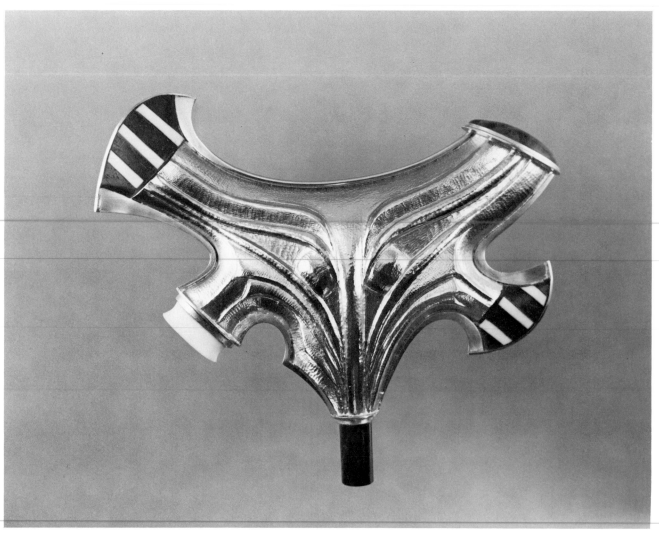

Marcia Lewis, *Clone Brooch #2*. Gold-plated silver with sodalite, ebony, and ivory; repoussé and construction. Courtesy of the artist. Photograph by Lewis-Hunter.

may reflect the owners' desire for individual expression. Others use tattoos to proclaim membership in a specific social group. Regardless of the rationale, direct adornment is personal, makes a statement, and evokes a reaction.

Tangible objects of adornment first appeared with Paleolithic humans. The materials used by these early cultures were nonmetallic objects gathered close at hand: stone, hair, bone, seed, wood, and other plant materials. Even approximate dating of the earliest nonmetallic pieces is difficult. The earliest metallic adornment is believed to have been made in Mesopotamia about 8,000 B.C. These pieces reflect a culture that had a relatively sound understanding of metalsmithing. Their work possessed an ornate quality incorporating chased and embossed surfaces on thin beaten forms. These forms provide evidence of what was perhaps the first metalsmithing technique: forging. As these Mesopotamian workers refined the elementary techniques, forms gradually became more sophisticated. Metal was combined with clay, stone, glass, bone, and other indigenous materials. Over the years, migration and trade provided sources of materials and offered broader design possibilities. By 2,000 B.C. craftspeople were traveling hundreds of miles to obtain materials.

The Bronze Age (circa 3,500 B.C.) saw a steady development in techniques. Museums throughout the world exhibit wonderful historical examples of filigree, relief work, granulation, and works of multiple units showing a mastery of forming and precision soldering techniques. To give our early counterparts their due, it should be noted that most of today's techniques were developed prior to the Iron Age. The era following the Industrial Revolution provided the next major influence on tools and techniques.

Jewelers throughout history have searched for unique materials. Creative impulses eventually became great enough to cause jewelers to seek materials suited to fulfilling their mental images. As with technique, early jewelers pioneered the use of most of the materials used today; obvious exceptions are space-age metals, alloys, and plastics. A look back at the work of Egyptian, Greek, Samaritan, and Italian jewelers offers an inspiring collection of precious and nonprecious materials from which to draw.

The images and forms produced in antiquity become quite intriguing when we consider underlying questions regarding their conception and execution. A review of historical work naturally provokes questions about why and how the pieces were created. The function of jewelry has changed with each era and culture and, along with this, the rationale for its creation changed. An examination of the functional changes in jewelry can add significantly to our understanding of the evolution leading to contemporary work.

The jewelry of early Egypt often included written script to relate a story, a message, or an image that served as personal identification. Some of these pieces gradually evolved into finely crafted signet rings, cylindrical reliefs worn as pendants, and pins used to emboss sealing wax. Many of the forms we know today were derived from functional needs: clasps, buckles, hairpins, buttons, pins. The early fibula changed in time to the decorative brooch, its front richly embellished, its pin stem generally hidden on the back. Paralleling the development of the brooch, the safety pin and kilt pin evolved from the fibula.

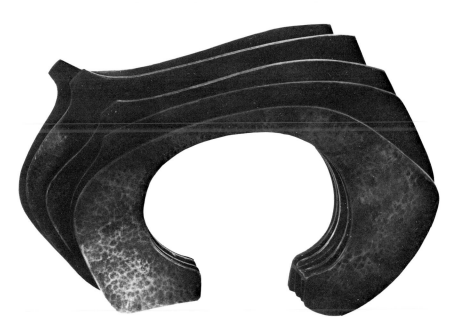

Sheena Thomas, *Finned Bracelet.* Forged, sunk, and constructed in copper. Courtesy of the artist.

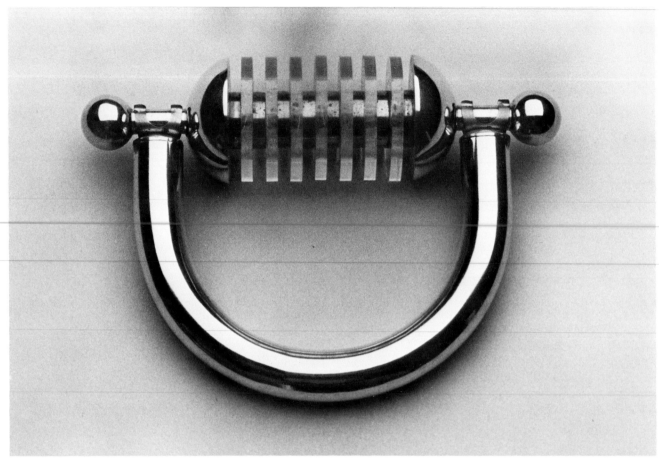

Greg Patrenos. Constructed bracelet of sterling, brass, acrylic, and light-emitting diodes. Courtesy of the artist. Photograph by Lynn Hudson.

Storage, transport, and exchange of wealth have been significant factors in the development of jewelry. Many cultures have looked on jewelry as bullion since it is easily transported, yet functional as personal adornment. This practice continues today: immigrants and refugees often arrive in new lands wearing their wealth on their arms, necks, and fingers. In parts of the eastern world, one's jewelry is a demonstration of wealth or social status, with even the poorest wearing a simple anklet of brass.

Several historical changes have played major roles in molding the role and attitudes of the modern jeweler. The control of steam and electric power were major steps to the present. Conversion from human power to almost total mechanical power resulted in greater productivity, mass production, more leisure time, and, most importantly, more thinking time. Along with the technical revolution came economic relief and, eventually, individual freedom for the working class. These changes touched our early counterparts, making their work less tedious. Mechanized buffing, improved alloying processes, steel die stamping, precision casting, cheaper basic materials, and the means to mass-produce grew out of early mechanization.

The jeweler's reliance on the machine and mass production, and the public's satisfaction with the resulting products, led to a gradual decline in creative expression with jewelry that reflected a cold, machinelike look. Generally, design concepts were governed by the capacity of the machine and production volume, with little regard for personal expression. The hand was no match for the machine and an economically free society demanding large quantities of inexpensive jewelry. But even at that, jewelry did function in satisfying the masses that earlier could not afford the luxury of adornment in any form. Nor was the production of expressive work completely dead. A handful of imaginative people was still providing beautiful work for those wishing (and able to afford) unique jewelry.

Near the end of the nineteenth century artists began to rebel against the lifeless machine aesthetic. At the same time, more people began asking for jewelry evincing personal effort. William Morris, an Englishman, was probably the first art critic of any influence to write and speak about these times. His critiques of the relationship between industry, the machine, and design were a major force in the birth of the Art Nouveau movement. In essence, Art Nouveau was a rejection of the past and a revolt against the humanless machine aesthetic. In other words, no more stamped-out Baroque, Rococo, or Victorian copies of the past. Swift in spreading through Europe and America, the ideals of Art Nouveau touched all the arts. Painters, architects, sculptors, and decorative artists seemed to jump on the bandwagon, which looked back, not at old styles, but to nature for inspiration. The common design element in Art Nouveau was the use of sensuous line to depict plant, insect, and human forms.

Morris envisioned a society of artists hand producing the objects of everyday use. Ideally, artists would create their work at a price the masses could afford. As a socialist, Morris felt that craftworkers had a social obligation to provide this service. The Morris dream lasted only a few years. Its decline was due in large part to the fact that only the well-to-do could afford high-quality handwork. Unfortunately, in some respects this problem exists today.

The idealism and individualism of the late 1800s left us a great deal to draw from. Nothing from the past has made as lasting a mark as Art Nouveau in terms of the freedom to create as we see fit, using any material or form we choose. Teachers and students of the Bauhaus School, the Dadaists, and the Surrealists freed us further from pressures and preconceptions of what art should or should not be.

Traditionally, jewelry has served its maker and its wearer on aesthetic, utilitarian, social, symbolic, and expressive levels, although not every piece fulfills all five functions.

The aesthetic consideration is generally the easiest for a viewer to comprehend and articulate. In addition to adorning the body, jewelry may stand alone as an aesthetically pleasing object. Currently there appears to be a trend in exhibitions and marketing toward using jewelry in dual roles. When a piece is not being worn it is displayed in a frame or case. Some craftworkers market small, limited editions mounted in display units. Modern jewelers tend to be as expressive and personal in transforming mental images to tangible forms as are painters and sculptors. Upon examination, all the design elements of modern art can be found in today's handcrafted jewelry: line, texture, form, and color.

Utilitarian functions and how certain jewelry forms evolved from these have been touched on. With the technological ability to make many of these forms unnecessary on today's clothing, our desire to expressively fasten, buckle, and pin supersedes the merely utilitarian applications.

Jewelry's social, symbolic, and expressive functions are closely allied and sometimes difficult to perceive separately. In an effort to analyze these functions, the viewpoints of the maker, the wearer, and the viewer must be considered. The maker may fulfill symbolic and expressive functions in creating a highly personal engagement ring. The wearer may feel all three functions have been fulfilled: the ring announces the person's engagement, the material value of the ring proclaims social status, and the selection of that particular ring expresses the wearer's self-image. A viewer may catch all of these meanings, or simply see a pretty stone in a setting the viewer may or may not like.

Regardless of the labels we attach, it is clear that adornment goes beyond hanging a stone around one's neck. The pleasure of creating and wearing jewelry goes deep. Perhaps we should simply say that the basic reasons for producing handcrafted jewelry are to express creative vision and to give the wearer a means of conveying self-image. Indeed, contemporary jewelers tend to focus primarily on the expressive function of their work. Unlike their predecessors, contemporary jewelers do not have to rely on their immediate surroundings for inspiration and materials. They do not have to create forms that speak to a specific culture, region, or status. Given the foundation of jewelry making's rich heritage and the help of modern communications and mobility, national styles have been eroded to the point that today handcrafted jewelry is truly a universal form of artistic expression.

JEWELRY

CONTEMPORARY DESIGN AND TECHNIQUE

CHAPTER ONE

The Jeweler's Work Shop

THE WORK SPACE

A well-planned, permanent workshop is a convenient advantage for the serious jeweler. Works in progress can be left out to avoid having to sort out materials and tools in preparation for another day's work—a great time-saver. This practice also provides a mental advantage; the stops and starts are less demanding since it is immediately obvious where work was left off.

Jewelers have shown considerable inventiveness in setting up permanent working environments in all sorts of locations: bedrooms, basements, attics, barns, garages, even closets. With a little legroom, almost any space can be made usable.

Before looking at specific shop needs, a few overall suggestions can be made. To intensify general lighting, the walls and ceiling should be light in color. Ideally, flooring should be constructed of a durable material: sealed concrete, tile, or heat-resistant linoleum. These materials are resistant to acids, water, and wear, and are easily cleaned. Equipment, benches, counters, and sinks should be installed in such a way to provide easy movement through the space. A traffic flow plan should be devised with the various processes in mind; **safety and efficiency should be major considerations.**

Ventilation

The location and amount of ventilation in a work space will depend on the size of the room, the arrangement of equipment, and the type of work carried out. **Generally speaking, any operation producing fumes or dust should be vented: soldering, annealing, pickling, etching, plating, enameling, casting, stonecutting and buffing.** Hooded vent systems with enclosed fans work well for most applications. These should be placed just above the contaminant source. Hoods can be purchased or fabricated to include vertically adjustable fronts to ensure complete fume entrapment. **Some processes, such as buffing, may require specially designed vents.** Many jewelers have forgone typical commercial buffing units and use a system that encloses and seals the front of the machine to prevent abrasive materials from being thrown into the atmosphere. These devices are usually constructed to fit the specific work requirements of the individual and most often incorporate an enclosed motor, fan, and filter.

To those not able to install proper vents, I can only say, "It's your life, at least open a window." Further information regarding the venting of individual areas will be covered in those chapters dealing with specific techniques and in Appendix 5.

Lighting
A properly lighted work area is essential to good work and, more importantly, to one's eyesight. General shop areas may be lit with fluorescent fixtures. These are relatively inexpensive to purchase and the cost of operation will be less than comparative incandescent sources. Individual workbenches should be equipped with adjustable, swing-arm incandescent lamps.

Electric Outlets
Considerable planning should go into the location and installation of wall outlets. They should be adequate in number and power capacity to serve the many tools and pieces of equipment available to the jeweler. **Check all equipment specifications to be certain that all power requirements match the available circuits.** Jury-rigged installations using extension cords could result in overloaded circuits and perhaps fire.

Water
Many jewelry-making techniques require water. For example, cleaning and rinsing are basic to almost any jewelry project. I can't imagine completing a piece of jewelry without having to use water at some point. A space plan should include a sink and counter made of acid- and heat-resistant material. Those making jewelry on a hobby basis may get along with just a container of water for rinsing work.

Workbench
The jeweler's bench is the primary setting for most handwork. A well-designed and properly installed bench is essential to the serious jeweler. The two major concerns of bench construction are function and durability. Commercially produced benches generally fall short in both respects. They tend to be hybrids that have evolved from the needs of the watchmaker, engraver, stonesetter, silversmith, and jeweler. An excellent bench can be constructed of hardwood using simple hand tools. Converted tables and desks are usually too short.

1–1   *Workbench of solid hardwood.*

Regardless of the type of bench eventually chosen, the work surface should be 34 to 36 inches above the floor. Proper height assures a comfortable seating position and the ideal relationship of the worker to the task at hand. The overall length and depth of the work surface should be such as to allow plenty of room for such things as files, pliers, saws, punches, and hammers. A top measuring 2 feet by 4 feet should provide ample space for most jewelers. Figure 1–1 illustrates the solid hardwood bench used in my studio. For extra stability it is bolted securely to the wall.

TOOLS

Jewelry-making tools have not changed as much through the years as one might expect. Modern materials and industrial processes have improved their variety and quality but the basic functions remain the same. Today's jeweler may purchase several specialized hand tools to do the work earlier jewelers had to accomplish with one handmade tool. There is no question that any given task is made easier today with so many hand and power tools at our disposal. This luxury does not guarantee a finer piece of jewelry since, in the end, the tool is simply an extension of the worker whose dexterity and creative insight determine the outcome.

Care and thought in selecting the proper tools for each step will make each task easier. Bargain hunting for tools is seldom real economy. High-quality tools will pay for themselves over time. Cheap tools tend to break or simply wear out and the craftsperson is faced with the additional expense of replacement and loss of time.

Routine maintenance of tools and equipment requires little time and generally involves only occasional wiping of surfaces and a thin coat of oil. The working surfaces of all metal tools must be kept free of pits and scratches. Marred tools will scratch the piece being crafted, requiring additional finishing time. Marred tools can be refinished with a file or emery and polished smooth. Tools should be stored in a moisture-free environment to prevent rusting. Proper care will prolong the life of tools; a jeweler can take pride in good, well-maintained tools and feel confident that they will operate effectively.

The optimum workshop with its equipment and tools varies with the jeweler. Arrangements and needs that might work for the hobbyist would fall far short for a professional. This section presents those tools most commonly used; each should be included in the average workshop. An excellent supplementary source of information on tools is one of the many catalogs available from jewelry supply firms. Large firms publish well-illustrated, technically informative catalogs covering practically every tool needed. Appendix 4 provides a listing of suppliers that I have found provide prompt service, quality merchandise, and competitive prices. Illustrations and detailed discussion of specific tools and equipment are found in subsequent chapters.

The following categorized tool listing covers several broad areas related to function. This is not meant to imply a tool cannot serve several purposes. Once a jeweler becomes familiar and experienced with a tool, he or she will find each tool has certain practical limits; with inventiveness and common sense, some tools are easily adapted to more than one task.

Cutting, Filing, and Piercing Tools

Jeweler's saw frame—adjustable length, throat depth 3 to 8 inches, 5 inches for general work
Jeweler's saw blades—number 3/0 for fine work, number 2 for general work
Hand files—cutting length 6 inches, medium and course cuts
  Half-round
  Flat
  Round
  Three square
  Crossing
Needle files—5½-inch length, number 2 cut
  Half-round
  Round
  Three-square
  Flat
  Knife
Riffle files—6-inch length, number 4 cut
  Knife edge
  Pointed half-round
  Spoon half-round curved
  Flat curved
File card
Hardwood emery stick—10 inches long by 1 inch wide by ¼ inch thick
Hardwood emery dowel—10 inches long by various diameters

Plate shear—scissor handle, 7-inch length
Aviation shears—10¼-inch length, universal cut
Diagonal cutters—5-inch length
Center punch—automatic or hammer struck
Drill bits—assorted small sizes
Flexible shaft machine
Assorted flexible shaft accessories: burrs, stones, emery drums, etc.

Bending and Holding Tools

Ring clamp—plastic or wood, leather jaws
Vise—for jeweler's bench, clamp on
Bench pin with V slot—3 inches wide by 5 inches long
Jeweler's pliers
  Round needle-nose
  Flat
  Half-round (one flat and one half-round jaw)
  Chain-nose
  Parallel jaw, flat nose

Shaping Tools

Stakes, assorted shapes and sizes
Hammers
  Planishing—3 or 4 inches, flat and domed face
  Rivet—3½ inches
  Raising—¾ or 1 pounds
  Forming—ball-shaped ends
  Ball-peen, 8 ounces
  Forging—1 to 2 pounds
Mallets
  Rawhide—2-inch diameter face
  Wood, flat, round, and wedge face
Anvil—tempered cast steel or iron with steel face plate, 50 to 250 pounds
Mandrels
  Ring with graduated sizes
  Bezel—round, square, oval
  Bracelet—round and oval
Dapping punches—assorted sizes ³⁄₃₂ to 2 inches
Dapping block—2½-inch square, steel
Disc cutter, block, and punches—⅛- to 1-inch diameters
Burnisher
Stone pusher—flat face

Pitch bowl—5- to 8-inch diameter, cast iron

Soldering, Annealing, and Melting Tools

Torch system and appropriate tips (one of the following):
  Natural gas/compressed air
  Natural gas/compressed oxygen
  Acetylene
  Propane
  Oxygen/acetylene
Flint striker
Dark goggles or face shield
Pickle (acid) pot—slow cooker with crockery pot or Pyrex pot with hot plate
Copper tongs
Silver solder flux—nontoxic paste or liquid
Silver solder—sheet or wire form
Fire extinguisher
Tweezers
  Soldering tweezer, bent tip
  Cross-lock
  Fine-point
Third hand
Tripod soldering stand
Steel mesh screen—4 inches by 4 inches
Soft firebrick
Charcoal blocks—7 inches by 4 inches
Annealing pan—12-inch diameter
Lump pumice—5 to 10 pounds
Solder pick—12-inch steel coat hanger wire
Binding wire—iron, 18 to 24 gauge
Pickle, Sparex or sulfuric acid and water

Surface Embellishment Tools

Chasing tools
Dapping tools
Torch
Chisels
Hammers
Files
Gravers
Drill bits
Rolling mill
Flexible shaft accessories
Scriber

Measuring Tools

Dividers
Calipers
Small square
Small steel rule
Ring sizer
Brown and Sharpe gauge plate
Compass

Additional Tools and Large Equipment

Drawplate
  Round
  Square
  Oval
Draw tongs
Rolling mill
Buffing machine
Machinist's bench vise
Troy or gram scale
Tube-cutting jig
Safety glasses
Sandblaster
Casting machine and accessories
Small belt sander—1-inch by 42-inch belt
Lapidary machine and accessories
Dust mask
Fire extinguisher

MATERIALS

The mind's eye is the only limiting factor in the search for materials to incorporate in jewelry. The natural and man-made materials that surround us provide a limitless source on which to draw. Recent art history records a freedom of expression that seems to have dropped all traditional barriers regarding which materials may be used, how to use them, and in what quantities. We now look at the expressive possibilities in many things that were historically taboo. At first glance some materials may appear restrictive, but this in itself is a challenge to spark the imagination.

If unique jewelry is to be created, the qualities and characteristics of each individual component must be looked upon as an expressive element of the total work.

1–2   *Materials: horn, plastics, wood, bone, and ivory.*

This section looks at a few of many of the materials in common use. In some instances, specific materials will be discussed in subsequent chapters.

Common Nonferrous Metals

Of all the available materials, metal is most commonly used by jewelers. Its characteristic beauty, versatility, and durability offer an ideal medium of expression. To understand the possibilities inherent in any material, its properties must first be studied. In times past, the primary attributes sought in metal were its luster, workability, durability, and rarity. Gold and silver were generally first choices.

Today, commercial suppliers offer many types of metal in a variety of forms, shapes, and alloys. This convenience provides a great savings in time that would otherwise be spent in refining and milling metals to workable sizes. Metal in sheet or wire form can be purchased in various sizes and thicknesses for constructed work; square and round rod forms are available for forging; and granular material is provided for casting.

Measurement of metal thickness is usually calculated and expressed in gauge sizes. Gauge is determined by the use of a Brown and Sharpe gauge plate (figure 1–3). The plate is made up of a series of numbered slots that indicate gauge size on one side and the equivalent decimal size on the other. For those wishing to express thickness in millimeters, a conversion table is provided in Appen-

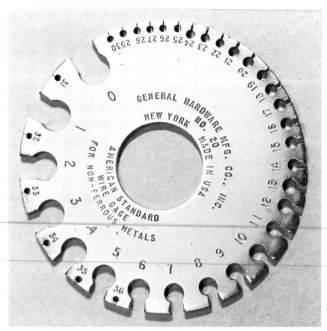

1–3 *Brown and Sharpe gauge plate.*

dix 1. Precious metals are generally purchased by troy weight. For specific technical information regarding alloys, weights, and measures see Appendix 1.

Platinum (melting point 3,224°F, specific gravity 21.45) Platinum, a silver-colored metal, is highly resistant to corrosion and generally used in expensive jewelry. Its cost has been a major factor in making it a little-used material for handcrafted work. Platinum fabrication requires a high-temperature welding technique and platinum alloy solders. Aside from its expense and high melting point, platinum is an excellent jewelry material. Its ductility and malleability lend themselves to most forming techniques. Platinum's hardness, durability, and lustrous quality make it especially suited to the setting of faceted stones. The metal's working characteristics and weight can be further enhanced by alloying it with palladium.

Gold (melting point, pure, 1,945°F, specific gravity 19.32) Just the word *gold* brings immediate thoughts of preciousness, richness, luster, and durability. Historically, gold has been one of the few metals used throughout practically every culture. In every sense, gold is ide-

ally suited for jewelry making. It is the most ductile and malleable of all metals. In wire form, one gram of pure gold can be drawn to a length of well over a mile. Pure gold is generally too soft for most jewelry uses and is therefore alloyed with other metals to provide the desired qualities for our work. Gold's corrosive resistance is unequaled. Pieces buried for centuries are simply brushed off to reveal surfaces as clean as the day the pieces were created.

A rich variety of colored golds has been developed over the years through alloying techniques. Today white, red, pink, green, blue, purple, and several shades of yellow gold can be produced. With each alloy there is also a resulting change in hardness, malleability, and melting point (see Appendix 1). Pure gold alloyed with palladium, platinum or nickel produces white gold with a higher melting point than pure gold. A green color is made with the addition of various amounts of cadmium, silver, or zinc to pure gold. Yellow golds are created by mixing differing ratios of silver and copper; with larger amounts of copper, a reddish pink gold is produced. A purplish alloy of gold and aluminum has been experimented with but thus far its brittleness has prevented significant use. With all the available alloys, we may choose the metal fitting a particular design color preference. For example, delicate prong settings might be of white gold, its tough, hard quality assuring the security of an expensive faceted stone, while the body of the piece may be formed of gold of a contrasting color. A softer yellow gold might be better suited for a bezel-set cabochon. The possibilities are unlimited.

Measurements referring to the relative pureness of alloyed gold are expressed in *karats,* which should not be confused with *carats* used in precious stone measurement. Pure gold measures 24 karats and alloys containing lesser amounts of pure gold are of a lesser karat. For example, an alloy containing one-half pure gold and the remainder of other materials is one-half 24: 12-karat gold. Alloys of less than 10 karats are not stamped and cannot legally be sold as gold in the United States.

Of the available alloys, 14-karat yellow gold is most commonly used. Its relative cost, color, and working characteristics make it an excellent choice for handcrafted work. Since it is harder than sterling or copper, the forging and manipulation of 14-karat gold requires a bit more force; with practice, the difference is hardly noticeable.

Articles sold as "gold filled" are constructed of a variety of base materials covered with a relatively thin layer of karat gold. The thin surface is clad to the base metal by means of sophisticated mechanical welding processes. To economize further, gold filled stock is extruded or rolled thinner. Electroplating is another means of creating a rich gold surface. For information on plating, refer to chapter 4.

Silver (fine—melting point 1,761°F, specific gravity 10.53; sterling—melting point 1,640°F, specific gravity 10.40)   Silver is the most widely used of the precious metals. Its qualities lend themselves to many household, industrial, and decorative uses. We are all familiar with some of its household uses: hollow ware, flatware, picture frames, photographs, and mirror backing. Industrially, silver is important for its capacity as a conductor of electricity and an excellent conveyor of heat. At one time silver was the prime source of reflective material for lighting. Until recently most automobile headlights used highly-polished, sealed reflector units to intensify their light.

Most people seldom see silver in its pure state. Unpolished, fine silver is white in color and second to gold in malleability and ductility. Its relative softness prevents its widespread use in jewelry. Some jewelers do prefer fine silver in wire form where considerable bending is required, as might be needed for fiber-related techniques. Others prefer fine silver when constructing bezel settings. The fine silver bezel is soft and easy to push over and smooth around a stone. Enamelists use fine silver because it is highly reflective, resistant to oxidation, and melts at a relatively high temperature.

Sterling is the most popular of the silver alloys. Sterling is usually composed of 92.5 percent fine silver and 7.5 percent copper. Jewelers prefer sterling for its hardness, malleability, and its capacity to take on and retain a high polish. These properties enable jewelers to use sterling for all types of jewelry forms embodying a wide range of techniques. Though considered precious, its price compared to gold and platinum is quite reasonable and surely accounts in part for its broad use.

Along with the attributes of sterling, we find a few bothersome points. First is the dark tarnish that occurs as a result of the metal being exposed to an atmosphere containing sulfur and moisture. This is not unusual in most households. Owners of sterling flatware often purchase special cases or wrapping material to store their silver. Another difficulty in using sterling takes place

during the working process. Upon heating, oxygen combines with the copper component of sterling and produces a copper oxide or fire scale over the surface layer. The oxide is evident as a dark gray color. In order to remove fire scale the piece must be dipped in acid or buffed until the underlying clean metal appears. In some instances, it is more expedient to simply electroplate a layer of silver over the unsightly surface.

Copper (melting point 1,981°F, specific gravity 8.96)   Contemporary jewelers have brought about the widespread use of copper and its alloys in jewelry making. While it has always been in use, it was often subordinate to other metals. Today we see many exciting works combining copper with silver and even gold. With the current expense of precious metals, it is not unusual to find jewelers working exclusively in copper and its alloys.

Copper possesses a number of characteristics that make it worthwhile for jewelry making. Its malleability is similar to that of silver and it may be forged, sawn, and refined as easily. The surface of copper takes on a lustrous red when polished and a wide range of patinas when oxidized. Enamelists have used copper as a prime material for many years because of its relatively low cost, durability, and high degree of brilliance beneath transparent enamels. Copper has a unique character that allows it to be alloyed with practically any metal. This capacity explains, in part, its current use as an important component in alloys being rediscovered in the research of ancient Japanese techniques. (Please refer to chapter 9.) The only significant drawback with copper occurs in casting. In its natural state copper oxidizes readily and, when heated, rapid oxidation often causes porous, pitted, or incomplete castings.

A large saving may be realized in purchasing copper and related alloys from industrial metal suppliers. Most large concerns offer materials in sheet, plate, and all forms of rod stock. Some prefer to sell standard dimension sheets or rods and may charge a cutting fee for partial sizes. Industrial suppliers use the decimal measurement in specifying thickness. This can be converted with the B and S gauge for our purposes. Suppliers are often willing to sell cuttings and scrap at reasonable prices.

Brass (melting point 1,630 to 1,850°F, specific gravity approximately 8.5)   Like copper, brass is becoming more widely used. An alloy of copper and zinc, the color variations and degree of hardness can almost be tailored to fit the jeweler's needs. Most brasses range from 5 to 40 percent zinc content. Those containing approximately 30 percent or less are sometimes called low brass and those above, high brass. Suppliers can generally provide alloys of specific ratios of metal content. For handwork, alloys of 30 percent or less of zinc are best suited. As zinc content is increased, the resulting alloy becomes more brittle and less applicable to cold working techniques. Alloys composed of higher zinc ratios are usually considered industrial materials and are hard and corrosion resistant. Commercial bronze, so called because of its color, is probably the best all-around brass alloy for handcrafted work. Brass surfaces easily take on a high polish.

Bronze (melting point 1,550 to 1,900°F, specific gravity approximately 8)   Bronze is another versatile copper alloy. Traditionally bronze was composed only of copper and tin but modern metallurgists have broadened the selection with alloys containing added phosphorus, lead, aluminum, beryllium, and silicon. Bronze may be given a high polish, is resistant to corrosion, and will take on beautiful patinas when chemically oxidized. Some of the bronzes are excellent metals for casting and cold working techniques. Basic colors of stock material range from brown to reddish yellow.

Nickel Silver (melting point 1,960°F, specific gravity approximately 8.9)   Nickel silver is one of the most deceptive metals the jeweler is likely to deal with. Although the name implies silver content, it contains none. It contains more copper than anything else but its color is silver gray. Nickel silver is a copper alloy composed of approximately 60 percent copper, 33 percent nickel, and 7 percent zinc.

Nickel silver surfaces are quite similar to sterling; when polished it is just a little darker than sterling. Manipulative qualities and hardness are similar to those of yellow brass; it is slightly harder than sterling. From a personal standpoint, the only problem encountered is the tendency of nickel silver to quickly oxidize during the processes requiring high heat. This problem has generally occurred while soldering several pieces at once when preparing laminations. Still, the pros outweigh the cons.

Nickel silver may be purchased in several alloy specifications. This should be checked closely when ordering material used specifically for laminations and torch texturing. Chapters 4 and 9 offer additional information concerning these techniques and the cleaning of nickel silver.

The metals reviewed here are readily available and particularly well suited to a variety of jewelry techniques. Additional information regarding lesser-used and space-age metals is given in subsequent chapters. Jewelers who have used only the more traditional metals are encouraged to explore the creative potentials of other metals.

Nonmetallic Materials

Gems and other stones are important in the work of many metalsmiths. To discuss these fully, however, a text in itself would be required. Those who wish to seek an in-depth study of stones and lapidary techniques may refer to the books listed in the bibliography.

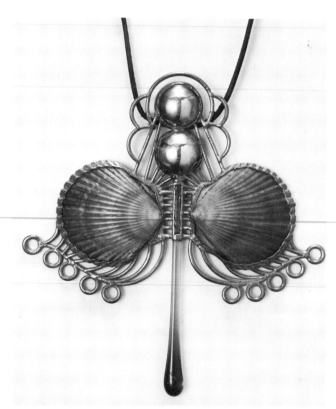

1–4 Lee B. Peck. *Pendant of copper, sterling domes, shell, and glass cane; electroformed and gold plated. Courtesy of the artist.*

Seashells   Although the shell has been used through history, contemporary jewelers have almost ignored its beauty. As many materials less rare, less beautiful, and less durable continue to be used, the expressive potential of shells is still overlooked except by a handful of jewelers.

Most shells can be cut and shaped with lapidary equipment or jewelry tools. Historically, the most decorative and popular use of shells has been as a carving medium in the production of cameos. Perhaps the tiresome cameo images of the past have made us regard shells as trite and not worth our interest. This in itself is reason to look further and begin applying carving or subtractive techniques in the creation of new forms in shell. In many instances, shells need not be altered, just uniquely integrated as accenting elements. Shells can be further enhanced by polishing and set or inlaid using techniques used with stones.

Fibers   If we were to examine trends in modern jewelry, the use of fibers and fiber techniques would be prominent. While fibers in one form or another have always been used in jewelry, today's jeweler has gone beyond historical and sometimes superficial applications and is using both synthetic and natural fibers in exciting ways. In some instances, jewelers are working almost entirely in fibers, using metal, stones, and other materials as subtle additions. Generally, fibers still tend to be subordinate, applied as accents that sometimes dangle as individual strands or small woven panels inset or wrapped in metal frames.

Fibers are grouped as three basic types: synthetic (rayon, nylon, acrylic); vegetable (hemp, flax, cotton, sisal); and animal (silk, wool, camel, human hair, etc.). These fibers come in an impressive range of colors and textures.

Some caution must be taken in selecting the proper

1–5 **Harold O'Connor.** *Constructed brooch of 18-karat gold and silver with red wool and white fur. Courtesy of the artist. Photograph by Ron Burton.*

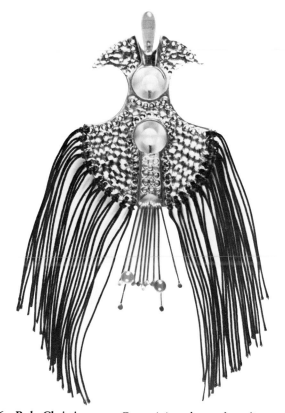

1–6 **Bob Christiaansen.** *Cast pin/pendant of sterling with pearls, carnelian, and fibers. Courtesy of the artist. Photograph by Charles Irwin.*

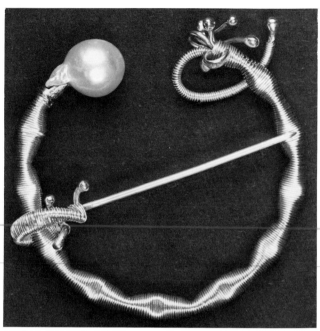

1–7 Frances Beis. *Brooch of sterling, fine silver, and pearl; fused and wrapped. Courtesy of the artist. Photograph by Anthony Monsarrat.*

fibers for a specific work. Each material's resistance to breakage, changes in shape and soiling should not be overlooked. Jewelers wishing to use fibrous mediums are referred to the many excellent texts dealing with the artistic application of fibers.

An offshoot of working with fibers is the application of fiber techniques to thin sheet metal and wire. Colors are often achieved by using plastic-coated electric armature wire. Spools of coated wire can be purchased in various colors from electrical supply firms. Thin wire and sheet strips in an annealed state are flexible enough to allow the jeweler to shape, knot, twist, wrap, and weave the metal into dimensional forms.

Plastics   Except for metal, few materials offer the versatility of plastic. It can be cast, carved, drilled, inlaid, laminated, machined, bent, and colored. Jewelry elements in a spectrum of colors can be cut on a lathe, bent to shape, or carved from a slab and the surfaces finely polished. Multicolored sheets can be laminated or colors cast in layers. Objects may be embedded or inlaid in plastic to create unique protective surfaces much like enamels. The common plastics (acrylic, epoxy, and polyester) can be purchased in liquid or solid form. While some workers make a considerable investment in equipment for working plastics, the average jeweler needs little beyond what is found in most workshops.

The same qualities that make plastic ideal for creative use have made it subject to abuse by artists and industry. Commercially, plastic is a popular choice in the production of a wide variety of objects, often as cheap imitations of other materials. Indiscriminate consumers can purchase plastic chrome, flowers, marble, knotty pine, and bathtubs. Artistically, the negative aspects of plastic stem not from overuse or imitation, but from superficial exploration into its creative possibilities. While most

1–8   Richard Helzer, G80-03P Landscape Brooch. *Constructed and carved in sterling, fine silver, copper, gold alloy, and acrylics using marriage of metals. Courtesy of the artist. Photograph by Don Pilotte.*

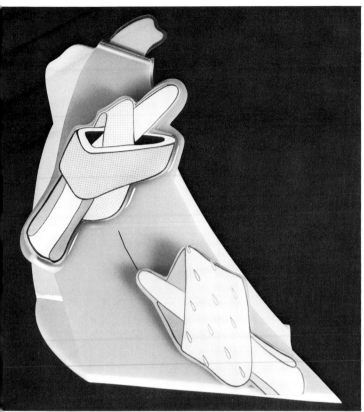

1–9 Amy Davison, Continuing Animation Series. *Acrylics, epoxy resin, and drawings. Plastic films and papers were illustrated, then embedded in acrylic sheet and poured resin. The elements detach to become pins. Courtesy of the artist.*

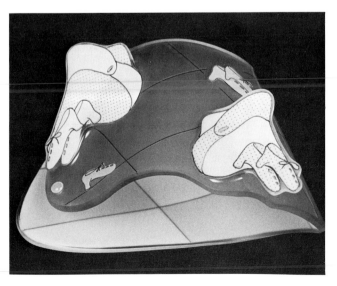

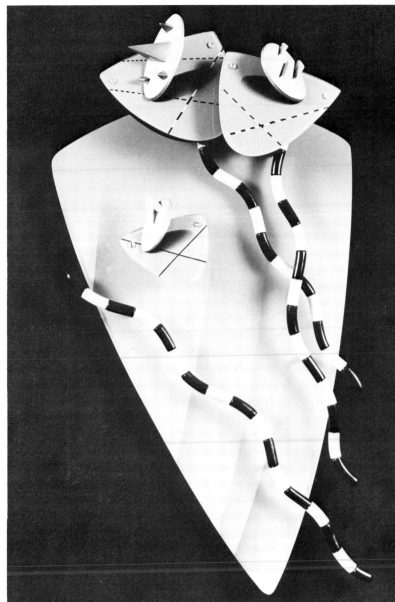

1–11 Bruce Metcalf, Three Pointy Pins with Long, Wavy Sticks. *Machined and constructed pins of brass, acrylic plastic, and enamel paint. Courtesy of the artist.*

1–10 Amy Davison, Bracelet Series. *Cast and constructed in epoxy, drawings, and plastic films. Courtesy of the artist.*

1–19   J. Robert Bruya, Preservation of the Species #35. *Constructed presentation and wearable neckpiece of pewter, bone, feathers, moonstone, and chain. Courtesy of the artist. Photograph by Gary Baun. Collection of Cecil Jarvis.*

In order to use unprocessed bone, it must first be cleaned.

1   Boil the bone in water, changing the water several times. Make sure all clinging material is removed. Boil one final time in a solution of water and a teaspoon or two of baking soda.
2   After cleaning and rinsing, bleach the bone in the sun for several days in a mild solution of 10 percent household bleach and water. **Wear eye protection when handling bleach.** Let the bone soak for 6 to 8 hours, then rinse it by soaking it for an hour or two in a solution of water and one teaspoon of baking soda.
3   Bleaching might result in a chalky surface that can easily be removed with emery cloth.

One drawback with bone and ivory is their tendency to flake and crack as they age. An occasional application of a thin coat of household floor wax will help retard drying and cracking.

Both bone and ivory are traditional choices of scrimshaw artists. This technique involves engraving or scratching an image into the material, rubbing an ink or other dark medium into the recesses, and then wiping away the excess from the raised surface. Contemporary jewelers, for the most part, have not taken advantage of scrimshaw techniques. Until we pick up and expand on this relatively simple process, we will continue to see it only in terms of yesterday's images of sailing ships and whales.

Horn   In terms or working characteristics, durability, and surface qualities, horn is quite similar to bone and ivory. The natural color of horn varies from black to cream; when bleached, lighter shades develop. The horn of a wild animal is generally solid. Domestic animal horn has a relatively thin outer layer of usable material and a soft inner core. Horn's distinctive grain pattern will vary with the angle at which the horn is cut.

To prepare it for use, the soft inner core can be scraped away after submerging the horn for several moments in boiling water. The outer material is then dried for a few days. Solid horn, when well-dried, may be used without special preparation.

Being a relatively flexible material, thin lengthwise slabs of horn can be shaped into curved forms. Place the slab in boiling water for a few minutes, remove the piece, and gently bend it to shape. Hold the shape until the horn is cool. Horn can be fastened to jewelry work by the same methods used with bone and ivory.

Additional Materials The number of usable materials is infinite. Imaginative jewelers should approach the creative use of materials with an open mind and apply them as honestly as possible. Simply dealing with unusual materials often poses the challenge necessary to broaden our focus and lift us out of old ruts.

Listed below are a few additional materials worthy of exploration.

Enamels
Glass
Feathers
Leather
Paper
Seeds
Animal teeth
Microelectronics that induce movement, light, and
    sound

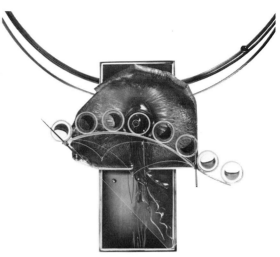

1–20 David Freda, Pacific Cruise. *Neckpiece of niobium, aluminum, sterling, brass, acrylic, steel, coral, and glass bead; constructed, cast, and granulated. Courtesy of the artist. Photograph by Bob Hanson.*

1–21 Joe Eddy Brown, Solitude Confederacy. *Constructed and fused pin of sterling, copper, and bronze with prehistoric horse tooth cabochon and printed circuit. Courtesy of the artist. Photograph by James Hagearty.*

1–22 Al Gilmore, Nu West Sidearm. *Neckpiece and pendant of bronze with rock, vinyl, and calculator; cast, photoetched, and constructed. Courtesy of the artist. Photograph by Lynn Hudson.*

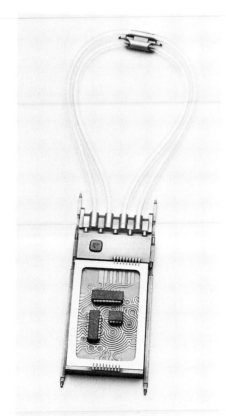

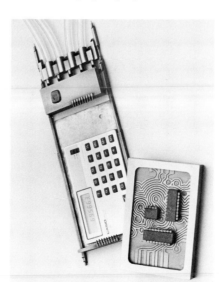

1-22

1-21

CHAPTER TWO

The Basic Techniques

Handcrafting jewelry is a highly personal endeavor, from design to selection of materials to the way the piece is worked. Even the basic techniques are adapted by individual jewelers. In any given number of technical resolutions, however, some will prove less frustrating or more expedient. The proven techniques presented in this chapter—and throughout the book—let the jeweler cut through a great deal of time, trial, error, embarrassment, expense, and frustration. Once these basic techniques have been mastered, however, the reader is encouraged to be bold and inventive in their application.

PATTERN AND DESIGN TRANSFER

After decisions have been made regarding a design and the shapes of the various components, lined patterns are generally transferred from paper onto the metal. Always keep in mind that sawing, filing, and finishing will result in some loss of material, which should be compensated for at the outset.

There are several ways of transferring lines from paper onto metal.

1 Carbon paper between the pattern and metal will work fine for simple shapes. Carefully holding the pattern and carbon in place, redraw the design over the original pattern.
2 Some jewelers brush a thin layer of light-colored water-soluble paint onto the metal. After it dries they transfer the pattern with carbon paper as previously outlined. The advantage of this method is that lines are more easily discernible on the painted surface.
3 Rubber cementing sketches directly onto the metal is

probably the most common transfer method. This approach is quite accurate since the saw blade pierces the pattern and metal on the same stroke.

4 Light-colored contact paper may be applied to metal as it is purchased, thus providing a protective cover against scratches and a drawing surface as needed.

5 Many jewelers forgo sketching on paper and draw directly on the metal.

SAWING AND PIERCING

Often one of the first steps in constructing jewelry components is cutting the appropriate shapes from sheet metal. With practice of the right approach the beginner is soon able to cut out intricate shapes and to pierce lines almost as if the saw blade were a pencil. Sawing quickly becomes routine and the saw an extension of the worker. Piercing or sawing in itself may be used as an expressive technique.

Saws are purchased with frame depths ranging from 3 to 8 inches. Because they are lightweight the smaller frames are a little easier to manipulate, but their shallow depth can be a limiting factor. A 5-inch frame works well for general use. Some jewelers purchase an extra-deep frame for occasions when greater depth must be reached.

Blades are sold in packets of twelve and sizes are indicated by a numerical scale with 14 the coarsest and 8/0 the finest. Number 2 blades work well for general use and occasionally a number 3/0 is needed for fine cutting. Most jewelers have several sizes on hand in order to accommodate each particular cutting requirement. All blades are manufactured in one standard length: 5¼ inches. You will find that blades break easily until you master the saw. Paraffin, beeswax, or soap serves as an excellent lubricant between the blade and the material being cut. Only a small amount is needed. It is applied by lightly rubbing the lubricant along the side of the blade. One swipe on each side is adequate. Excess lubricant will gather with the cuttings and clog the teeth of the blade. With experience, you will recognize when to apply lubricant.

2–1 Mark Knuth. *Constructed and laminated pin of brass and Damascus steel. The artist's linear use of the piercing technique and the linear quality of the lamination's striations help to visually unify the top and bottom elements. Courtesy of the artist. Photograph by Peter Krumhardt.*

2–2 *Saw frames and blades.*

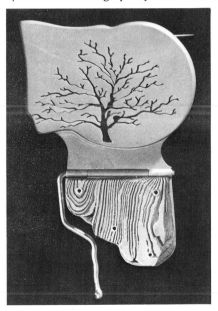

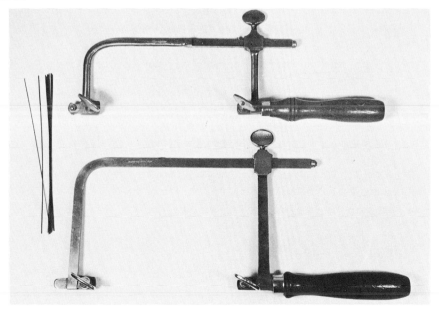

Initial Blade Attachment

1 Loosen the wing nuts (A, B, and C in figure 2–3).
2 Relative to the saw frame, the blade will be installed as illustrated in figure 2–4.
3 With the saw frame lying on the bench, set the blade alongside the bottom of the frame at points A and B.
4 Use the slide fixture at point C and adjust the frame until the ends of the blade rest at approximately the centers of A and B. Tighten C firmly by hand. Never use pliers for frame adjustments. Overtightening will strip the wing-nut threads.
5 Sitting upright at the bench, place the frame with C down, A braced against the bench, and the handle against your body. Bracing between the body and the workbench frees both hands for adjustments.
6 Insert approximately ¼ inch of the blade's end at A and tighten.
7 Gently compress the frame against the bench and secure approximately ¼ inch of the opposite end at B.
8 Take care to compress the frame just enough to create tension but not enough to bend the frame permanently. The return action of the imposed tension tightens the blade. Properly set, the blade will produce a musical pinging sound when plucked with the finger.
9 Since blades are a standard length and the frame is initially set, there is no reason to ever loosen C. Subsequent blade installations are now only a matter of proceeding as outlined in steps 5 through 7.
10 Attempts to use short sections of broken blades are false economy that results in ineffective cutting and loss of time.

The workpiece is braced and supported over a wooden bench pin. Figure 2–5 illustrates a pin and one method of attachment to the bench top. The use of bolts through the pin and top tends to secure the pin more firmly than commercial clamping devices. Most handwork requiring that the piece be braced or stabilized can be held against the pin. Bench pins can be further shaped or grooved to fit a particular workpiece or tool. Pins are expendable work surfaces; do not hesitate to file or reshape them to expedite the work.

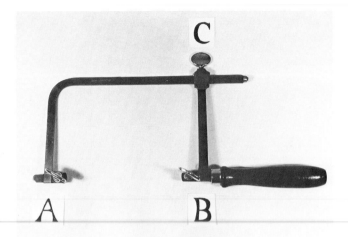

2–3   *Installation of the saw blade.*

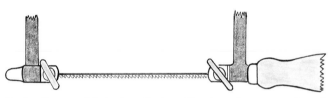

2–4   *Correct blade installation. Teeth point outward and toward the frame handle.*

2–5   *A ½-inch bolt is used to secure the bench pin to the bench top.*

Cutting

An important aspect of learning the techniques of any craft is the ability to skillfully manipulate the related tools. Basic to this is the direct physical interaction between the worker, tool, and material. Sawing is no exception. A clear understanding of what is necessary prior to cutting will make subsequent work much easier.

Proper body position should allow the saw blade to be placed perpendicular to the metal and permit a comfortable, vertical stroke of the saw. Deviation from the vertical approach will most likely break the blade. Work should be held firmly over the bench pin's V slot to give support on both sides of the cut as the blade travels through the metal. Hold the saw handle with a relaxed grip and let the wrist and fingers act as a mechanical joint between the arm and saw. A firm, stiff grip will make it difficult to maintain a vertical, rhythmic action. Soon you will find the most comfortable seating position relative to your height and angle to the work. After working just a short time these points will become second nature and sawing will require little energy (figure 2–6).

To start the cut, bring the blade down against the metal's edge with no forward pressure against the saw. Allow just the weight of the frame alone to create the initial thrust starting the blade's teeth into the metal. On the next down stroke apply a gentle forward pressure; from this point on you will begin sensing the correct rate of forward pressure as the blade cuts. Since the blade cuts just on the down stroke, sawing becomes a series of up-and-down movements of alternating gentle forward pressure down and a relaxed stroke upward. Soon the hand stabilizing the metal and the saw's motion begin working together and the blade will cut intricate curves and straight lines with ease.

Initially, the cutting of angles and tight corners may be difficult. As the blade reaches the apex of an angle, remove all forward pressure while continuing the up-and-down motion and slowly turn the saw in the new direction. Some find it easier to slowly turn the metal and keep the saw on its original path. Once the turn is made the forward pressure is again applied. If a blade becomes stuck, simply release the top thumb screw and pull the frame straight down, releasing the blade without breaking it.

2–6 *Worker sits upright, shoulder and arm aligned with the bench pin and the saw frame held in vertical position.*

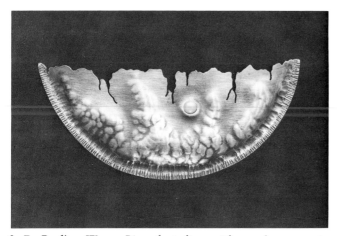

2–7 **Pauline Warg.** *Pin of sterling with pearl; repoussé, piercing, and hammer texturing. Pierced upper edge gives the balance needed for the highly textured lower edge. Courtesy of the artist. Photograph by A. Edgar.*

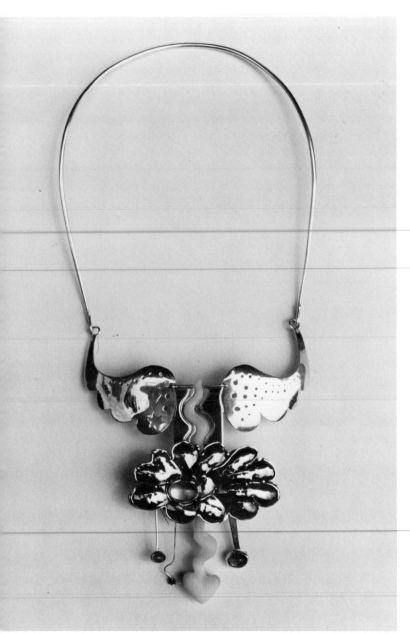

2–8   Diana Taylor. *Pendant of sterling, 14-karat gold, Delrin, and stones; repoussé, piercing, forging, carving, and construction. Courtesy of the artist.*

Piercing

To pierce a negative shape in sheet metal without cutting through its outer dimensions, a small hole slightly larger than a saw blade must be drilled just inside the shape for insertion of the blade. Before drilling, a shallow indentation or prick mark is placed in the metal as a starting guide for the drill bit. Overlooking this step will usually cause the drill bit to skitter around and mar the surface. A center punch and a light tap with a hammer are used to make the mark (figure 2–9). The aim is to make a shallow mark and not to force the punch through the metal. When using a center punch, place the metal on the table of an anvil or steel bench block. Do not use bench tops or wood of any kind as punching surfaces. Wood is relatively soft and will allow the area immediately surrounding the punch mark to bend inward. After drilling, insert the blade through the hole, retighten the saw's thumbscrew, and begin sawing.

2–9   *Center punch and ball-peen hammer.*

FILING

Filing is one of several finishing processes that, if completed properly, will save time and energy in subsequent steps. Trueing and refining metal surfaces is generally accomplished through a series of techniques using first a coarse abrasive, a file, and then successively finer materials. Abrasives remove metal; therefore, the coarser the abrasive, the greater the amount of metal removed. Polishing compound is used in the final step to remove microscopic particles and leave a uniform, brilliant surface.

This section examines a few points that are almost universally accepted regarding files and their use. As with all techniques, each worker gradually develops an individual way of filing. Most often, the aim of filing is to true a surface: make it flat, undulating, straight edged, curved, or a combination of these.

From a side view, an uneven surface appears as a series of high and low points. To make it smooth, the highs are filed down to the level of the lowest low spot. This in itself creates a surface of less pronounced highs

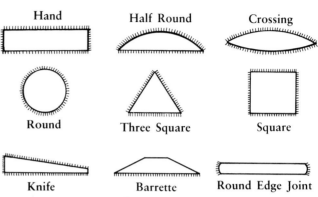

2–11 *Cross sections of common file shapes and their cutting surfaces.*

2–10 Marjorie Schick, Fan Brooch. *Constructed in sterling and nickel. Final detailing that resulted in the precise angularity and crisp linear qualities of this piece consisted of careful filing, emering and buffing. Courtesy of the artist. Photograph by Larry Long.*

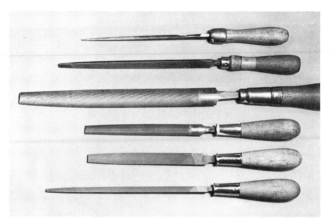

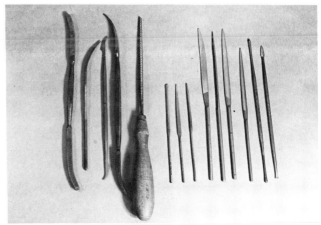

2–12 *Files used for general shop work.*

and lows caused by the file. These become less and less pronounced as finer abrasives are used.

Files are available in many shapes, sizes, and cuts. The beginner may want to purchase a few to start (see the tools list in chapter one). Specialized shapes and sizes can be added as required. In many instances you will find a file to fit a particular job perfectly. At times, several files will be needed to complete a particular task. The important concern is to use the file that best fits a particular shape or surface (figure 2–11). Figure 2–12 illustrates a typical variety of files. Lengths range from approximately 2 inches for the miniature needle files to 10 inches for hand files. Domestic files are generally manufactured in three grades of cut: fine, medium, and coarse. European files are identified numerically in a broad range, with 00 the coarsest and 6 the finest.

The cutting area of a file is quite similar to that of a saw. An exaggerated view reveals many rows of small teeth pointed in one cutting direction (figure 2–13). With the file held by its tang end and pushed forward, the hardened steel teeth cut into and remove metal. Regardless of how one eventually develops the filing stroke, the important thing to realize is that the tool is designed to cut on the forward movement. Downward pressure is exerted on the forward stroke to give the teeth positive penetration into the metal. Movement on the backstroke accomplishes little, if anything. Some craftspeople prefer to lift the file on the return stroke, others drag it back. Over a period of time, dragging the tool, especially over ferrous metals, will dull the teeth. When working in areas of critical fit or precise edges, it is wise to lift the file on the backstroke and take careful, deliberate cutting strokes. This technique permits constant visual evaluation as the desired surface or shape develops. On large or less critical areas I take fast strokes and do not lift the file. Personally, I view a file as a consumable tool, like saw blades and bench pins. At the same time I make every effort to avoid senseless abuse of any tool.

When filing keep the following suggestions in mind.

- Files are most effectively used with handles. **Installing a handle on each file prevents the possibility of injuring the hand or wrist with the tang** and allows full use of the cutting surface.
- When a significant amount of metal is to be removed, it is more expedient to first use a medium or coarse cut and then a fine cut. Some jewelers mistakenly use only fine-cut files.
- Flat files should be used on flat surfaces, straight edges, and outside curves. Rounded files tend to follow existing irregularities (figure 2–14).

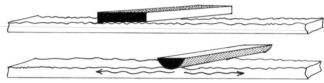

2–14 *Flat files remove peaks. Rounded shapes will follow peaks and valleys.*

- Round, half-round, and crossing files are used on inside curves.
- Where possible, use the largest file that will fit a given surface.
- Use needle and riffle files on delicate and hard-to-reach areas.
- Take full, diagonal strokes across the work.
- Hold the workpiece securely against the bench pin or in a ring clamp (figure 2–14a).

2–14a *A ring clamp provides the craftsperson a means of holding small pieces.*

- Small files used on broad areas tend to leave a series of facets.
- Occasionally brush the file clean with a file card or steel wire brush.

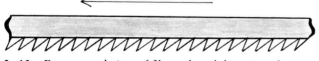

2–13 *Exaggerated view of file teeth and direction of cutting stroke.*

- Use separate files for white metals, steel, and precious metals. If this is not possible, clean files well before changing metals.
- Many jewelers mount a tray or spread a cloth or leather apron just below the work surface to collect precious metals that may fall.

SANDING

Sanding often seems overly time-consuming and tedious. In reality it will save time and effort by preparing a relatively smooth surface for buffing. Beginners often make the mistake of spending too much time buffing when a few additional moments sanding would reduce the total finishing time.

Sanding removes scratches through the abrasive action of the hard, granular particles that cover the paper or cloth sanding material. After filing, a coarse or medium grit sanding material is used for further refinement and removal of the file marks. A fine grit is then used in preparation for buffing.

Emerying is a term used by some jewelers in lieu of *sanding*. This evolved from the material most often used, emery cloth or emery paper. Though usually more expensive, emery cloth is an excellent material. The cloth backing makes it more durable and resistant to tearing. Emery in 9- by 11-inch sheets can be purchased from jewelry suppliers, hardware stores, and paint stores. Several grades of cloth should be at hand as finishing work progresses, generally from coarse or

medium to fine. Abrasive grades are 160 grit for coarse work, 220 grit for medium, and 420 grit for fine finishes. This is a basic range with many other grades available.

The actual emerying process is quite similar to filing. A back and forth motion over the work surface cuts and removes metal. The emery should cross the work surface from several angles to avoid the development of visible grooves and deep scratches. When uniformly applied, an emery surface can provide a pleasing finished surface.

Here are several suggestions on emerying.

1 Where feasible, emery should be supported with a hard backing to enable firm, uniform contact with the metal. Strips of emery can be held lengthwise against flat pieces of wood, dowels, files, or almost any hard object fitting the workpiece contour (figure 2–15). Emery in several directions.
2 Emery can be rubber-cemented or taped to the work table and the metal rubbed over its surface.
3 Specially shaped and slotted fixtures may be purchased or fabricated to attach to a flexible shaft. Strips of emery are inserted through the slot and wrapped around the tool.
4 Preformed cones and cylinders of emery material are also available for use on similarly shaped fixtures that attach to a flexible shaft or buffing machine.

The basic components of a flexible shaft machine are a high speed one-tenth horsepower motor, a flexible drive shaft, and a handpiece in which any one of many small cutting, grinding, buffing, and piercing tools may

2–15 *Emery or polishing board.*
2–16 *Abrasive cloth cemented to a work table.*

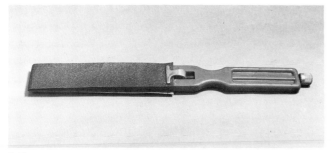

2-15

2-16

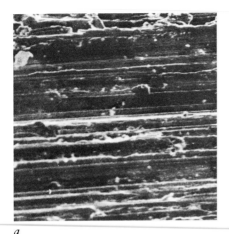

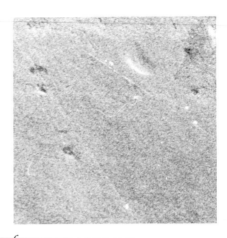

a   *b*   *c*

be attached. Most flexible shaft units are purchased with a foot operated rheostat for motor control. Most jewelers hang the machine within easy reach of their work bench.

2–17 *Magnified views of copper finished with: (a) 220 grit emery, (b) 360 grit emery, and (c) tripoli buffing compound. 500× magnification. Photographs by Peter Grigg, Ph.D.*

ADDITIONAL FINISHES

The following is a brief introduction to several additional finishing methods. Though used less frequently than filing and sanding, they meet special finishing needs and should not be overlooked.

Scraping
A three-sided scraper of finely honed steel is used to shave away metal surfaces (figure 2–18). Figure 2–19 illustrates how it is held to bevel edges, remove burrs and excess solder, and form depressions in a metal surface. The blade's edge is held at a slight angle and firm pressure is applied to cut away thin layers. Maintenance of the tool's cutting edges is extremely important in order to achieve accurate and uniform results. Cutting edges are sharpened with a fine oil stone by laying the flat sides of the tool on the stone and moving the tool back and forth at approximately the same angle used in cutting. Rotate the scraper until the three sides have been stoned. Store the scraper away from other tools that might mar its edges.

2–18 *Triangular bladed scraper.*
2–19 *Scraper's cutting position.*

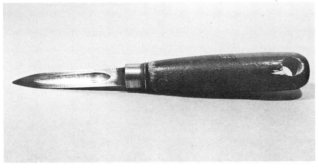

2-18

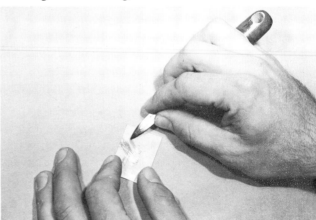

2-19

Burnishing

Burnishing is a polishing or smoothing process. The burnishers commonly used by jewelers are 5 to 6 inches in length and short handled (figure 2–20). The blades are straight or curved and generally oval in cross section. Blades are most often made of hardened steel but occasionally one might find a blade tipped with agate or other hard stone. Blades are highly polished and must be free of scratches and pits. The burnisher's smooth, polished surface is rubbed across the work surface using considerable pressure. Given the relatively minute amount of metal-to-metal contact, the blade compresses and redistributes the underlying metal. To burnish out a scratch, the blade is moved across the depression at a slight diagonal path (figure 2–21). Light oil or spittle is used as a lubricant to ease the burnisher's movement. Burnishers are often used to push and smooth bezels and to polish hard-to-reach areas.

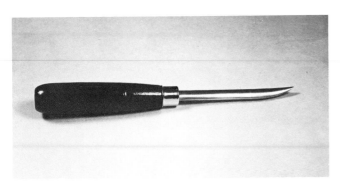

2–20 *Curved burnisher.*

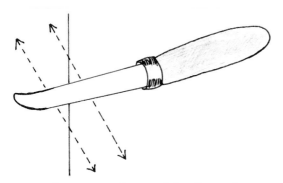

2–21 *Burnisher is moved at a slight diagonal across the scratch.*

Stoning

Scotch stones can be used in areas where files or emery cloth will not fit. Stones may be purchased from jewelry suppliers in various sizes and cut to approximately 6 inches in length and their ends ground to fit the specific task. When stoning it is best to hold the work under running water to prevent metal particles from clogging the stone. Pumice stones may also be used, but they leave a coarser surface. These can be purchased at the local drugstore.

Pumice Powder

A derivative of volcanic stone, pumice powder is used in several ways in jewelry making. It is rubbed directly on surfaces to give a matte finish, added to buffing mixtures as an abrasive, or brushed on with water as a cleaner. Pumice is also added as a binder in pitch mixtures (see page 54). Small quantities of pumice can be purchased from drugstores or in pound quantities from jewelry suppliers. Powder is graded in three grit sizes: fine, medium, and coarse.

Sandblasting

For those fortunate enough to have access to a sandblaster, interesting surface effects can be created. Sandblasting also provides an effective means of cleaning hard-to-reach areas. Operation of a sandblaster is fairly simple. It is usually enclosed in a sealed, boxlike structure incorporating the appropriate compressed air hoses, fittings, and a nozzle. Sand is blown through the nozzle at a high velocity. Blasting removes minute quantities of the surface onto which it is aimed, creating a texture and cleaning. Masking tape or contact paper placed over the workpiece allow a precise, selective means of stop-out. Unique surface qualities can be created with other blasting media: crushed walnut shells, glass beads, and steel shot are just a few. A word of caution: prolonged blasting will warp thin sheet metal, especially flat surfaces. A quick, uniform blast pattern will prevent warpage (figure 2–22). **Be sure to use adequate ventilation when sandblasting.**

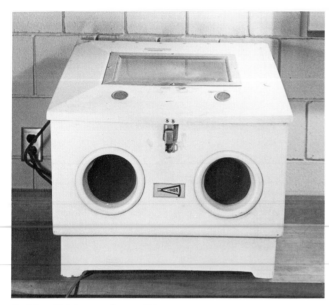

2-22   *Cabinet style sandblaster.*

Flexible Shaft Accessories

The range of small accessories available for use with the flexible shaft machine is too numerous to list completely. A few are shown in figure 2-24. Their functions vary from coarse grinding to polishing. An almost infinite number of shapes, sizes and materials can be found. The following is a list of only a few.

Type	Shape
Mounted emery points	Cylinder
Hard rubber impregnated	Round
Steel burrs	Flame
Emery drums	Oval
Hard felt wheels and bobs	Pear
Rotary files	Cone
Rotary stones	Pointed
Bristle brushes	Inverted Cone
Wire brushes	Knife edge
Cotton and muslin buffs	Round edge

Safety glasses should be worn while operating the flexible shaft, particularly when grinding or cutting any metal. A breathing filter should also be worn to prevent the intake of particles.

2-23   **Todd Noe.** *Constructed and sandblasted bracelet of acrylic and bronze. The artist achieved a dramatic, crisp-edged surface pattern by stopping out areas prior to sandblasting. Courtesy of the artist.*

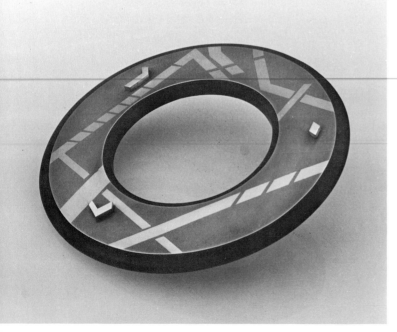

2-24   *Flexible shaft machine and accessories.*

SOLDERING

Solder is by far the most common means of joining individual elements composing a piece of jewelry. It is therefore essential for novice jewelers to learn the fundamentals of soldering. This section covers the practices and materials one might find in the average shop. The major emphasis is on silver solders and their joining of silver- and copper-based metals. Other specialized soldering techniques and materials are discussed in subsequent chapters.

Solder is generally composed, in varying ratios, of silver, copper, and zinc. Most contain at least 50 percent silver and are referred to as *hard solder*. Jewelers perform most of their work with three types of silver solder: hard flow, medium flow, and easy flow. Their melting points are: 1,425° F (hard); 1,390° F (medium); and 1,325° F (easy). The variation of melting points allows the jeweler to safely solder several joints that may be relatively close to one another without danger of melting the first joint during subsequent applications. Generally, a piece is soldered with hard solder first and the other joints with medium and easy solder. This is not saying that all three grades of solder must be used in a piece. It is quite possible to create some forms having multiple joints with only one type of solder. This process sounds a bit complicated in print but with planning and a little practice the selection of solder is quite simple.

Successful soldering requires careful attention to four basic points, any of which, if ignored, can cause problems. It is important that the worker know how—and why—to accomplish each of the following steps. (Specific soldering instructions are given later in this section.)

1. Joining

In some respects, soldering is like assembling an object with glue. The parts to be joined must be clean and well fitted or they will not adhere to one another. Prior to soldering, it is best to give some thought to how pieces should be placed for the most effective appearance and strength. Rather than having a solder seam visible, it is often possible to work from the back or flow solder between pieces, ending with hidden joints. In any case, the point where it is placed must touch and fit well. A few moments with emery cloth or a file is usually ade-

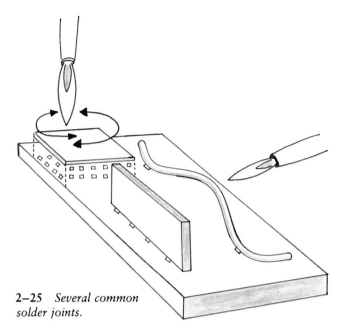

2–25 *Several common solder joints.*

quate to provide a good fit. No single rule covers how solder joints should be fitted.

As work progresses, the jeweler may find the need to employ several basic joints in one piece of jewelry. Figure 2–25 shows several common joints. Regardless of the joint used, the joining surfaces should make adequate contact to ensure a complete flow of solder through the entire joint. As solder melts, a molecular attraction is created, pulling liquid solder through the seam by capillary action. The heated mating surfaces are metallically diffused with the solder and become essentially one metal. Poorly fitted areas generally cause gaps and retard an even flow throughout. If solder is used as a filler to compensate for poor fit, an uneven or broad line of solder will appear on the finished work. The phrase, "Solder will not fill a gap" simply is not true. Instead, follow this rule: "Solder should not fill a gap."

2. Cleaning

Contaminated surfaces prevent the flow of solder. Usually, solder will just ball up and not flow across areas contaminated with oxidation or oily fingerprints and buffing compound. Joints bonding oxidized components are generally not as strong as those bonding clean metal. Chemical cleaning of oily and oxidized surfaces in most pickle solutions is not adequate. Pickle is excellent for removing flux and scale, but the solution often leaves either a thin oxide layer or metal flashing over the surface of the workpiece. Surfaces should be abrasively cleaned with pumice powder and water or clean emery cloth. These remove residue and oxides, plus a thin layer of metal. Cleaning down to virgin metal permits the molten solder to diffuse into the material being joined. Scrapers, stones, and files are also excellent cleaning tools. After cleaning, pieces can be held by their edges to avoid leaving fingerprints and further contamination.

3. Flux
One of the most common difficulties encountered in soldering is the formation of oxides in and around joining surfaces. Left unprotected, the cleaned areas to be soldered will begin to oxidize as soon as heat is applied, which will almost certainly prevent bonding. Flux serves as a barrier between the clean metal and surrounding oxygen. A number of types of flux are available from welding and jewelry supply firms. A borax-based paste flux is probably the most widely used. It provides a glasslike covering over the metal and dissolves oxides as they develop.

Prolonged heating will eventually burn away all flux. Those unfamiliar with the soldering process are often a little hesitant to apply a strong flame to their work or tend to heat the work slowly. This, of course, contributes to the oxidation of the metal. Always use an intense flame and complete the process quickly.

Prior to heating the workpiece, the joint—or the entire piece—should be covered with flux. Once soldered, the work is cleaned by pickling. Many jewelers, particularly those working in sterling silver, will cover the entire piece with flux to inhibit the formation of cupric oxides or fire scale over the surface of the metal. Beginners may ask, "Should I flux it?" When in doubt, flux it.

4. Solder Placement and Heating
After deciding which joint to solder first and which solder to use, the joint is prepared and solder snippets or paillons are placed along the joint. Solder should be set at points that can easily be cleaned in the event the solder flows (or "spills") in the wrong direction. Figure 2–25 shows examples of typical placement. Solder is generally available in thin sheet and wire of various gauges. Either form will work in most instances. For illustrative purposes, small paillons of sheet solder are used in the following applications.

Setting up work prior to soldering can be a real challenge at times. Again, forethought and experience will

2-26

eventually lessen this task. An excellent support for work and one worth its price is a soldering or annealing pan. Pans may be purchased in 6-, 12-, and 18-inch diameter sizes (figure 2–26). Pans are mounted on ball bearings to permit the worker to rotate the piece as needed. The bed of the pan may be filled with pea pumice, firebrick, or Carborundum grain. Bed surfaces serve to align work and reflect heat. Where a pumice stone surface will not work, soft firebrick, charcoal blocks, or commercially prepared magnesia blocks may be needed.

The worker should be inventive and be ready to employ a combination of supporting devices in order to complete the task. It may also be necessary to secure pieces together with iron binding wire, steel sewing pins, or cotter pins. Simple clamps can be fabricated from short sections of coat hanger wire (figure 2–27). Quite often pieces can simply be propped against one another. Employed sensibly, a tweezer device or third hand is a useful tool (figure 2–28). It should not be used as a ridged clamping device holding pieces together near the area being heated. Work clamped in this manner can easily collapse or crumble. The third hand is best used to clip near an edge in order to stabilize one of the joining elements. A soldering tripod and steel screen provide a surface to support work being heated top and bottom, as might be needed while attaching pin findings, bezels, or sweat soldering laminations. In other instances, the tripod may be an inefficient means of support. It should not be used for annealing or general solder work. The steel screen acts as a heat sink and gives little, if any, reflective heat. Figure 2–29 illustrates other methods of aligning or securing work to be soldered.

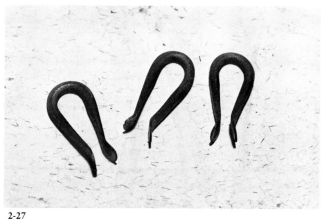

2-27

2-28

2–26 *Soldering and annealing pans.*
2–27 *Sections of coat hanger wire with ends flattened and bent to form soldering clamps.*
2–28 *A third hand device used to aid in soldering.*
2–29 *Several aids used in soldering: binding wire, drilled hole, graver stitches, and steel pins.*

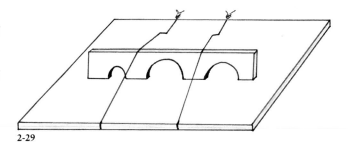

2-29

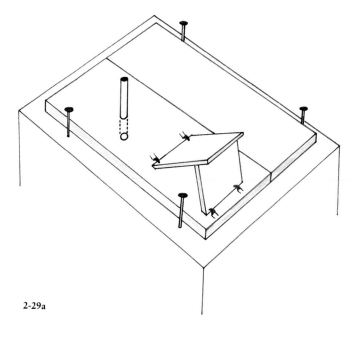

2-29a

Heat Sources

A complete look at all the available torch units could in itself fill a chapter. Some schools and professional shops use several different systems, each for specific operations. The following discussion examines a few of those in general use and points out the ones particularly suited to the techniques discussed in subsequent chapters. **Always use caution when working with gases that are under pressure.**

Propane   Small propane units can be purchased in discount and hardware stores. The unit's small tank may be hand held or fitted with a short hose and attached to the reusable single-valve torch. Tanks are disposable and new ones are inexpensive. These units are generally satisfactory for occasional jewelry work. For the serious jeweler, propane may be a false economy. Over time the initial investment plus the cost of tank replacement might be greater than that needed for a more effective system. The major drawback and frustration that I've experienced with these units is their uncanny knack for blowing out when most needed.

Natural Gas/Compressed Air   Probably the most versatile system available, the natural gas/air unit with a proper torch may be used to solder very delicate jewelry or large hollow forms. The intial installation is relatively expensive, requiring a gas line and compressed air system comprised of piping, regulator, air storage tank, and compressor. Besides its versatility of heat range and flame size, the flame's quality may be changed for each task by adjusting the gas or air volume. Varying the volume of gas and air results in a new mixture ratio that may provide a flame ranging from small, intense oxidizing heat to a soft, voluminous reducing flame. With a little experience, attaining the correct ratio is only a matter of minor valve adjustment. Once the basic system is installed, further versatility may be attained by using larger or smaller torch heads. Gas/air units are most often used in schools and professional shops that make jewelry and hollowware (figure 2–30).

Natural Gas/Compressed Oxygen   Many jewelers without access to compressed air employ this system. Gas/oxygen units function much like the gas/air system; slight valve adjustment provides the appropriate mixture ratio and flame intensity. While not as versatile as gas/air in terms of flame size, this system is adequate for

any jewelry need. Some torches come with interchangeable tips that allow the capability of soldering small work, annealing, and melting metal for casting. One drawback is the periodic expense of recharging and rental of oxygen cylinders (figure 2–31).

Acetylene   All things considered, acetylene units are perhaps the best choice for most shops. The basic unit consists of a tank, regulator, hose, and torch. Torches are designed to accept several sizes of tips to give the jeweler a wide choice of flame size. Tanks are small enough to be easily moved around the shop. The initial cost of the complete outfit is considerably less than a natural gas installation and tank refills are relatively inexpensive. Fuel and air adjustment is primarily a one-valve operation at the torch handle. The gas-to-air mixture is preset by means of an orifice at the connecting end of the torch tip. As gas flow is increased, a proportionately larger amount of air is drawn into the orifice, creating a hotter flame. Acetylene gives an extremely hot, clean-burning flame. Units may be purchased from welding and jewelry supply firms (figure 2–32).

2–30   *Natural gas/compressed air torch.*

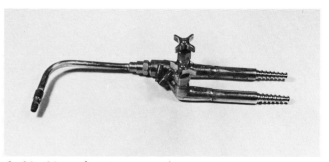

2–31   *Natural gas/compressed oxygen torch.*

2-32

2-33

2–32 *Acetylene torch system: tank, pressure regulator, pressure gauge, hose, and torch handle assembly.*
2–33 *Oxygen/acetylene system: tanks, pressure regulators, gauges, and hoses.*

Oxygen/Acetylene Oxygen/acetylene units may be luxury items in some jewelry shops. To some jewelers their expense weighed against their probable use generally does not justify the investment. For most of us, the one instance in which these units might be needed is for casting. Their operation is a bit more complex than the units previously discussed. Gases under high pressure in the tanks are reduced by regulator valves to a lower pressure in the hoses. The worker adjusts the low pressure gases by two valves on the torch assembly to achieve the required flame. Oxygen/acetylene gases produce a heat in excess of 6,000°F (figure 2–33).

Soldering Guidelines

As in so many instances, seldom do two people solder alike. The important thing is to satisfactorily complete the workpiece, in this case without its melting or having solder spilled over its surface. Regardless of the heat source chosen, the following guidelines are fundamental to each. Keep in mind that guidelines are just that—guidelines. For illustrative purposes, an acetylene torch is used.

1 Before lighting the torch, be sure all preliminary steps have been observed: joints fitted, cleaned, and fluxed.
2 Paillons of sheet solder may be cut with hand shears.

First cut straight lines 1/16 inch wide and approximately 3/4 inch into the sheet and then cutting across the strips at intervals of 1/16 inch to produce paillons 1/16 inch square (figure 2–34). Paillons are generally precut and set aside in small containers marked "easy," "medium," and "hard." Each sheet should also be well marked. When using wire solder, a small brass tag can be attached to appropriately identify it.

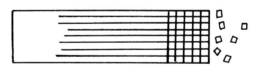

2–34 *Sheet solder and snippets.*

3 Given the nature of our work, it is difficult to provide a rule of thumb on the amount of solder to use. While a well-fitted sheet metal joint 1 inch long might require three or four paillons, attaching a wire's end to a piece of sheet may require only one-half a paillon. Too much solder will spill over or leave an unsightly fillet, both of which will have to be removed later. Remember to plan so that, if needed, solder with successively lower melting points may be used.
4 After applying flux, set the solder between and

touching both parts to be joined. In some instances, solder can be placed directly over a seam, allowing gravity to aid the flow. Ring bands are soldered in this manner. Some jewelry makers use a fine pointed brush saturated with flux to pick up and place paillons. The brush fluxes the solder as it is being placed. I find this method awkward and prefer to use tweezers, dipping each piece in a shallow container of flux.

5 Fit the acetylene torch handle with a number 3 or medium tip. This size tip is adequate for general soldering. Open the torch valve slightly, light the torch, and adjust the valve to produce a flame with a light blue inner cone surrounded by bluish violet flame. Continue to open slowly and listen for a harsh hissing sound; then close the valve a bit to eliminate the harsh noise. Once adjusted, the valve will be open approximately one-tenth of a turn. The noise and valve placement are mentioned only as references for those beginning. After a few tries, lighting the torch will become second nature.

6 Judging flame quality and size is often difficult for inexperienced jewelers. The placement of the flame relative to the workpiece is important. One-half to one inch beyond the tip of the blue cone is the hottest portion of the flame. This area should be played over the work surface. Generally, overall flame size can be increased or decreased proportionally with the size of the jewelry piece. This may entail changing tip sizes or torches.

7 Another factor to consider is that solder flows to the hottest point. This means that components or joints to be bonded should rise to the solder's melting point at the same time. On work composed of elements of differing sizes or masses, heat must be played over the larger mass for a proportionately longer time. For example, in joining a section of thin wire to sheet metal, heat can be concentrated on the sheet. The sheet will come up to the correct temperature by direct heat and the wire by conductive and reflective heat from the sheet metal.

8 As heat is applied, flux will boil and take on a white, crusty appearance. Continued heat will stabilize the flux as it becomes vitreous. Although it is frustrating, solder paillons can become dislodged by boiling flux. Always have a solder pick at hand to nudge paillons back into place. Picks may be fashioned from a length of tungsten rod or coat-hanger wire.

Cut a piece approximately 10 inches long and file one end to a point. When solder becomes displaced, continue to play partial heat over the piece while sliding the paillon back. Removing the heat at this point will allow the flux to solidify and bind the solder out of place. In some instances it may be less frustrating to first heat the workpiece until the flux stabilizes and then set flux-wetted paillons in place. This tends to make them stick in place. The more experienced jeweler might prefer to heat the joint to the temperature at which solder flows and carefully apply paillons to the joint with the tip of the solder pick or directly feed in wire solder.

9 Difficulty often arises in soldering because of insufficient or slow heating. Ideally, the most effective way to join two pieces is to heat the two masses at once until the melting temperature of the solder is reached. This concept usually works fine if the pieces are relatively small. The neophyte often falls into the trap of trying to heat the workpiece slowly and evenly with a gentle flame, apparently believing that in doing this the flux will not boil and that eventually the temperature will rise to the proper point. In theory, perhaps this is true. In practice, metal and solder begin to oxidize when heat is applied and the longer it takes to reach the desired heat, the more oxides develop to reduce the chances of succesful bonding. Some overall heating is fine. Overall heating can relieve any stresses within the structure of the metal, may help align joints, and, to some extent, help alleviate the rapid boiling of flux. After a brief initial overall heating, place the major portion of heat around the solder area to quickly bring it up to temperature and let the solder flow. As soon as flow occurs, remove the heat. Additional heat may result in a textured or molten workpiece. Keep in mind the points outlined in number 7 of these guidelines.

10 On pieces requiring multiple joints, it is not always necessary to pickle and clean after each soldering. Work can be set up so that joints can be soldered successively and all pickled at once. Flux all joints prior to heating. (For information on pickling, see pages 40 to 41.)

The preceding guidelines must be general, since each piece may pose a unique challenge. The intent is to provide an overview with emphasis directed on areas of particular difficulty to the novice.

Safety Precautions

1 Inherent in flame is the potential for burning hair, clothing, flesh, and fixtures found in and around the soldering area. Tie back clothing and hair. Loose clothing made of synthetic fibers is particularly susceptible to fire. Keep a fire extinguisher and a source of water near the soldering area.

2 Follow the manufacturer's instructions regarding the handling of fuel tanks and the operation of pressure regulator valves.

3 Always work in a well-ventilated area. A vent system should pull harmful elements away from the worker. Figure 2–35 shows an excellent method of venting. It is not an exaggeration to say that almost every material encountered in jewelry making presents a potential hazard, especially when heated. The construction of a functional ventilation system is time well spent.

4 Avoid the use of solder containing cadmium. The toxic elements in cadmium fumes accumulate in the body. Cadmium is sometimes alloyed to make low-melting silver solders. Suppliers can provide the technical data on the solder being ordered.

5 Observe the manufacturer's label on flux containers. Some, especially the borax-based types, contain toxic elements. Again, have the area well vented and avoid leaning over the workpiece.

6 In the event lead-based solder is being used, avoid the fumes. Lead fumes are toxic. In addition to the fume problem, lead will erode, pit, and possibly destroy the surface of any silver or gold piece it comes in contact with in the presence of high heat. Work contaminated by lead should be scraped absolutely clean before heat is applied. Pitting occurs just below the annealing point.

2–35 *A vent system designed to pull fumes back and out of the worker's breathing space.*

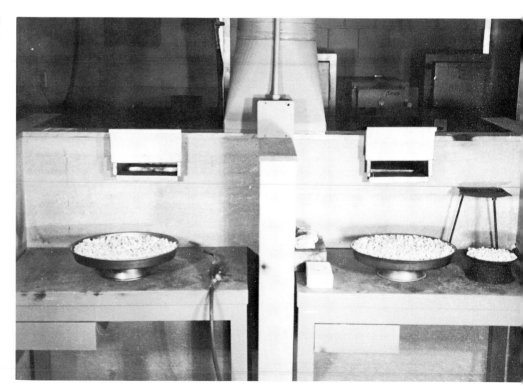

BUFFING

Today's jewelry makers enjoy the convenience of electrically powered buffing tools. For centuries the jeweler had only his or her hands and loose abrasive powder to smooth and polish metal surfaces. We cannot be sure of all the ancient processes, but we do know that in general polishing involved the use of leather stropping devices impregnated with fine granules of stone. The stone was applied dry or mixed with water and oil and applied as a paste. Using great physical pressure, strops were rubbed across the metal again and again, successively cutting away minute bits until finally, perhaps days later, the effort resulted in a polished surface. Burnishing devices were also widely used in years past. Many of these were unique in design, having a variety of shapes and sizes. To increase downward pressure on the work surface, an ingenious leverage system was devised. Employing a leather thong wrapped around the forearm and secured at the end of the burnisher's handle, the worker was able to multiply downward force and ease the task. Despite this somewhat easier method, hand polishing still required a great deal of time and physical effort. Thanks to electric power, there are few instances when hand polishing is required today.

Buffing Machines

Ideally, a buffing machine is designed with built-in lighting and a dust-collection system. Most commercial machines come with these features plus a means to recover filtered dust and metal particles. Shops doing work in precious metals save the collected matter for sale to metal refiners. Occasional work in gold or silver may not warrant the expense of handling and shipping the material to the refiner for reclamation. **Machines with a vacuum and filter system do not prevent small amounts of particulate from being thrown outward by the centrifugal force of the wheels.** Some jewelers have overcome this problem by fabricating box or drumlike enclosures on the front of the buffing unit. The enclosure has an opening on each side large enough for the worker's arms to penetrate and a safety glass or plastic window in front for viewing. To further aid in sealing, the side arm openings may be partially covered with sheet rubber cut into radiating strips that lie against the worker's arms, as in figure 2–36.

Jewelry suppliers can provide many types of buffing units. Generally, two types are sold for jewelry work: the cabinet model with filters below the buffing area and a compact table model with the filter enclosed behind the buffing area. The cabinet type is usually more expensive but tends to contain contaminants better. Both units may be purchased with two-speed motors and tapered spindles. Buffing units should sit approximately 42 to 44 inches from the floor to the spindle (figure 2–37). Homemade buffers may be unsafe, too slow, or create a dusty environment.

The actual buffing or polishing process occurs as an abrasive-charged wheel passes across the metal's surface at a high speed. As buffing compounds of diminishing grit sizes are used, the surface gradually becomes smooth as the microscopic high points are cut and burnished smooth.

Buffing is no different from the previous finishing processes in that the tools, in this instance buffing wheels, are manufactured in a variety of materials, shapes, sizes, and qualities. Henceforth, the term *buffs* includes buffing wheels, polishing wheels, and felt laps. Generally speaking, buffs are manufactured of either a soft flexible material that will mold itself to the basic contour of the surface being worked or a hard, unyielding compressed felt best suited to working flat surfaces or high points. Specific guidelines as to which buff should be used for particular tasks are difficult to give. Generally, close-stitched and hard-felt buffs are used for cutting or buffing with coarse compounds and to buff hard-to-reach areas, while loose or unstitched cotton and other soft materials are used for fine polishing. The di-

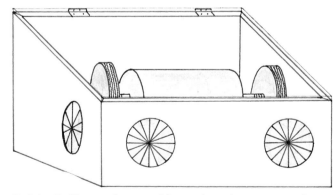

2–36 *Buffing enclosure with a safety glass cover and arm openings.*

ameter and shape of the buffing wheel will in part be determined by the shape and size of the jewelry piece and type of compound to be used. For example, to achieve a high polish on a large, bulbous form requiring a broad, dispersed effect, a large, unsewn cotton buff could be used; on small, flat work, a wide, hard felt buff could be used. Motor speed is yet another consideration. In general, the slower the motor speed, the larger the wheel diameter should be. A high polish requires high surface speed. With coarse compounds, low wheel speed may be used.

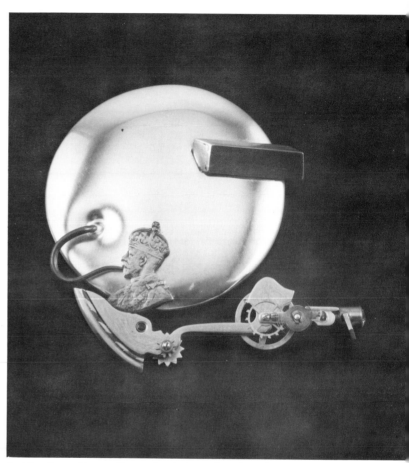

2-38 **Anne Owens-Stone,** Evolution of a Thought. *Brooch of sterling, copper, brass, and 14-karat gold with ruby and spinel using marriage of metals and assemblage. The buffed circular element provides a strong focal point and variety to the total forms composition. Courtesy of the artist.*

2-37 *Cabinet and tabletop style buffing units.*

A partial list of buffing wheel shapes and materials follows. All come in various widths and diameters (figure 2–39).

Shapes	Materials
Wheel	Muslin
Goblet	Cotton flannel
Pointed cone	String
Round cone	Canvas
Cylinder	Felt
Tapered ring	Wool
Knife edge	Leather

Fortunately, selection of the right buffing compound is not as complex as wheel selection. The process is simple: work progressively from coarse to fine compound or to final polish. Surfaces need not have mirror finishes; the decision to stop at any point, even while filing or emerying, is up to the worker's sense of design. File textures, emery, and matte pumiced surfaces could well be the answer as long as the choice is true to the form. Buffing compounds are most often purchased in cake or stick forms. Compounds are generally hardened mixtures of abrasive powder and a binder of tallow, wax, or heavy oil. Many types of natural and synthetic abrasive materials are used; corundum, iron oxide, silica, pumice, flint, and aluminum oxide are just a few. Generally, the compounds used most frequently for jewelry work are bobbing, tripoli, and rouge. Work is begun with bobbing, the coarsest, and progresses to rouge, the final high polish.

Before a buffing motor is started, a number of safety factors and technical points must be understood. Of all the machines jewelers work with, the buffer is most likely to cause bodily injury and damage to the workpiece. The speed with which the wheel spins, combined with its weight, create significant kinetic energy. Held incorrectly, jewelry is easily dislodged from the hand and sent sailing. This is minor compared to what can happen through inattentiveness. Every teacher and practicing jeweler has a tale of a buffing-room horror. The following are basic guides regarding safety and operation.

1 Neckties, long hair, and loose clothing must be secured to prevent hanging near and possibly becoming entangled in the buffing wheel. Reaction and correction time in buffing is zero; damage is instantaneous.
2 Eye protection should be worn. At the very least, machines should be equipped with a plastic viewing shield above the spindle area. Dust and solid particles are constantly being thrown outward and can easily enter the eyes.
3 When using a poorly vented machine, a respirator should be worn. Inexpensive respirators may be purchased from paint and hardware stores.
4 Always work on the lower front quarter of the wheel. Working above will likely cause the wheel to snag and fling the work outward. The lower quarter spins away from the worker (figures 2–41 and 2–42).
5 Always place the buff on the spindle with the motor at rest. Trying to center a buff on a moving spindle can result in hand injury.

2–39 *Assorted buffing wheels.*

2–40 *Buffing compounds.*

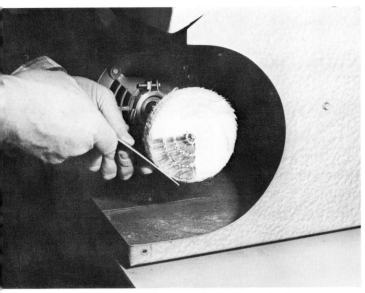

2–41 *Workpiece relative to the buffing wheel.*

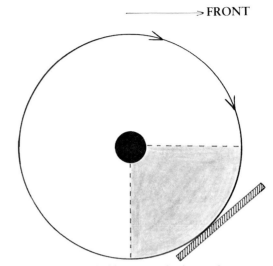

2–42 *Workpiece is held against the lower front quarter of the buffing wheel.*

6 As the work is placed against the wheel, always try to buff from the center outward, slowly pulling the work outward. Difficulty often occurs when the worker extends the piece in beyond its center and catches the nearest edge as the wheel comes around.

7 When polishing chain or flimsy wire forms, wrap the work around stiff cardboard or wood and buff with a gentle pressure. Buff along the axis of the chain. Go slowly and finish a little at a time. Be sure both ends are held and not allowed to flop around.

8 If an object becomes entangled, step back and turn off the machine. Do not attempt to retrieve tangled work with the machine spinning.

9 The greatest cause of buffing mishaps is the worker's inattentiveness. The lethargic daydreamer is asking for trouble. The mind must be centered on the task and on nothing else.

The actual buffing process is quite simple providing the previous guidelines are understood and followed. Polishing is begun after the work is emeried to a fine matte finish, cleaned with soap and water, and dried. New, loosely stitched buffs should be dressed by spinning against the side of an old file. The sharp edge of the file cuts and pulls out loose fibers and threads. Further trimming with scissors may be necessary. The file may also be used in the event wheels become impacted with compound. Too much compound will clog and make

the wheel less effective. An excellent cleaning tool can be made with a few nails and a piece of wood (figure 2–43). With the wheel spinning, hold the compound against it firmly until the wheel's surface is covered. This requires only a second or two. A firm, consistent pressure should be maintained on the work as it is held against the wheel and moved in varying angles to prevent cutting grooves into its surface. As buffing progresses from the coarse compounds and wheels, the work must be thoroughly cleaned before using the finer compounds. Failure to clean the piece will contaminate the polishing wheels with coarse compounds. Storing buffs separately with their related compounds will help

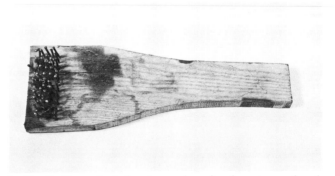

2–43 *Buffing wheel cleaning tool made of scrap wood and nails.*

prevent contamination. If wheels do become contaminated, soak them in kerosene or solvent for several hours, wring out excess solvent, and wash them several times in a strong solution of detergent, ammonia, and hot water.

METAL CLEANING

Pickling

Generally, the first cleaning process after soldering or heating is immersion of the work in a water/acid pickle solution. Pickling dissolves surface oxides, scale, and the residue of flux. Usually, the piece is placed in the acid immediately after heating. On large forms it is best to allow the work to air cool before pickling, thereby avoiding the possibility of warpage or stressing solder seams.

Although several types of pickling solutions are available, Sparex, a commercial product, is probably the most widely used. Sparex comes as a dry, granular compound and is dissolved in water. The solution may be used hot or cold but its action is quicker when heated to approximately 140°F. Sparex is an excellent substitute for sulfuric acid solutions and is relatively safe and easy to use. Refer to Appendix 5 for additional information regarding safety precautions and the mixing of pickle solutions.

Some jewelers prefer to use a sulfuric acid pickle. The bath is usually mixed one part acid to ten parts water (slightly stronger for pickling gold). **As in all instances when acids and water are mixed, the acid is poured into the water. Otherwise the results can be excessive fuming and spattering. The mixing and use of acids should always take place in a vented area with water and baking soda at hand. In the event of spattering, the affected area of skin should be flushed with water and, if needed, medically treated.**

A number of containers work well for mixing, heating, and storing pickle. For occasional jewelry work, a Pyrex bowl heated by a hotplate is adequate. A crockery slow cooker, with a variable heat setting, is an excellent, inexpensive, self-contained unit. The longevity of these units can be extended significantly by sealing all openings and seams with silicone-based bathtub caulking material. Large pickle baths are constructed of stainless steel or lead and usually heated by natural gas.

2–44 *Slow cooker pickle container and soldering implements.*

Iron-based materials such as binding wire and tweezers should not be placed in pickle solutions. The introduction of iron, combined with the metal being pickled, will create an electrolytic action in which the acid solution essentially becomes a copper-plating bath. Metals present in the bath will become plated by copper salts that were previously dissolved in the pickle solution through normal use. Copper, brass, or wooden tongs can be used safely in pickle.

Contrary to what some jewelers believe, the accidental introduction of iron into pickle does not necessarily mean the solution is permanently contaminated. If the iron-based materials (binding wire, tweezers) are totally removed, the acid may be used as before. Electrolysis only occurs while the iron is in the solution.

Through normal use over a period of time, dissolved oxides in solution will saturate the acid and its color will become dark blue, an indication that it is time to discard the bath.

After the workpiece has been pickled, rinse it thoroughly in water. Hollow forms that are difficult to rinse should be soaked in a neutralizing solution of about one tablespoon baking soda per cup of water. Where practical, the back of hollow forms should be drilled in at least two points to permit draining after pickling and cleaning. Vents at opposite sides of the backing will help assure complete drainage. Unvented enclosed forms can become bombs when heated. Unless vented, air or moisture trapped inside the piece will expand upon heating and blow the work apart, possibly causing serious injury.

Stripping Fire Scale

On sterling silver, the removal of heat-induced cupric oxides, commonly referred to as fire scale, is often necessary. Usually fire scale is not apparent until the piece is completely soldered, cleaned, and buffed. Generally, fire scale develops uniformly over the surface and appears as a grayish color over the silver. The problem becomes obvious only after part of the surface is removed, as might occur while emerying or buffing. With a portion of the surface buffed through, a contrasting light and grayish surface results. To achieve a uniform, light silver finish, the remaining gray areas must be removed, either mechanically or chemically. Some workers, particularly those creating large forms, prefer their work to be finished with a gray-silver surface. In this case, in final finishing the goal is to polish carefully and not break through the accumulated fire scale.

Abrasive materials are generally used to mechanically remove fire scale. Even with all the devices at our disposal, abrasives may not completely remove oxides. Attempts to buff away hard-to-reach areas may result in loss of detail or crisp edges. Complete removal of fire scale might best be accomplished by immersing the workpiece in a solution of one-half nitric acid and one-half water. Again, **take care to pour the acid into the**

2–45 *Ultrasonic cleaning units.*

water, and place the bath in a vented area. Wear eye protection. Acid removal or stripping is accomplished as follows:

1 Clean the work thoroughly with pumice powder and water.
2 Using plastic or wooden tongs, dip the piece into the acid solution for a few seconds until blackened areas appear. Remove, rinse in water, and again clean with pumice and water.
3 Continue this process until no black areas appear. This indicates that all fire scale has been removed.
4 Prolonged immersion can cause etching of surfaces and erosion of solder seams.

Another effective method of stripping is by deplating the work in an electrolytic bath. The process requires additional equipment and therefore may not be practical for occasional use. Details of this process can be better understood through a study of chapter 4.

Ultrasonics

Small ultrasonic cleaning units can ease the task of having to remove buffing compounds from finished work and clinging mold compounds on castings. The ultrasonic process works on the principle of electronically induced high frequency sound waves passing through a liquid cleaning agent. Sound waves cause an accelerated cleaning action by the liquid. Most jewelry suppliers can provide concentrated solutions tailored to most needs. Precautions should be taken when cleaning objects containing nonmetallic materials. Always follow the manufacturer's recommendations concerning the operation and maintenance of the cleaning unit and solutions (figure 2–45).

Soap and Water

The most common method of cleaning is by soaking and scrubbing the piece with soap and water. In day-to-day work, soap and water is generally sufficient.

First, soak the piece in a solution of a couple of ounces of liquid detergent in a pan of water. After soaking, scrub thoroughly with a soft toothbrush. Use plenty of liquid on the brush and workpiece. To clean recesses and small cavities, use a sliver of wood or a toothpick. The soap solution may be further strengthened with an ounce of ammonia or household cleanser. After cleaning, rinse the workpiece thoroughly and dry it with a soft cotton cloth.

OXIDATION COLORING

Oxidation coloring is by no means necessary to finishing a piece of jewelry. It is one of many interesting options. Darkened or oxidized areas may provide visually pleasing contrasts to highly polished areas or may be quite effective by themselves. When properly applied, chemical oxidation can be used to color areas that would otherwise be oxidized by natural elements. Chemically applied, the colors can be developed evenly and in selective areas. This section focuses primarily on silver and copper. The basic points covered apply to most metals containing copper. Appendix 2 outlines a variety of data relative to chemical coloring.

Oxidation is generally applied after a piece is completely finished, buffed, and cleaned. Cleaning is an essential step; if overlooked the oxidation will be spotty or unevenly colored. After a thorough cleaning with soap and water, the piece should be scrubbed with a slurry of fine pumice powder and water on a soft toothbrush. Do not be disturbed at this point by the matte finish left by the pumice. Later, a light buffing with rouge will renew the surface if desired. Usually the matter of selective oxidation is a subtractive process, first oxidizing the entire piece and then buffing the oxidation from selected areas.

The coloration of silver and copper occurs through a process of oxidation, in this case caused by the reaction of oxygen and a solution of potassium sulfide (liver of sulfur). Colors are created by a residue of silver or copper sulfides that develops on the metal surface as the oxidation occurs. The following are step-by-step guidelines for developing a variety of colors. See Appendix 5 regarding the safe use of liver of sulfur.

1 Liver of sulfur is purchased in lump form from jewelry and chemical supply firms. It should be stored in dry, dark, airtight jars. For convenience, a strong premixed concentrate may be made up by dissolving a 1-inch chunk of liver of sulfur in 12 or 13 ounces of water and storing the solution in a jar. Ready-to-use solutions are made by dissolving flakes or small chunks of liver of sulfur into a pint or two of cold tap water. An inexpensive plastic bowl can be used to contain the mixture. Add enough liver of sulfur to make a light yellow mixture. If necessary, a stronger solution can be made by adding more liver of sulfur. The premixed concentrate may be used instead by pouring it into the water until the light yellow color is reached. A relatively weak, cold solution is used in order to bring out the oxidation colors gradually. Hot solutions or the placement of heat directly on the piece will bring on colors so rapidly that the work instantly becomes slate gray or black.

2 If possible, work near a sink so that as the piece is oxidized, it can be quickly rinsed. With the solution mixed, dip the work in for one or two seconds and then rinse in cold water. As the colors come forth, the cold rinse will stop the chemical reaction and retard further coloring. A hot rinse will sometimes quickly darken the piece. Keep in mind that as the metal dries, it will darken slightly.

3 Repeat the previous step of dipping and rinsing until a suitable color appears. Some jewelers take the extra precaution of brushing the oxidized surface after each rinse with a soft brass brush. The brush and work are covered with soap and water for lubrication. Brushing helps to remove any film that might appear after dipping and also enhances the overall appearance.

4 The three factors that usually govern the effects of oxidation are the strength of the solution, its temperature, and the preparatory cleanliness of the surface of the metal. Variations in any of these will have an effect on the result. The perceptive jeweler will quickly learn to experiment with these qualities and bring forth colors unseen in shortcut methods. When a jeweler decides that a form calls for an oxidized finish, the coloring process should be approached with as much concern as any other part of the work. It is often necessary to reoxidize a piece several times before achieving the desired effect. In the event the work becomes too dark or spotty, reclean the entire piece with the pumice slurry and repeat steps 1 and 2. For copper, an excellent aid in cleaning is one of the commercial household copperware cleaners. This is followed by pumice and water.

5 After final coloring, the jewelry should be thoroughly dried. Ideally, compressed air is the best method to assure an absolutely dry surface. Air pressure provides a positive means of drying out hollow or recessed areas and alleviates the possibility of leaving water marks often left by wiping dry. If an air source

2–46 **Barbara W. Stanger.** *Ceremonial wedding ring of sterling, 14-karat gold, and copper with adventurines; constructed. This concept incorporates highly symbolic forms that relate directly to the ring's function. Courtesy of the artist. Photograph by Ralph Heigl.*

is not available, a soft cotton cloth is the next best choice. To expose underlying metal or to highlight areas, carefully rub away oxidation with moistened pumice powder and rinse well. Exposed areas can be polished with gentle pressure against the rouge buff or a rouge cloth.

6 Left unprotected, treated surfaces will darken with time and may be marred by fingerprints and moisture. A light coat of household floor wax will provide a protective film for a considerable time. Buff the wax dry with a soft cloth. Some jewelry suppliers offer a protective wax compounded specifically for metal protection. Clear lacquer sprays are not recommended as coatings. They invariably peel.

Jewelry made of gold or brass is generally difficult to oxidize. To avoid this problem, a thin layer of copper may be plated over the piece. The copper will take the oxidation. After oxidation, unwanted oxidation and copper plate can be carefully buffed away to expose the base of brass or gold.

Plating may be applied by conventional means or unconventionally by wrapping the piece with binding wire and immersing it in a copper-rich (blue) pickle solution for a few minutes. Be sure no other work is in the pickle container and that the binding wire is removed after plating; otherwise, plating will occur as other pieces are dropped into the solution.

CHAPTER THREE

Forming

Being creative individuals, jewelers soon tire of applying a few basic techniques to flat sheet metal. The possibilities of jewelry making can go far beyond the basically graphic images and shapes often expressed in work composed entirely of flat sheet material. To fully express the natural qualities of metal, its form may be manipulated from flat sheet and given dimension or depth by bending and stretching. The process employed to both bend and stretch metal is called forming. The individual techniques discussed in this chapter are only a few of many forming methods. Later chapters reveal how metal is forged by hammer, melted and cast, and electrodeposited into new forms.

ANNEALING

Though not a shaping or forming technique, annealing is an essential step in these and many other processes. In its natural state metal is more malleable compared to the hardness it reaches while being worked. Through normal work processes (flexing, bending, hammering, and stretching) the structure of the metal compresses in the areas being moved. This action applies force to the inner structure, compressing and elongating the material, which eventually becomes brittle and stressed to the point of fracturing if compression continues. Heat treatment or annealing will return the metal to a relatively soft state. As work progresses, the time for annealing will become apparent. With just a little experience the worker will begin feeling a definite resistance to the tools being used and gains a sense of how far the material can be bent, stretched, or compressed before breaking.

Every metal has a specific temperature at which its crystal structure is realigned in an optimal malleable

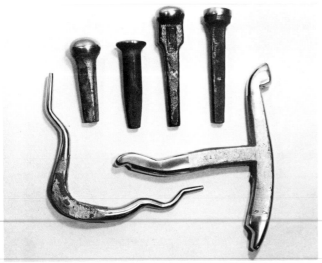

3-1

3-2

arrangement. In practice, measurement of precise temperatures is generally not feasible, therefore jewelers learn to identify the annealing range by color changes in the metal as heat is applied with the torch. For commonly used metals the color indicating the annealing point is a dull to faint red. Some refer to this as "cherry red." The annealing color should not be confused with the colors of surface oxidation. (Annealing temperatures are listed in Appendix 1.) Some jewelers prefer to anneal in a darkened area or with lights out in order to see the annealing color sooner. After annealing the work is generally quenched in pickle to facilitate the removal of surface scale. Large forms should be allowed to cool for a few minutes and then pickled. A sudden quench will sometimes distort a shape or fracture solder seams. Ferrous metals must be air cooled. Painting the workpiece with a borax-based flux prior to annealing will help alleviate oxide and scale formation while heating.

BENDING

Bending, or curving, metal is perhaps the most direct method of forming. Bending generally does not change the thickness of the materials, at least that is not the aim. Wire and sheet metal are often bent with pliers or with mallets and hammers over appropriate mandrels, anvils, or stakes.

3-1 *A few of the many steel forming stakes. Stakes may also be fabricated of hardwood and plastics.*
3-2 *Rawhide mallets.*

3-3 *Just a few of the many pliers available to the jeweler.*

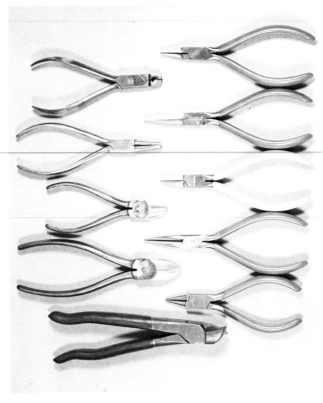

Whenever you work with metal, keep in mind that all tool marks and scratches applied in the working processes will result in additional finishing time and effort unless such marks are part of the design. Scratches can be avoided by using the correct tools. Use rawhide or wooden mallets over steel stakes or mandrels. Steel hammers used over metal stakes will create unneeded marks, thinning of the metal, and possible distortions.

The application of pliers in bending can be misunderstood by the novice. As noted in chapter 1, many types of pliers are available—far more than the average jeweler would ever need. At times, it appears that jewelry suppliers, dental suppliers, and die makers have conspired to bombard us with every conceivable gadget. If purchased as needed, five or six pliers should be sufficient. Before using them to bend metal, consider the shape of the jaws, the desired curve, and the effects of the jaws against the metal as pressure is exerted in bending. Jaws should be absolutely smooth and free of pits and scratches. The use of tape or leather around the plier's jaws is an inadequate substitute for the proper tool. This practice is usually poor protection against mars or scratches and usually leaves a mess of torn and sticky tape on the pliers. Again, the best protection against mars and scratches is the tool that properly fits the desired bend. Figures 3–4 and 3–5 show a variety of jaw shapes and their appropriate applications. In gen-

3–6 Debra Lynn Gold, Hollow Bracelet. *NuGold and sterling with dot inlays of iron; constructed. A strong line quality was achieved by bending sheet strips and allowing the edges to overhang. Courtesy of the artist. Photograph by David Wagenarr.*

eral, flat, angular shapes are formed with flat jaws and curves are bent with round, half-round, and combination flat and round jaws. A rounded jaw is placed on the inside of the bend and, ideally, a flat jaw against the outside. Use of a flat jaw on the inside of a curve will certainly indent the surface of the metal. A round jaw placed against the outside of a curve will also mark the surface.

Remember, bending hardens the metal, even wire. As complex or tight bends are developed, it may be necessary to anneal several times before completion.

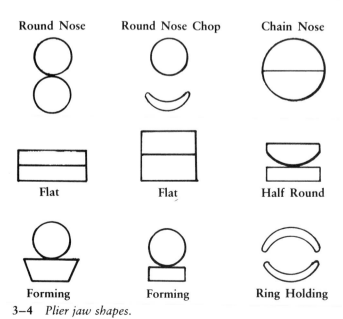

Round Nose Round Nose Chop Chain Nose

Flat Flat Half Round

Forming Forming Ring Holding

3–4 *Plier jaw shapes.*

3–5 *Application of various plier jaw shapes.*

3–7 Susan Hamlet, Neckpiece/Flexible Column #18. *Constructed in stainless steel. Shown as a neckpiece and sculptural presentation. Courtesy of the artist.*

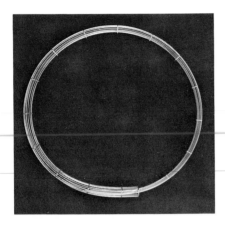

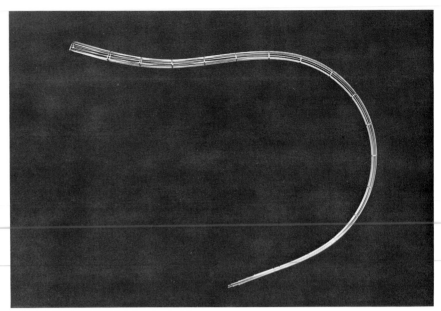

3–8 Ann Owens-Stone, Intricate Armed Capers. *Steel; assemblage. Courtesy of the artist. Linear elements of this type can be accurately bent with half-round, flat jawed pliers.*

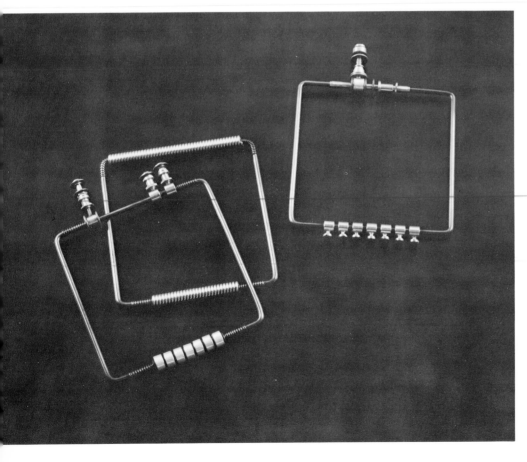

STRETCHING

Stretching curves flat sheet metal, as does bending. However, the stretched sheet does not maintain its original thickness. As the form develops, its cross section becomes thinner as the piece is given greater and greater depth and dimension. Stretching normally involves depressing sheet stock downward into a negative space.

The stretching methods covered here (sinking, repoussé, and die forming) can be thought of as scaled-down silversmithing techniques. Jewelry making and smithing naturally overlap; craftpersons fortunate enough to be versed in both disciplines have an unlimited technical capacity to draw upon. Additional smithing techniques occasionally applicable to jewelry forms are covered in several of the volumes listed in the bibliography.

3–9   David Freda, Parker Pin. *Brooch of sterling, 14-karat gold, glass, beads, garnet, mica, and acrylic; turned, etched, and constructed. Flat sheet metal was stretched or raised, giving this piece greater dimension. Courtesy of the artist. Photograph by Bob Hanson.*
3–10   Bonnie Gwaltney, Marine Series: Pin #7. *Pin of sterling and copper and Shibuichi mokume-gane; repoussé and construction. Courtesy of the artist.*

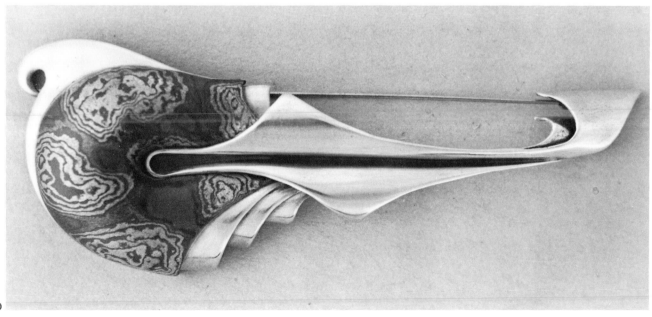

3-10

SINKING

In sinking, forms are generally produced by forcing sheet metal into depressions precut in a hardwood block or tree stump. Tree stumps cut with their ends parallel make excellent work surfaces. In addition to use in sinking and general metal forming, the stump provides a sound foundation for mounting anvils and vises. For basic shop needs, a stump approximately 20 to 25 inches high and 15 to 20 inches in diameter works fine. Depressions are cut into the stump with a woodworker's gouge or with a large round rotary file mounted in an electric hand drill. Shallow depressions can be made with sharp blows of a round-faced forming hammer.

Stumps and wooden blocks are recommended for sinking. They are easily attained, basically maintenance-free, and inexpensive. The physical characteristics of wood are ideal: giving yet relatively hard, easily shaped, and durable. In general, lead blocks, preformed steel blocks, and sandbags are not as practical in day-to-day use. Sand-filled canvas and leather bags work fine as resilient and relatively secure means of holding pitch bowls (page 54), but for sinking they are not firm or secure enough and inevitably leak sand and split open. Lead is pliable but lifeless with no spring. Once indented, the impression is permanent until the block is

3–11 *Hardwood work stump.*

melted and recast. Lead blocks are also prone to flaking and splitting. Lead is unsafe and is always a possible contaminant of other metals. Dishlike steel blocks give little latitude in form possibilities. Their surfaces are extremely hard and the edges are often sharp and likely to mar the metal being sunk. Steel dapping blocks are another choice; they are discussed on page 63.

After the desired outer shape of the workpiece is determined and cut from sheet metal, the piece is held over the depression and with a rounded hammer, mallet, or

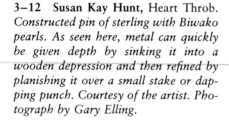

3–12 Susan Kay Hunt, Heart Throb. *Constructed pin of sterling with Biwako pearls. As seen here, metal can quickly be given depth by sinking it into a wooden depression and then refined by planishing it over a small stake or dapping punch. Courtesy of the artist. Photograph by Gary Elling.*

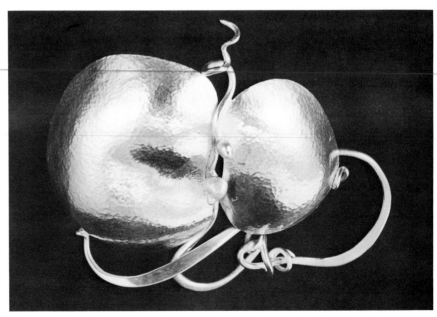

punch is gradually forced downward by a series of blows. Small, shallow depressions may be formed in sheet with just a few hammer blows but deeper, complex work will require slow going, and annealing several times. The beginning diameter of the chosen shape will remain essentially unchanged as the metal is forced downward. Work is begun in the center and gradually moved outward to the form's edge. The thickness of the piece decreases as work progresses, requiring caution to avoid overthinning and eventual tearing of the metal.

Some distortion or twisting is quite common in sinking. The problem can be corrected by first annealing and then giving the piece a vigorous twist by hand. The piece can also be placed face up on the anvil and its edges tapped gently back in shape with a mallet. When cutting out the original shape, some jewelers allow an extra amount of metal around the perimeter, sink the desired form, and then trim away the extra. The perimeter provides a relatively rigid circumference and a means of holding the metal. Another method, which wastes mate-

rial, is to use the center area of a square sheet to develop the form and to trim away the excess. The square may be nailed in place over a wooden depression to eliminate distortion.

Finishing a sunken piece is usually a matter of planishing or smoothing over small stakes with a hammer or mallet. Again, the jeweler can choose from the full gamut of hammer surfaces and finishing processes. Generally, finishing work is begun in the center of the shape and moved outward using a supporting tool face closely matching the form's inner curve. On areas requiring more precise refinement, smaller tools should be used. The work may be set up for final detailing as discussed in the next section on repoussé.

3–13 Barbara Anne Nilaūsen, Hollow Form #2. *Pin of sterling and Delrin formed over dapping punches and stakes. The form was conceived to fit the body in a manner that allows the tendrillike element to curve along the breast. Courtesy of the artist. Photo by Stephanie Karakas.*

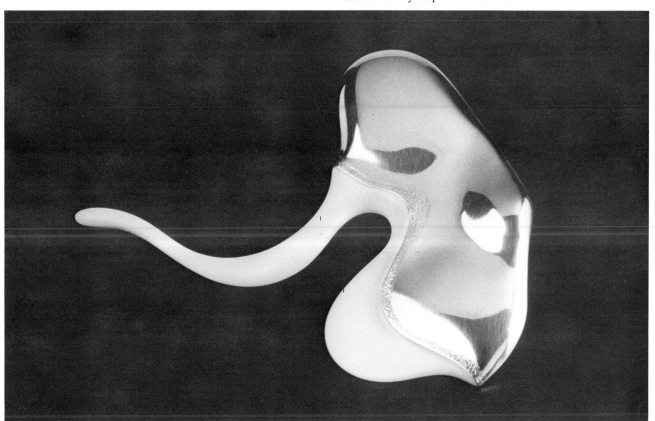

REPOUSSÉ

Repoussé offers the means to create lightweight relief forms in relatively thin sheet metal. Repoussé is that work performed from the back of a piece causing relief to develop on the front. This may be a bit confusing since typically most jewelers work a piece front and back using the same tools and actions on both sides. Strictly speaking, the process of working the front of a relief is referred to as chasing.

The following general points are necessary to create small relief forms in jewelry.

1 In practice, relief work might be thought of as a scaled-down sinking process. Consideration regarding overstress and annealing the workpiece are the same.
2 Because the work is relatively small in scale, the sheet metal can be held secure in a pitch bowl or over the end grain of a wooden block.
3 With a hammer and punches with variously shaped faces, selective depressions are made in sheet metal. The resulting depressions correspond in cross section to the shape of the punch faces (figure 3–14).

Repoussé Tools

Punches   Most commercially produced repoussé and chasing punches are approximately ¼ inch thick and range from 3 to 6 inches in length, and are made of square, round, or rectangular tool steel rod stock. Punch faces are hardened and polished and shaped to create specific effects: doming, cutting, patterning, delineating, and texturing. A jeweler may purchase any number of punches needed for a particular task. Some craftworkers prefer to make their own tools as specific needs arise. This technique is discussed in Appendix 3. Punches may be categorized by basic function into four groups: matting, modeling, curving, and tracing (figure 3–15). Along with the specialized punches, a standard set of

3–15

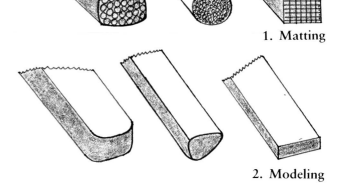

1. Matting

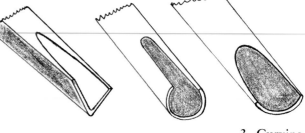

2. Modeling

3. Curving

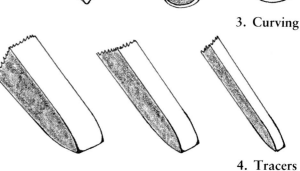

4. Tracers

3–14   *Repoussé and chasing punches.*

3–16 *Dapping punches.*

steel dapping punches offers a wide range of form possibilities. These are excellent tools for forming broad domed areas and may also be held in a vise and used as small stakes (figure 3–16).

Hammers For shallow or finely detailed work, chasing hammers are ideal. They are designed in shape and weight for light, delicate work (figure 3–17). A good, inexpensive substitute for a general repoussé and chasing hammer is the local hardware store's 4-ounce ball-peen hammer. The less expensive, cast ball peens have softer faces so are not as apt to deflect or slip on impact with a punch. Hammers are used with a rhythmic series of blows while the worker focuses on the work surface. This sounds more difficult than it really is. After just a few taps, the hand and hammer seem to work automatically as the punch is moved along. Be sure to rest the punch-holding hand solidly, near the work.

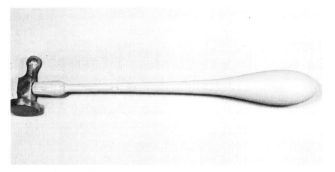

3–17 *Chasing hammer.*

Pitch Bowl Hemispherically shaped cast-iron pitch bowls may be purchased from most jewelry supply firms. Sizes range from 5 to 8 inches in diameter. Some suppliers offer bowls partially filled with cement or lead to add weight and stability. The remainder of the bowl contains pitch whose adhesive and resilient qualities make it ideal as a work surface in which to set the metal. Suppliers also sell doughnut-shaped rubber or leather bases designed to cradle the bowl at any angle needed (figure 3–18). For those not wishing to purchase a commercial bowl, a used cast-iron frying pan is a good alternative. Thin pie pans are not recommended because they lack rigidity and allow the pitch to crack and break away. For work too large for a bowl or pan, a suitable container may be constructed with ½- or ¾-inch plywood.

Preparing Pitch
Pitch is a by-product or residue in the distillation of crude oil, coal, and conifer wood sap. In its pure state, it is too hard and brittle for the jeweler's purposes. Other ingredients are added to give it the qualities needed.

3–18 *Iron pitch bowl and base.*

Ready-mixed pitch can be purchased in several grades tailored to the jeweler's need. The various grades generally range in degrees of hardness and resilience. The cost of petroleum products is reason enough to purchase raw pitch and blend your own mixtures. A typical mixture is:

> 6 to 8 parts pitch
> 1 to 2 parts oil
> 8 to 11 parts fine pumice

Increasing or decreasing the proportions of the three ingredients will result in a harder or softer work surface. The adhesive quality will also change.

Only heavy oils should be used, those which vaporize slowly and have low volatility. Rendered animal fat, linseed oil, vegetable oil, and motor oil are a few possibilities. Instead of pumice, plaster of paris or brick dust may be substituted.

To mix the ingredients, slowly heat the raw pitch in an old pan until the pitch is molten and then stir in the pumice and oil. The pitch must be heated slowly to avoid boiling or burning. Some experimentation with varying ratios may be needed to find the ideal mixture. In heating during the working stages, the pitch mixture should be heated with a gentle gas flame. Overheating causes vaporization and burning of the pitch surface which leaves chunks of charred matter in the pitch. After repeated heating during the working process, the mixture will naturally change in quality. Adding a little of one or two of the ingredients usually corrects the composition. Work in a well-ventilated area.

Hollow forms are sometimes worked by first filling them with pitch and then manipulating their structures with hammers and punches. **Special precautions must be taken in removing pitch from these forms. If the opening is smaller than the overall diameter, expansion from heat and gases given off by the contents can create extreme pressure and cause the form to explode or shoot molten pitch from the opening.** To avoid this, the piece can be suspended with the opening down and slowly heated around the opening. The mixing pan can be set beneath the piece to catch the dripping pitch (figure 3–19).

Repoussé Technique

After the pitch has been mixed and poured into a bowl or other suitable container, these basic steps can be followed.

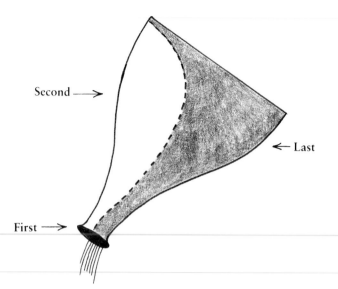

Second →

← Last

First →

3–19   *The order in which pitch is evacuated from a hollow vessel.*

1 When feasible, layout of the general shape should be drawn or lightly scratched within a rectangular or square piece of sheet metal, 18 to 24 gauge. Eventually the finished form will be cut from the square or rectangle (figure 3–20). Using a piece larger than needed provides increased adhesion and a secure workpiece. Figure 3–21 illustrates a corner of the square sheet bent with pliers. Corners serve as locks in the pitch. On other shapes, the outer edges can be slotted with a saw and then bent to lock.

2 Using a soft flame, slowly heat the pitch until its surface is smooth and soft. This may be tested with a length of coat hanger wire or an old pair of tweezers. At this point the annealed workpiece is set into place and allowed to settle just enough for a little pitch to flow over the edge of the sheet metal. If the pitch is too hot, the metal may submerge completely. Too little heat and the workpiece will not adhere. The movement of pitch around the edges can be retarded with cold water in the event of overheating. With practice, recognition of the correct heat will be a simple matter. Some metalsmiths heat the pitch until pliable, set the metal in place, and push pitch around the edges with the tweezers.

3 Pitch must cool completely before work begins. Warm pitch does not have the resilience necessary for repoussé and usually work will bend or sink through the surface.

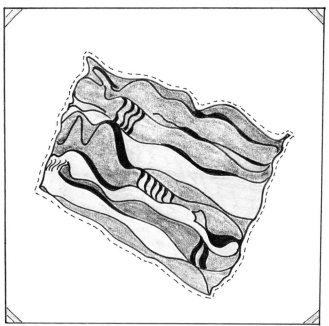

3–20 *Tooled shape is cut from within a square sheet.*

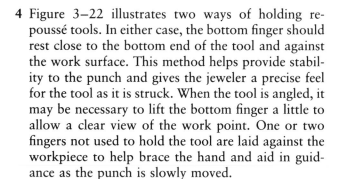

3–21 *Corner locks.*

3–22 *Two common methods of holding repoussé/chasing punches.*

4 Figure 3–22 illustrates two ways of holding repoussé tools. In either case, the bottom finger should rest close to the bottom end of the tool and against the work surface. This method helps provide stability to the punch and gives the jeweler a precise feel for the tool as it is struck. When the tool is angled, it may be necessary to lift the bottom finger a little to allow a clear view of the work point. One or two fingers not used to hold the tool are laid against the workpiece to help brace the hand and aid in guidance as the punch is slowly moved.

5 At this point, the novice should work on a practice piece to become familiar with the position of the hand and tool while striking with the hammer. The practice should incorporate areas worked with a variety of punches and surfaces stretched to differing depths. Hold each tool perpendicular to and angled against the metal and observe the tool marks that occur. The proper rate of hammer blows and tool movement will quickly become apparent. Punch marks should overlap one another almost as if planishing (see chapter 5). Rather than repeatedly lifting

the tool, the punch is advanced by slowly sliding it over the metal. The rate and rhythm of hammer blows also resemble those used in planishing.

6 Once familiar with the capability of each punch and the action of the hammer, set the work in place. Generally, those areas to be worked the deepest should be stretched first. On relatively deep and broad areas, the hammer's peen end may be used directly in order to quickly form the initial shape and depth. Remember, the metal is being thinned and will tear if pushed too much. At the first indication of resistance in the metal, remove the piece and anneal it. If the design allows, time may be saved by working each area of the design at least once before the metal is removed for annealing.

7 It will be necessary at times to remove and reset the metal. Play a soft flame over the entire piece until pitch along the edge is softened and then lift out the workpiece with tweezers. If the repoussé is complete and is to remain work-hardened, soak the piece in kerosene to remove the clinging pitch. If the metal needs further work, set it on an old firebrick and heat until annealed. While annealing, surface pitch will burn away, leaving a white ash. The ash will flake away with a water quench.

3–23 Marcia Lewis, Aquatic Form #3. *Brooch of silver and garnets using repoussé, chasing, and construction. The artist's expertise in applying the repoussé and chasing techniques allowed her to execute this exciting literal interpretation of an aquatic form in lightweight sheet metal. Courtesy of the artist. Photograph by Lewis-Hunter.*

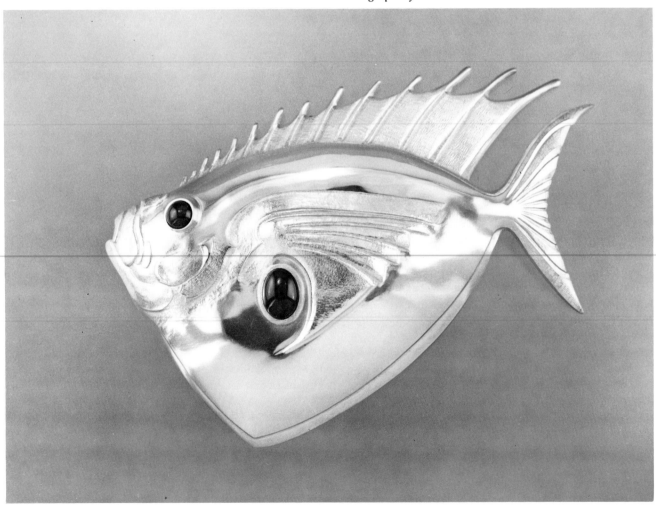

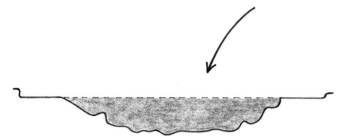

3–24 *Filling a back recess with pitch.*

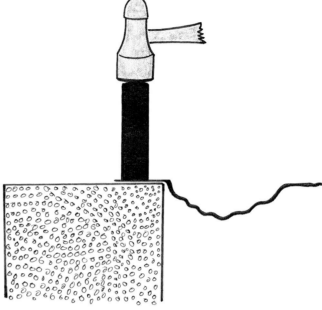

3–25 *The correction of edge distortions with a punch.*

8 In reversing the work, its shape is quite often composed of deep areas of undercuts or domes developed earlier. Before resetting, lay the piece face down (figure 3–24) and slowly pour pitch onto the back area to fill the deeply depressed areas. Allow the piece to cool. Proceed as in step 2. Prefilling depressions precludes the possibility of air spaces and the denting or collapse of these areas in subsequent work.

9 Bends or distortions along the outer edges can be corrected in either of two ways: using a modeling punch over a wooden block (figure 3–25) or a wooden mallet over an anvil's edge (figure 3–26). Minor irregularities can be adjusted by hand or carefully with pliers.

10. Finishing is of course a personal choice that may include one or more of the previously discussed methods. If there is a need to planish, a dapping punch, repoussé tool, or small hammer face might be used as stakes.

Relative to the metal's thickness, a jeweler working the front and back of a form can create extreme contrast in high and low areas. Domes worked inward can be reversed and their centers pushed back out (figure 3–27). Details and dimensional lines can be accentuated by using smaller tools held at a slight angle.

Some jewelers fail to take advantage of the unique possibilities of repoussé. Too often, results are overworked, shallow, bimorphic forms or superficial explorations involving a lumpy dome. Just a glance at historical relief and repoussé work should suggest what can be accomplished in terms of the interplay of positive and negative surfaces.

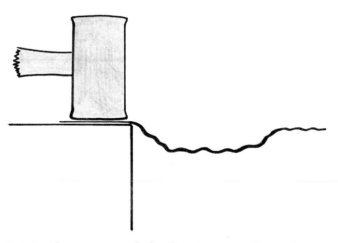

3–26 *The correction of edge distortions over the anvil.*

3–27 *Reversed dome form.*

CHASING

In a strict technical sense, chasing means to ornament by engraving or embossing. As previously mentioned, chasing is often used in conjunction with repoussé, generally to further define or delineate the front of a piece. Chasing may also be used on solid forms to define, indent, or carve areas. Crude castings are often cleaned up and detailed by chasing. Matting punches are commonly used as embossing tools to create interesting patterns and background areas. Physically, the processes of chasing and repoussé are the same.

For chasing on sheet metal, the supporting surface should be relatively hard. A resilient backing will allow the metal to bend or stretch, countering your efforts.

With a hard backing the metal can be embossed or compressed with little, if any, stretch or distortion to the workpiece. Some jewelers advocate the use of pitch bowls as supporting devices, but in my experience pitch has been too resilient or, when mixed hard with little or no resilience, it becomes brittle and the work invariably breaks away. Pitch works well for hand engraving because the tool's pressure is steady and usually parallel to the support surface.

Steel blocks, stakes, or anvil faces work well as a backing. Small pieces can be held and stabilized over these steel forms by the same hand guiding the chasing tool, although this tends to be awkward. Figure 3–28 shows several alternate holding devices. Variations of these can be easily fabricated.

3–28 *Holding devices.*

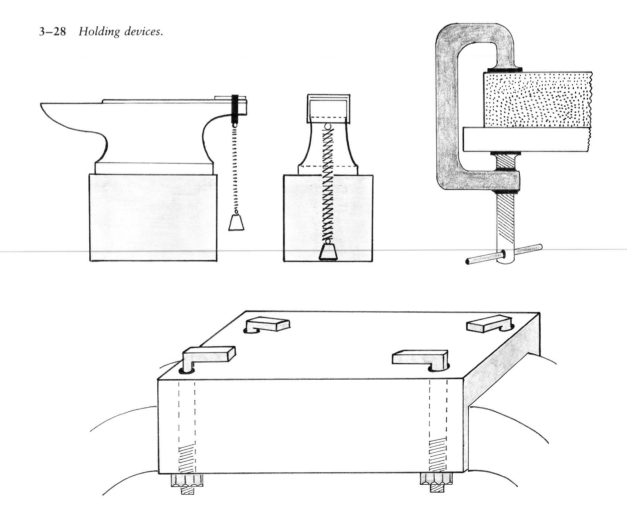

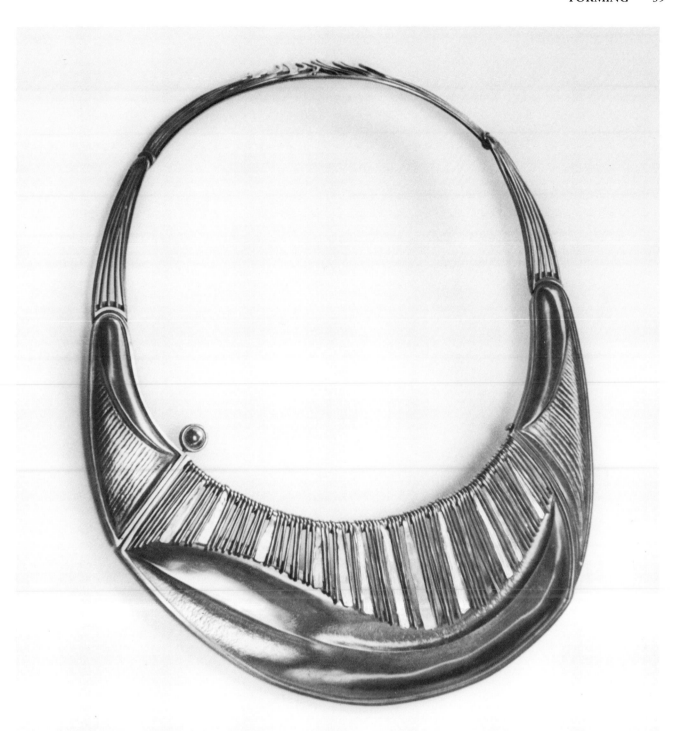

3–29 Frances Pickens. *Chased and constructed neckpiece of oxidized sterling and gold. Chased lines were an effective means of achieving a visual transition between the front verti-cal wire elements and the wire neckpiece sections. Courtesy of the artist. Photograph by Francis Haar.*

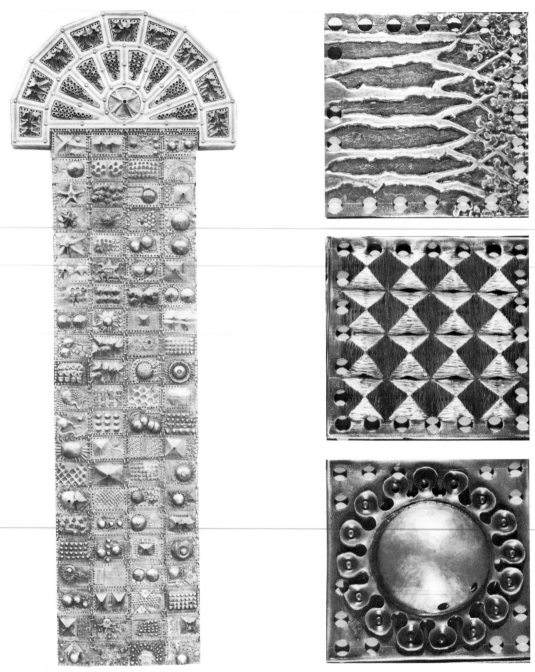

3–30 **David Luck,** Sideshow Sorcery. *Copper, nickel silver, and brass. Courtesy of the artist.*

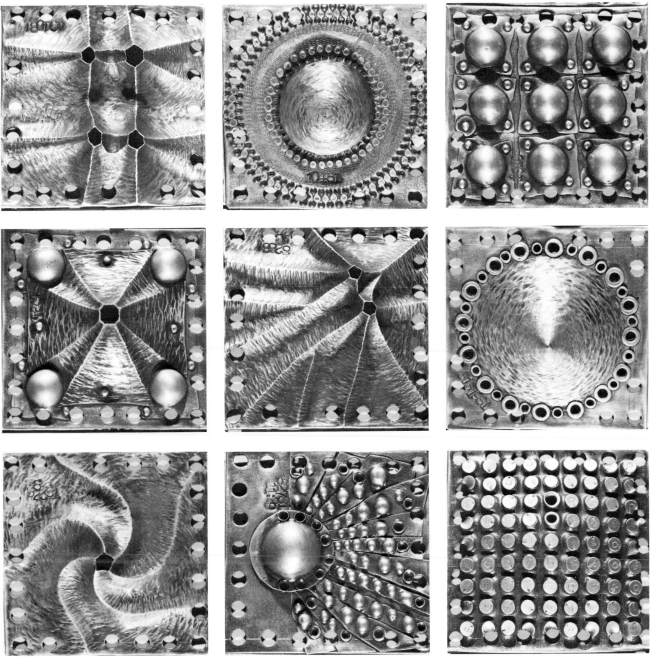

3–31 *Examples of various surface treatments employed in the work by David Luck. The pieces were formed by a combination of hammer forming, dapping, embossing, repoussé, perforation, and appliqué with rivets. Each sheet was worked over an anvil, metal stake, wood, die, or air. Pitch was not used. Courtesy of the artist. Photographs by the artist.*

3–32 David Benedek, Bracelet 6. *Repoussé and constructed in 14-karat gold and sterling. Besides the obvious visual effect achieved by the repoussé and chased lines, the tooled sides become physically strengthened. Courtesy of the artist. Photograph by Bob Hanson.*

3–33 Thelma Coles, Enduring Production. *Bracelet of silver and gold; stamped and constructed. Courtesy of the artist.*

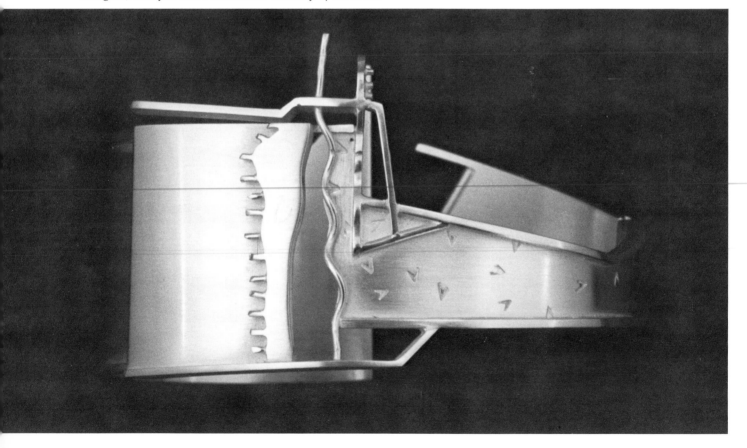

DOMING

A steel dapping block is an effective tool in making precise hemispherical or domed pieces. Jewelry suppliers offer several types of blocks (figure 3–34). The most versatile is a 2½-inch polished steel cube having hemispherical depressions of varying sizes in each of its six faces. Steel dapping punches (figure 3–16) in sizes corresponding approximately to those of the block are used to sink circular discs of sheet metal into the block's depression. In practice, the punch and block become a male and female die. Flat sheet metal discs are cut to fit just inside the appropriate depression. The disc is centered in the depression and struck in its center with a dapping punch whose diameter is slightly smaller than the block's depression. The punch's diameter must be such as to allow for the disc's thickness, otherwise the ball of the punch will not fit properly. The use of a punch that is too large can mar the block's edge or the face of the punch.

Half spheres may be formed from discs having a radius approximately one-third greater than that of the depression being used. After dapping inward to achieve the initial depth, the disc should be tilted slightly so that

3–34 *Steel dapping block.*

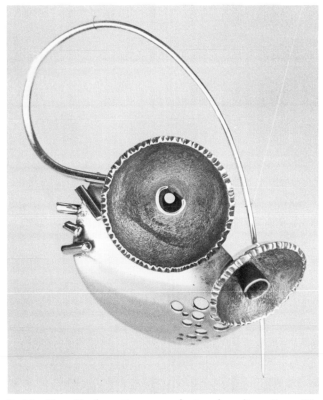

3–35 **Ron Verdon.** *Constructed pin of sterling silver. The graceful, sweeping curve of the pin stem balances the curved and dapped pieces making up the body of the form. Courtesy of the artist.*

its edge is below the top edge of the depression. Then the punching is continued until the disc has been punched around the entire edge. Minor marring may occur that is easily corrected with a file and emery cloth. Semispheres may also be developed by punching a disc into successively smaller depressions. Dome forms can be created directly in sheet metal by laying the sheet over a depression and dapping inward. Again, be careful to select the proper dapping punch.

Along with the block and punches, many jewelers enjoy the convenience of a disc cutter (figure 3–36). Most cutters can cut discs ranging from ⅛ to 1 inch in diameter. One end of the disc-cutting die punch is precision-machined and hardened to impart a shearing action against the sheet metal as it is struck squarely with a hammer. The cutter should be backed with a piece of hardwood or annealed copper to prevent possible dam-

3–36 *Disc cutting set.*

age to the cutting punch. Double-check to ensure that the correct end of the punch is placed down, otherwise the hammer blow will damage the cutting face. Discs up to 16 gauge may be cut from nonferrous metal.

DIE FORMING

Die forming is the process of using similarly shaped positive and negative dies to press relatively thin sheet metal into dimensional forms. The use of dies is not new. Early dies were carved from stone or wood and the metal pressed into or around the form. Industry has used die forming for many years to produce countless decorative and useful items. The Statue of Liberty is perhaps the world's largest artistic undertaking. Created in sheet metal, each component of the statue was hand formed in 3/32-inch copper sheet over or into large dies.

The recent revival in die forming by jewelers and metalsmiths has brought forth an exciting array of objects. For our purposes, die forming is an expedient process permitting the creation of work difficult to achieve by other means. A major advantage of this process is the production of multiple mirror images. Contemporary metalworkers have borrowed an old technique and adapted modern materials and tools to create objects reflecting our times.

Two types of die forming are presented here. Many possible die forming uses are left for the creative jeweler to explore.

Outline or Silhouette Die

Figure 3–37 illustrates this rather simple yet effective die frame. The die's inner edge corresponds to the outer edge of the desired form. Workpieces are given dimension or depth by stretching selected areas with a hammer or punch. Frames can be made of many materials: hardwood, masonite, aluminum, brass, steel, nylon. The inner shapes are cut away with a coping saw, hand saw, or jeweler's saw. If a band saw is used, it may be necessary to fill or plug the saw's cut between the outer edge and the cutaway shape. Care should be taken in cutting the inner edge so that when the workpiece is sunk, its outer edge will be crisp and well defined. Forming is begun by cutting out a piece of sheet metal, 16 to 24 gauge, whose

3–37 *Silhouette die.*

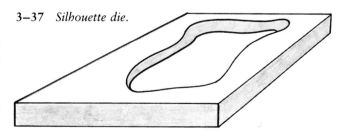

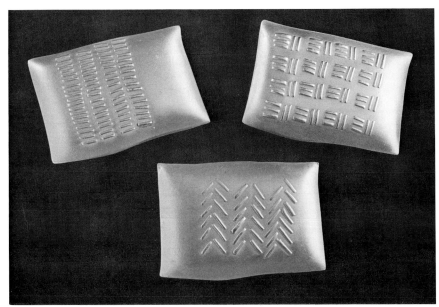

3–38 Jan Yager, Silver Pillow Pins: Whomp and Puff Series 1981. *Fine silver; embossed, pressed, and constructed. Courtesy of the artist.*

3–39 Jan Yager, Scarab Pendant: Whomp and Puff Series 1981. *Embossed, pressed, and constructed of silver. The artist's choice of material and techniques resulted in a soft, billowy form with crisp, linear detail. Courtesy of the artist.*
In 3–38 and 3–39 surface details were first stamped and embossed into pierced and machined sheets of steel. The forms were backed by lead and struck with a drop hammer. The detailed sheets were then puffed or pressed outward in steel, aluminum, and tempered masonite silhouette dies. A rubber backing may be used to back the metal as it is pressed to shape. The negative dies define the forms' contours.

silhouette corresponds to that of the desired form with approximately 1 inch extra left on all sides. The extra material serves as a flange to be secured to the die frame. The flange's size and shape can be varied to suit individual designs. Many jewelers take advantage of the flange by incorporating it into the finished work. The workpiece is held to the die with nuts and bolts placed through the flange and frame.

Dies can be placed in a vise or clamped to the bench top while being worked. Metal is forced inward from the edge and worked gradually toward the center. Keep in mind that the metal is stretching so it will have to be annealed periodically. Hammering or punching is best accomplished in a systematic path of overlapping blows around the workpiece from the edge inward (figure 3–40). Maximum depth of a form can be roughly calculated as equal to the radius of the workpiece.

Combination Male/Female Dies

A male/female die may be thought of as a positive and negative form that when sandwiched around and pressed against sheet metal, develops a duplicate of the dies used. Commercially, this process is used to manufacture items ranging from knives and forks to auto bodies. Industrial dies are usually made of steel, which allows them to be used many times under extreme hydromechanical pressure.

Again, today's jewelers have adapted an industrial process to fit the needs of their craft. A simple home-

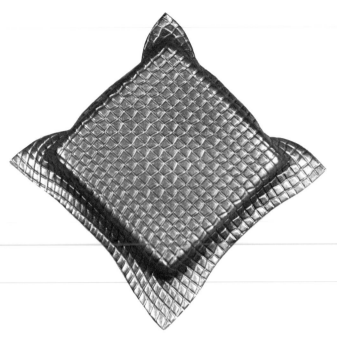

3–41 Ann Wright. *Pin of copper. Roller embossed and die formed.*

made hydraulic press or vise will supply the force needed to shape the sheet into jewelry-size forms. Jewelers have been quite inventive in adapting many materials to build die units. A major consideration in selecting materials is that they be durable enough to withstand the pressure required to stretch the sheet metal. To make the effort worthwhile, dies should be strong enough to create multiples of a piece. Figure 3–42 illustrates one method of constructing aluminum dies.

Additional information on die forming may be found in several of the articles and texts listed in the bibliography.

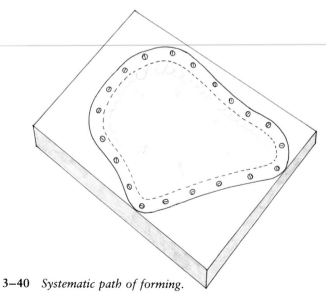

3–40 *Systematic path of forming.*

3–42 *Aluminum dies. Provided by Ann Wright.*

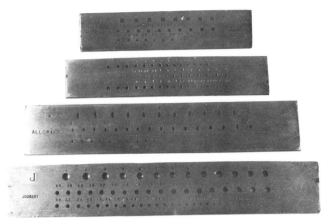

3–43   *Drawplates.*

3–44   *Correct mounting of the drawplate.*

DRAWING WIRE

Wire can be drawn, or reduced in thickness, through a drawplate. This tool is a rectangular steel plate ¼ to ½ inch thick with graduated sizes of tapered holes through which wire, rod, and tubing can be formed into successively smaller diameters. While wire and tubing are readily available in many sizes and shapes, it is often necessary to draw down a larger size to fit the need at hand. By pulling the metal through decreasingly smaller holes in the plate, the craftworker is able to literally see and feel the material compress and stretch (figure 3–45). The steps in drawing wire follow.

1 File one end of the wire to a point starting about 1 inch from the end. Shaping the end is made easier by first filing a small groove along the edge of the bench pin and laying the end of the wire in the groove while filing. Use a 6- or 8-inch flat file to shape heavy wire and a needle file on fine wire. It is a serious mistake to use a sander or grinding wheel to shape wire. The possible entanglement of the wire in the machine makes it a gamble not worth taking.
2 Drawplates should be mounted firmly in a vise bolted to a secure bench or work table. The plate is set in the vise horizontally with the line of holes approximately ¼ inch above the vise jaws. Mounting the plate vertically or with the holes too far above the jaws can cause the plate to flex slightly and make the task more difficult.

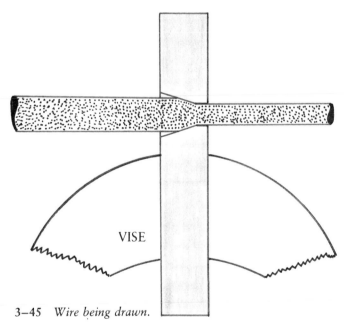

3–45   *Wire being drawn.*

3 Drawing is begun by first trial fitting the wire into holes until resistance is felt. Holding the tongs with the curved end around the side of the hand, firmly grasp the wire's pointed end and pull steadily. Rubbing a little paraffin or beeswax along the wire will provide lubrication. Continue drawing the wire through successively smaller holes until the desired size is attained. To reach the correct diameter, it may be necessary to repoint the end of the wire. While

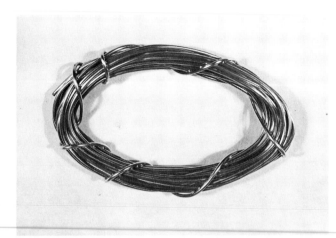

3–46 *Wire coiled in preparation for annealing.*

heat evenly over the coil, being cautious that loose ends or individual strands of the coil are not overheated. To anneal thick coils you may find it easier to heat one side, then turn the coil over and anneal the other side.

5 Annealed wire is easily straightened by tightening one end in the vise and taking a firm, steady pull on the other end with the draw tongs. A slight stretching will be felt as the wire straightens.

TUBE MAKING

Jewelers occasionally have a need for tubing in sizes not available through suppliers. Some jewelers simply enjoy the satisfaction of making their own tubing. From a technical standpoint, the major advantage of handmade tubing is that generally its wall thickness is greater than that of its commercial counterpart. This feature makes it especially well suited for hinges and findings.

Starting with annealed sheet metal, 18 to 24 gauge, cut it to shape as shown in figures 3–47 and 3–48. The width of the strip should be approximately 3 times greater than the desired finished diameter. The end of the strip is tapered as shown, the sides parallel and filed clean.

pulling, be sure the wire is drawn perpendicular to the plate; otherwise it is pinched through the hole and may break.

4 Elongation and compression may make it necessary to anneal the wire. Heating a length of wire is best accomplished by first wrapping it into a tight coil around the palm of the hand and using a few inches of one end to wrap along the coil to prevent its opening while being heated (figure 3–46). Lay the coil over pumice stones and heat with a soft flame. Play the

3–47 *Flat strip prepared for tubing. Strip will be formed to a furrowlike section.*

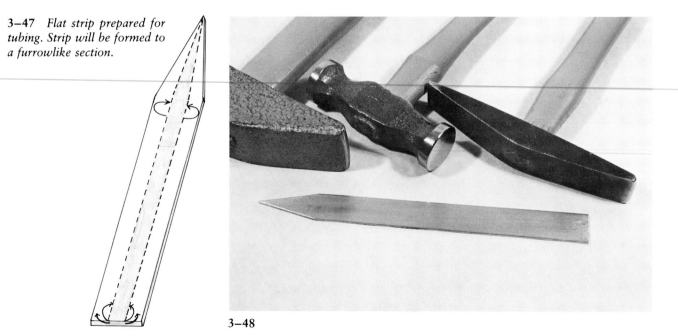

3–48

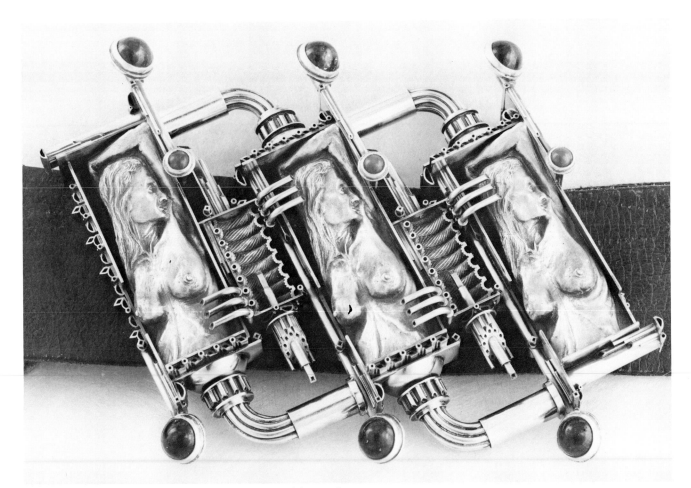

3–49 Richard Mawdsley, Goneril, Regan, Cordelia. *Belt buckle of sterling with lapis lazuli and coral; constructed and cast. While tubing is obviously a wise choice because of its light weight and strength, the artist has creatively applied it to frame the cast forms with a variety of detail and contrast. Courtesy of the artist.*

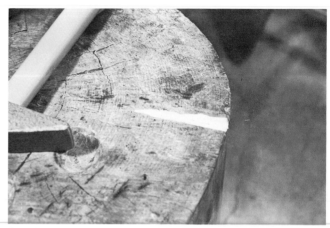

3–51

3–50 Harold O'Connor, Heat Exchanger. *Constructed brooch of 18-karat gold with ruby. Courtesy of the artist.*

Forming is begun with the strip held over a V groove filed into a hardwood block or tree stump (figure 3–51). A narrow cross-peen hammer is used to carefully form the work along its axis as the piece is moved through the groove (figure 3–52). The aim in hammering is to develop a furrowlike cross section that, when pulled through a drawplate, will become round (figures 3–53 and 3–54). Continue using the cross-peen hammer all along the inside to gradually bring the side edges closer together (figure 3–55). When the cross-peen no longer fits, the form can be further closed from the outside with the rounded face of a planishing hammer (figures 3–56 and 3–57). End-to-end distortion can be corrected by annealing, and it can be bent straight by hand. Close the strip's entire length, including the tapered portion (figures 3–58 and 3–59). When the sides almost touch, the tube is ready to be drawn.

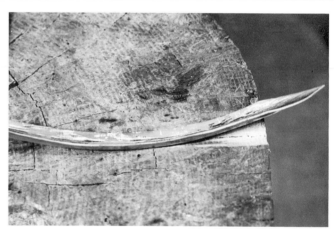

3–54

Pulling a tube is similar to drawing wire. The precut taper avoids the need to file a tapered end, however. As before, trial fit the tube through the holes in the draw-plate until a slight resistance is felt. If the finished seam must remain straight, a thin knife blade or piece of hard brass can be inserted in the seam and braced against the back of the plate. As the tube is pulled, the inserted blade acts as a guide, steering the seamed area straight through the hole. Any end-to-end curve can be straightened by hand or gently hammered on the anvil after a final annealing.

3–57

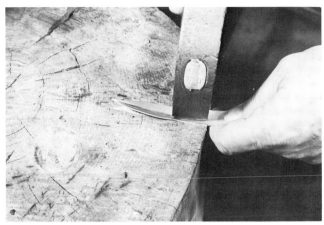

3–52

3–53

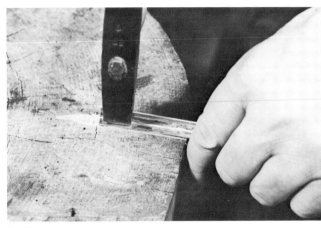

3–55

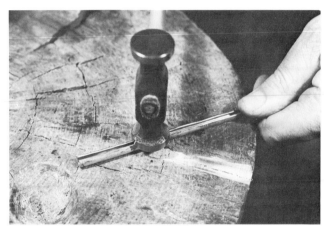

3–56

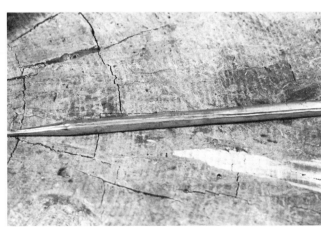

3–58

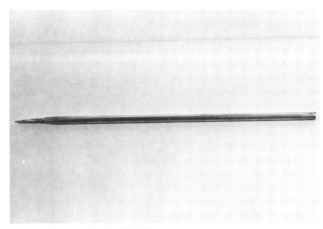

3–59

3–60 *Draw frame.*

Those wishing to draw heavy-gauge wire and tubing might require the use of a draw frame (figure 3–60). A drawplate is fixed at one end and the tongs attached to a chain or belt that is hand cranked through a set of reduction gears. A suitable alternative can be fashioned over a work table with a section of angle iron at one end, as the drawplate fixture, and a small hand-powered cable winch at the other (figure 3–61).

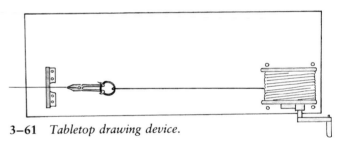

3–61 *Tabletop drawing device.*

3–62 Ann Owens-Stone, Linear Departures #1. *Brooch of sterling, gold, nickel, and steel; marriage of metals and construction. Courtesy of the artist.*

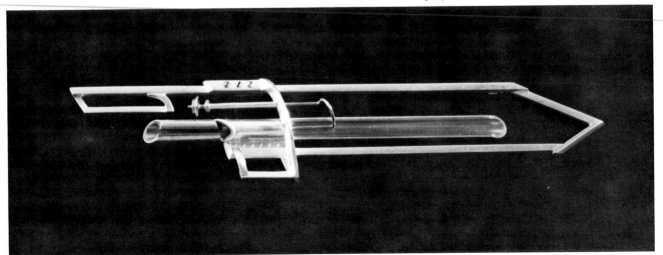

FORMING CYLINDERS AND CONES

To the novice, the forming of small cylinders and cones can be mystifying. Little more than the techniques thus far discussed is needed. The creation of small cylinders is relatively simple and, in many instances, nothing more than pliers and a soldering torch are required. (Refer to the section on bending.) Those requiring thick metal can be formed from the inside with the cross-peen hammer as discussed in the section on tubing. In any case, the cylinder is first rough formed until the edges touch evenly, they are then soldered and the cylinder trued over a ring mandrel or small steel rod. Some jewelry makers mistakenly think it is necessary to have the cylinder perfectly round prior to soldering. Rounding is easier with the ends joined; otherwise the cylinder becomes springy and may be difficult to solder. On very small cylinders, the round jaw of a pair of needle-nose pliers can serve as a mandrel. After rounding, excess solder is filed away. Figure 3–63 shows the fitting of a butt joint. In some instances iron binding wire may be needed to hold a joint closed. A small tab of paper between the wire and seam leaves an ash that prevents solder from flowing onto the binding wire.

Figure 3–65 illustrates the graphic layout of a cone pattern. After the shape is cut from sheet metal (16 to 24 gauge) and annealed, the two straight edges are trued with a flat file. The small end of the cone should not be cut to a sharp point. Leave this slightly flattened (figure 3–66). A point end is difficult to close.

Using the small cross-peen hammer once again, the basic forming step is identical to that of tubing. This time greater care must be taken to avoid excessive denting of the metal. Unlike in tube construction, the drawplate cannot be relied on to remove surface irregularities. With the cone bent and edges soldered, the form may be refined. Round and half-round plier jaws secured in a vise can be used as minimandrels to planish

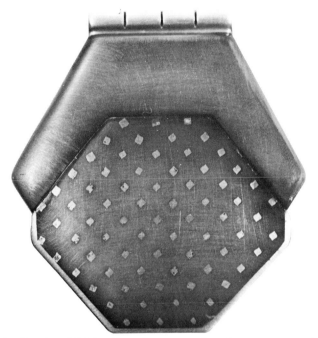

3–64   Ann Wright. *Pin of copper and sterling; constructed, die formed, and solder inlaid.*

3–63 *Butt joint. Mating surface should be 90 degrees to the top and bottom plane.*

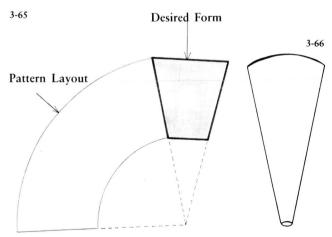

3–65 *Simple cone layout. The desired shape is extended approximately three times.*
3–66 *Cone form.*

tiny cones. For those fortunate enough to have a well-fitting mandrel or stake, finishing is only a matter of smoothing the cone with a mallet or planishing hammer and filing or emerying minor irregularities. Completion of the form without a mandrel is a little more difficult. Some workers fill the roughly shaped piece with pitch and use its resilience as a mandrel. In using this approach, the cone is laid on a flat wooden block or anvil face and gently worked with a planishing hammer. Blows should overlap concentrically as the cone is slowly turned. Continuing this will gradually round the form at least to the point where minor bumps can quickly be filed away. An alternative that I generally prefer when a mandrel is not at hand is to planish the work "over air." While slowly turning the cone over the anvil's face, the piece is lightly planished with no inside support. This must be done carefully to avoid the cone's collapse. Regardless of the forming method used, finishing is generally a matter of routine filing, emerying, and buffing. Figure 3–67 illustrates several cone variations.

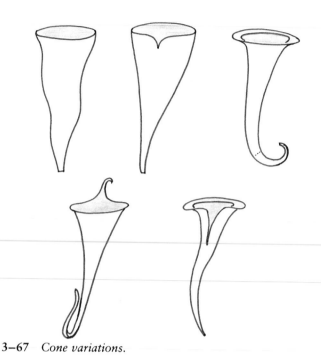

3–67   *Cone variations.*

3–68   **Hannelore Gabriel.** *Constructed pin of sterling and copper. The technique of cylinder construction may be employed in many ways in jewelry making. Here the artist has incorporated cylinder elements to visually carry over the curving, yet crisp opposing forms. Courtesy of the artist.*

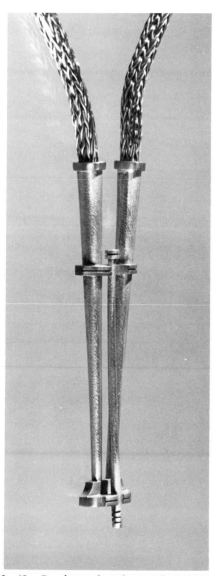

3–69 *Pendant of sterling and copper; woven, constructed, and file textured. Photograph by Peter Krumhardt.*

3–70 **Laurie Peters.** *Necklace of sterling and natural crystal using hollow construction. The segmented hollow cones make the piece lightweight and give it an overall visually pleasing form. Courtesy of the artist.*

TWISTING WIRE AND ROD

Twisting is an often overlooked means of transforming simple linear elements into visually complex and rhythmic decorative components. Single or multiple strands of wire, rod, and sheet stock can be twisted in infinite patterns. Mixing the sizes, cross sections, and materials further expands the range of possibilities. A finished twist can be drawn through a drawplate or rolled through a mill to further alter its cross section or exaggerate its pattern.

The process of twisting is quick and simple. Strands are first annealed and cleaned. One end or set of ends is fastened in the vise, their lengths are made equal, and the strands are twisted by pliers, a hand vise, hand drill, or vise-grip pliers. Figure 3–71 illustrates the process. A light backward tension is held while twisting. This pre-vents the twist from knotting or buckling. To twist together multiple strands, the process can be facilitated by soldering the tips of the work ends together. This can then be chucked directly in a hand drill.

In addition to direct twists and those generally viewed in the jeweler's realm, a few jewelers have miniaturized twisting techniques heretofore only used by the blacksmith. Reverse twists, basket twists (figure 3–75), and incised rod twists are just a few. For this last twist, a sharp chasing punch or chisel can be used to incise a straight line down the center of each side of a square rod; when twisted, the rod appears as a spiraling network of multiple strands (figures 3–72 and 3–73). Segments can also be filed away from a rod; twisting the rod then produces still more possibilities. This brief example carried further should provide an endless number of possibilities. Figure 3–74 shows a bracelet created by the segmented filing of a round rod.

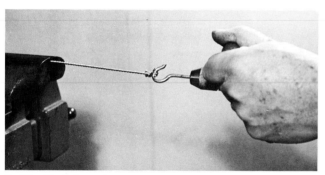

3–71   *Twisting wire.*

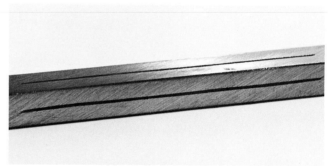

3–72, 3–73   *A shallow line is incised into four sides of a section of square wire and twisted. If the edges are rounded off prior to twisting, the twist area will appear to be made up of four round wires.*

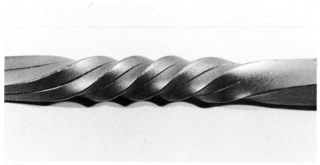

3-73

3–74   *Bracelet of sterling silver. Round rod was filed, twisted, forged, and file textured. This technique results in a twist quite unlike that produced with a square rod.*

3–75 William Fiorini. *Pendant of sterling silver and moonstone; constructed, twisted, and forged. The artist scaled down a blacksmithing technique to provide the focal point of this piece. Six lengths of wire were bound together radially and soldered carefully at the ends. The bundle was twisted one way and then the twist reversed. The reversal opened the basket. Courtesy of the artist.*

CONSTRUCTING FRAMES AND SMALL BOXES

The need to construct precise, hard-edged, boxlike pieces often arises. Applications can range from container jewelry and small square bezels to frames for insetting enamels or laminations. The basic approach detailed here can be used as a springboard for creating many effects. By changing the given dimensions and angles and adapting the general process, an infinite number of applications can be created.

These steps detail the construction of a rectangular frame of 18 gauge metal measuring 1 inch by 1½ inches by ¼ inch.

3–76   Marjorie Schick. *Constructed brooch of sterling silver. Strong linear, frame-like shapes are joined to develop a pleasing dimensional form. Courtesy of the artist. Photograph by Larry Long.*

1   Cut a strip of metal 5½ inches long by ¼ inch wide. Be as accurate as possible to assure the edges are straight and parallel. Avoid bending the strip while sawing and trueing with the file. The metal is less apt to bend if it is not annealed.

2   Use a divider and small square (figure 3–77) to measure and scribe five lines as shown in figure 3–78. It is absolutely essential that the lines be square to the edge and their distance, one to the other, be accurate. Double-check measurements with the divider. A visual check with a ruler is not as precise as physically checking length to length and width to width with the divider. The extra ¼ inch at each end will be removed later.

3   Use a triangular needle file to score each line to approximately seven-eighths its depth. The triangular file offers a relatively sharp cutting edge and its shape provides a flat surface on which the worker may place the index finger as cuts are made. Held in this manner the file is stabilized, resulting in less chance of slip-

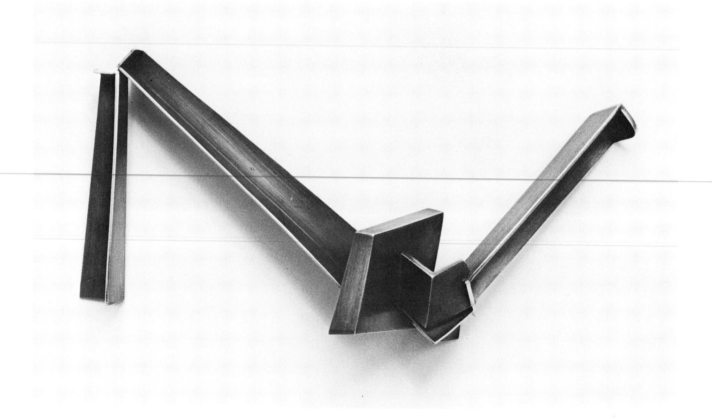

3–77   *Square and divider.*

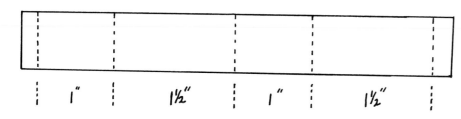

3–78   *Frame layout.*

ping. To further alleviate chance of slipping, start the score at the extreme edge with the file at a steep angle and gradually lower it with each stroke. File carefully to maintain a straight line, otherwise the finished piece will be out of square. The depth of the score is also critical. Too shallow and the bent corners will become rounded; too deep and the corners may break during bending. Occasionally check the work with the square to ensure precision.

4 After the correct scoring depth is reached, use a 6- or 8-inch flat or equaling file to open the upper portion of the scores to 90 degrees (figure 3–79). The objective is to file away just enough metal so that when the corners are bent their angle will be square. Do not allow this second filing to increase the depth of the scored line.

5 Holding the strip flat on the bench, extend the ¼-inch ends over the edge and flex them with pliers until they

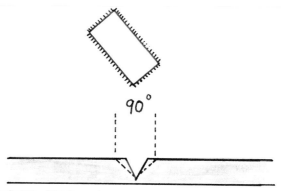

3–79   *Final scoring.*

3–80 *Laminated and constructed pin of sterling, copper, brass, and NuGold.*

break off. File away any remaining burrs. The breakaway ends will form a square corner when joined.

6 The strip can now be bent into a rectangle, corners checked with a square, and minor adjustments made by hand. A length of binding wire can be wrapped around the frame to help retain its shape while soldering. Flux each corner and flow solder through each score. Remove the binding wire and pickle and clean the piece. Any spilled solder can now be filed away.

7 The frame can be finished to suit the particular jewelry piece. A bottom plate or bearing can be added to support stones, enamels, plastic resins, or any number of decorative materials. With little more than an applied top and bottom plate, the frame becomes a box.

FUSING

Fusing should be viewed as a direct and creative way of joining metals without the use of solder. Too often this technique is approached haphazardly or with shallow interest, as shown by resulting pieces that are little more than puddled masses of metal. This need not be the case.

Looked at creatively, this process can go beyond joining scraps of sheet and bits of wire, although these pieces are good for practice or for casting. New shapes can be cut and integrated into unique jewelry forms by carefully joining areas made to touch or overlap.

While great care should be taken, the process is difficult to control with absolute surety. Fusion occurs an instant before pieces melt together. At this instant, a molecular transfer and bonding occurs. The next instant, pieces are molten and dissolve into free-form, organic designs.

Fusing may be completed in the following manner.

1 Clean and flux each piece. Lay the pieces in the desired arrangement over a soldering surface. Soft firebrick is an excellent surface that will aid the process by reflecting some of the heat underneath.

2 Light and adjust the torch as if to solder. Play the flame over one joint at a time, equalizing the heat so that both sides of the joint reach fusion temperature at the same time. A faint shimmer around the joint will indicate the moment of fusion and just beyond, surface textures begin. Quickly remove the torch.

The most exciting qualities of fused forms occur at the fusion point and an instant beyond, when surface textures appear and in some cases edges begin to draw back leaving the basic shape intact. For example, using fine silver over sterling results in a fused piece having relatively crisp upper surfaces over a textured or "orange peel" base. There are many variations of the process, encompassing the spectrum of metals, their fusion points, and their colors. All metals sharing similar alloy components may be fused to one another.

Use scraps at first to experiment and to become used to the torch's effect on several types of metal. Then begin cutting shapes to fit the form desired. You may wish to combine fused areas within formal, constructed, and soldered frameworks. This is just one of many possibilities.

3–81 *Fused fine silver over sterling.*

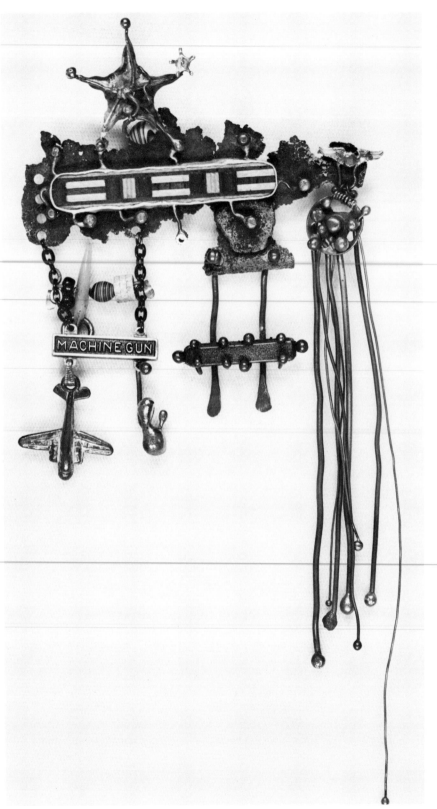

3–82 Joe Eddy Brown, Woodfield Warrior Relic. *Constructed pin of found steel fragment, wood, glass, sterling, plastic, bronze, brass, and bar magnet. Courtesy of the artist. Photograph by James Hagearty.*

CHAPTER FOUR

Surface Enrichment

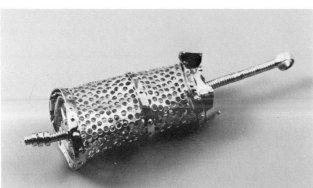

4–1 **Joe Muench.** *Belt buckle of brass. Textured with chasing punches and constructed.*

4–2 **Harold O'Connor,** Ore Breaker. *Constructed pendant of 18-karat yellow and white gold. While this profusely pierced surface provides the artist a literal interpretation of subject matter, it also creates an exciting texture. Courtesy of the artist.*

TEXTURES

Textures offer the jeweler many exciting surface applications to draw upon. There are several good reasons we might choose to embellish metal surfaces. A functional consideration is that textured surfaces are less apt to show the results of normal wear and fingerprinting. From a visual standpoint, texture can be used as contrast, to create an illusion of greater dimension, to soften and dull contrast, or to draw one's focus. Textures may also be used to define formal pattern or compositional elements in harmony with other devices. Regardless of the texture used, its surface should be true to the total form and work in unison with the overall design concept. In other words, texture applied just for the sake of texture is merely a gimmick.

Many of the common textures are created with punches, stamps, dapping tools, chisels, and matting tools. As they are struck with a hammer, their faces leave marks on the metal. Textures can also be applied mechanically using the flexible shaft machine and rotary stones, steel burrs, and drill bits. A small electric stipple machine can make interesting effects (figure 4–3). These tools are available in most hardware stores.

The term surface texture is admittedly broad. Most of the processes covered in this chapter and many from other chapters (hammer textures, inlay, and overlay, for example) are means of producing surface texture. A few examples not covered elsewhere are shown in figure 4–4.

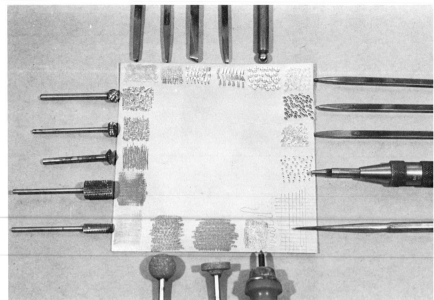

4–3 *Electric stippler.*
4–4 *Tools and related texture samples.*

ROLLER EMBOSSING

Roller printing or embossing has been used by contemporary jewelers for a relatively short time. Industry has applied the technique for many years, producing products ranging from wallpaper to auto components. The basic process is simple, requiring little more than a sheet of metal being pressed and indented by an object under the force of a rolling mill (figure 4–5). Results are positive or negative mirror images of the embossing material. Choices can range from coarse random textures to precise repeat patterns.

Sheet metal patterns used for embossing will eventually distort with rolling. The distortions and elongations, particularly in pierced patterns, become quite interesting and often well suited as decorative surfaces.

A few common-sense precautions must be observed during the embossing process. Too much pressure against the roller assembly can cause gear teeth, roller housings, and even rollers to break. Several trial pieces can be rolled with increasing roller adjustment until the proper setting is determined. Never use corrosive materials against the rollers. Vegetable material may release

4–5 *Rolling mill.*

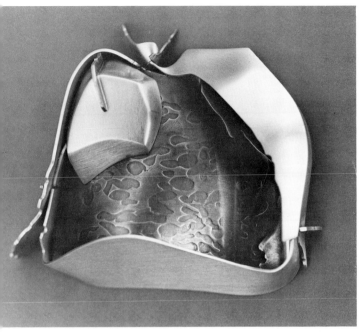

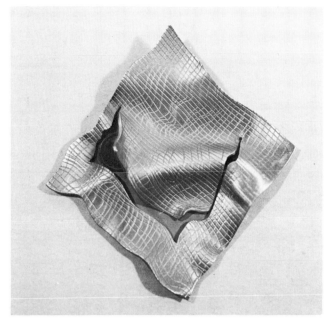

4–8 Ann Wright. *Roller embossed and constructed pin of copper and agate.*

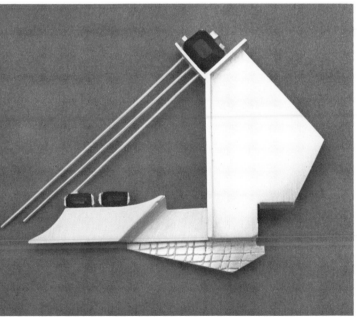

4–6 Lynda Watson-Abbott, Merced River in Winter. *Embossed and constructed sculpture frame of sterling and pewter. Courtesy of the artist.*

4–7 Thelma Coles, Dependent Systems. *Constructed brooch of silver with garnets. A relatively small section of roller embossed metal adds texture to an otherwise smooth form. The textured element's contrast, shape, and size lends balance and greater interest to the overall form. Courtesy of the artist.*

acidic chemicals that, if allowed to remain on the roller, will etch the polished steel. Rollers should be wiped clean and given a light coat of oil. Hard or abrasive material must never be used directly against the rollers. Used improperly, these materials can imprint the roller surfaces. A cushion layer of hard brass can be used above or below questionable materials to protect rollers.

Here is the basic procedure.

1 Almost any material will leave an imprint on annealed, nonferrous metal. Simply stated, sheet metal and a textured medium are sandwiched and rolled through the mill. For example, cloth lace could be placed between two sheets of metal to imprint them simultaneously.

2 Sandwich the medium and sheet metal in the desired arrangement. Open the rollers wide enough to easily slip the stacked pieces through and tighten down until resistance is felt against the rollers. Note and mark the setting index. Open the rollers just enough to remove the stack and then turn the rollers back to the noted index setting. As the rollers are now set, the opening distance roughly corresponds to the thickness of the workpiece, any decrease in the opening

4-9

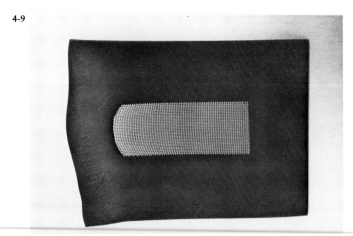

will be the depth to which the print medium will emboss. This is generally dependent upon personal preferences and the thickness of the pieces being used.

3 Several sample pieces can be rolled through, noting the settings of the index before rolling. The rollers may then be readjusted closer for each pass until the embossed depth is correct.

The photographs on this page show examples of printing mediums, embossed metal, and finished jewelry incorporating embossed areas.

4-10

4—9   *Fine-mesh brass screen roll inlaid in copper.*
4—10   *Rolling mill adjustment mechanism and index.*

4—11   *Embossed samples using plastic and metal mesh. Provided by Ann Wright.*

4-11

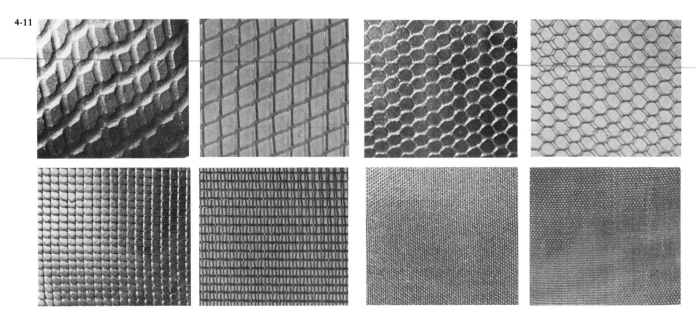

4-12

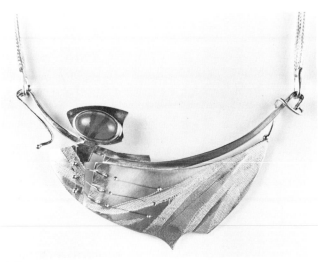

4-13

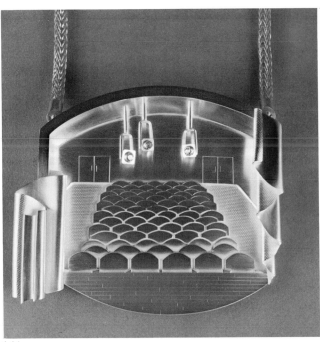

4-14

4–12 Heikki Seppä. *Pin of 14-karat gold; roller embossed, forged, and constructed. Courtesy of the artist.*

4–13 Ann Grundler. *Pendant of sterling and 14-karat gold with Mexican opal; roller embossed and constructed. Courtesy of the artist.*

4–14 Avigail Upin, Looking Out From Within. *Constructed pendant of sterling and fine silver with spinels and loop-in-loop woven chain. Roller embossing softens the ground, giving the "seating" section greater dimension and crispness. Courtesy of the artist.*

ETCHING

Printers and printmakers have used the etching process for many years to selectively create recessed lines in metal plates that are then used in presses to produce multiple images in ink. For our purposes, the technical process is relatively simple.

A piece of metal is painted over with an acid-resistant material (resist) and allowed to dry. Then those areas to be etched are exposed, usually by scratching away the resist. The metal is then submerged in acid and allowed to be corroded or dissolved in the areas in which the resist was scratched away.

As in any instance requiring the use of acids, safety precautions must be observed. Appropriate safety glasses, apron, and rubber gloves should be worn and the work area well vented. Ideally, open acids should be placed immediately in front of or below an exhaust opening to ensure the removal of fumes or vapors. In mixing, always pour acid into water. Reversing this procedure can result in violent and dangerous bubbling and splattering. In the event there is an accident, affected areas of the body should be immediately flushed with cold water and given medical attention. Baking soda should be kept at hand to neutralize acid spills or acids being discarded.

An etch may be very precise, often largely dependent upon the worker's skill in the removal of the resist. Areas are sometimes stopped out ahead of the resist application and removed as the resist dries. This can be accomplished with stencils, contact paper, or tape. These preparatory steps can be a real test of one's drafting and layout skills. Patterned or textured surfaces can be developed in intaglio, a recessed image, or relief, depending on the resist's placement in the background or foreground. Many acid-resistant materials are suitable as resists; the most common are asphaltum and varnish.

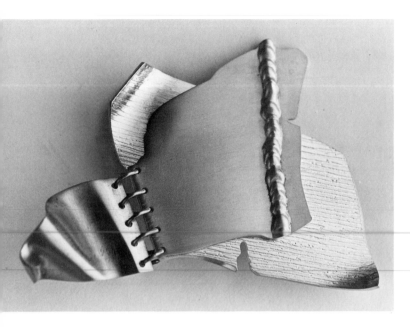

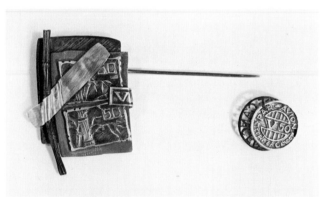

4–15 **Lynda Watson-Abbott,** Joined Like Paper. *Pin of copper and sterling; T.I.G. welded and etched. Courtesy of the artist.*

4–16 **Paula B. Garrett.** *Stick pin/brooch of copper, sterling, Kuromido, 18- and 14-karat gold; etched, roller embossed, carved, and constructed. Etching brings forth a precise, highly detailed image. Courtesy of the artist. Photograph by Cynthia Myrdek.*

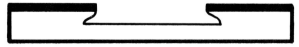

4–17 *Etched undercut.*

These substances dry slowly, however. Automobile spray primer also works well and dries more quickly. This is an area open to individual experimentation. The most important consideration is that the chosen resist be durable enough to withstand the acid's action. Premature lifting or dissolving will permit the acid to attack areas you would otherwise want unaffected.

Acid mixtures (mordants) most commonly used by jewelers are varying ratios of nitric acid and water. Refer to Appendix 2 for information on other mixtures. To etch silver, brass, copper, bronze, and nickel silver, a ratio of one part acid to three or four parts water is sufficient. Observing safety precautions, pour the liquids into a glass tray in quantities great enough to cover the workpiece.

The actual etching process follows these general steps.

1 Before applying the resist, the workpiece should be thoroughly cleaned. Soap and water followed by water and fine pumice powder are usually adequate. If the finished piece is to have its raised surfaces polished, the metal should be buffed now. Mechanical buffing after etching might erase delicate lines or crisp edges.

2 Apply the resist. If liquid brush-on resist is used, better coverage can be achieved by applying several thin coats, allowing each to dry before adding subsequent coats. Be sure to cover the edges and back. Let the resist dry completely. Again, other stop-out devices should be examined. Be leery of paper stencils, lace, and spray, however. The results are often trite or overbearing.

3 Place the prepared workpiece into the mordant and allow the acid to work until the exposed areas are etched to the desired depth. (This, of course, is dependent on the effect or particular design being sought.) Greater depth and undercutting may be required for the eventual application of enamels or inlay materials (figure 4–17). As the acid attacks and dissolves the metal, bubbles will tend to lie over the workpiece and should be gently brushed away with a feather or soft bamboo paint brush. Removal of the bubbles assures a uniform acid bite.

4 After the etch is finished, remove the metal and rinse it. Then burn off the resist or dissolve it with the appropriate solvent. The piece can now be cleaned.

ENGRAVING

Fine, controlled engraving comes only with extensive study and much patient, hands-on practice. Simply the selection and proper preparation of the tools (figure 4–18)—and learning their capabilities—requires considerable time. Even so, the deft manipulation of cutting edges through metal is a skill many jewelers feel is well worth mastering for the singular qualities of the engraved line.

For those wishing a brief look at the graver and particularly its possibilities as a texture device, a few points are offered here.

1　For handwork, gravers are fitted with round or hemispherical-shaped wooden handles. The graver should extend ½ to 1 inch beyond the fingertips during use. New gravers are generally too long for most purposes. They are sized by being set in a vise, tang protruding, and snapped off with a hammer. A tang can be reground. The graver is driven into the handle with a mallet.

2　Graver cutting faces are angled at approximately 45 degrees for general work. Angled less, the cut tends to be deeper and require more force. Angled greater, the cut will be shallow but need less force. The greater angle also results in less material at the apex of the angle, often causing the hardened cutting edge to break off. The cutting end of the tool should be tempered to a straw-yellow color (Appendix 3).

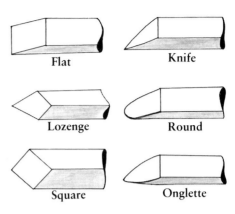

Flat　Knife
Lozenge　Round
Square　Onglette

4–18　*Graver shapes.*
4–19　**Tim McCreight.** *Pocket watch container of sterling silver. Constructed and engraved. Courtesy of the artist.*

4–20　*Gravers.*

4–21　*Graver sharpening fixture.*

3 The initial face angle can be shaped on a belt sander or grinding wheel. A horizontal, water-cooled wheel works best. In any event, the tool should be water cooled to prevent overheating. If the straw-yellow color turns brown, purple, or blue, the graver must be hardened and retempered. A fine Arkansas stone can be used for final shaping and sharpening. Use a light oil as a lubricant on the stone. The angled face must be held parallel along the stone's surface and pushed back and forth to sharpen. Figure 4–21 shows a graver fixture whose adjustment is calibrated in degrees. The fixture's supporting surface must also be parallel to the stone in order to achieve true angles at the graver face. A piece of plate glass or a steel surface plate can be used for this purpose. Keep in mind that this is a simplification of the shaping and sharpening process. The serious engraver treats each graver tip's shape with respect to the specific task. In practice, graver tips are *heeled* or given an additional angle (figure 4–22) and some are *relieved* (refer to Line Inlay, page 183).

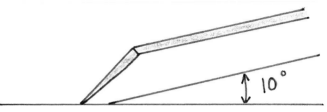

4–22   *Heeled graver angle.*

4 Many of the methods described elsewhere can be used to secure the workpiece. An engraver's ball is traditionally used but is rather expensive. Pitch bowls are adequate for many applications; the work is inset as detailed on page 54. My personal preference is to mount the work over a wooden block set into a swivel table vise. This method frees both hands for tool control and alleviates the worker's need to focus attention and energy toward stabilizing the work surface, as might be needed by a novice using the pitch bowl or engraver's ball.

4–23 **Marcia Lewis,** Lionfish Neckpiece #1. *Constructed of silver, acrylic, and tigereye with forged neckpiece. Engraving, repoussé, and carving produced the undulating lines that give texture and suggest movement. Courtesy of the artist. Photograph by Lewis-Hunter.*

4-24

5 Gravers are held with the handle against the heel of the hand, thumb along the blade and the blade tip firmly against the workpiece (figure 4–24). The index finger lies on top or along the opposite side of the blade and the other fingers stabilize the handle against the hand. To aid in control, the thumb of the opposite hand lies in front and against the thumb of the work hand. Force is put on the graver with the muscles of the hand directing the pressure to drive the tool through the metal. Controlling the tool by this method allows the thumbs to remain stationary, securely braced together on the workpiece as the graver moves past the thumb of the driving hand. At the start of a cut, the thumb tip of the working hand is close to the end of the graver (figure 4–25). The hand muscles force the tool past the thumb as pressure is applied and the graver's face comes to a new position (figure 4–26). The thumb position is changed to continue the cut. After a little practice, instead of inching along, cutting will become a single, smooth action. With this approach mastered, work can begin on the engraver's ball; the work is moved with one hand into the tool's cutting edge. Intricate curves can thus be created.

4-25

4–24   *Hand-held graver position.*
4–25   *Position at the start of a cut.*
4–26   *Position at the end of a cut.*

4-26

For further information related to this section, refer to chapter 8. Additionally, the reader is directed to *The Art of Engraving* by James Meek (Brownell and Sons Publishers) and *The Jewelry Engraver's Manual* by R. Allen Hardy (Van Nostrand Reinhold).

TORCH-INDUCED TEXTURES

Flame-induced textures offer the jeweler a variety of rich metal surfaces. The process is relatively simple and the results may range from subtle wavelike striations or herringbone effects to tiny cratered perforations. Little in the way of preparation or tools is required, only the metal and a torch. Textures develop over the metal's surface as a hot flame is slowly and carefully moved across the metal.

Of the silver-based alloys, one comprised of 180 parts copper and 820 parts fine silver is the most commonly used for torch texturing. Excellent results can be achieved with 18 to 22 gauge sheet. Heat treatment prior to actual texturing causes a melting point differential between the metal's inner and outer structure. The inner material has a lower melting point apparently because of the relatively high copper content. As texturing heat is applied, the inner structure becomes molten. Upon heat removal solidification and shrinkage occur, drawing the outer skin into a reticulation or network of ridged, rippled striations.

Preparation is begun by annealing a sheet of 820 alloy, letting it air cool, and then immersing it into hot pickle. Rinse and repeat this step once. Annealing and acid cleaning develops a thin surface layer of copper-depleted silver and causes a change in the material's inner mass critical in bringing forth the texture. Metallurgical studies indicate that the annealing and cleaning also forms a critical layer of copper oxides just below the outer skin. It is this layer that contains the inner mass upon melting and shrinkage. In light of this, a long process of annealing and cleaning is not as important as previously thought. One or two annealings prior to actual texturing of silver alloys is sufficient to bring forth rich textures.

Place the prepared sheet on a clean, flat soldering surface. Some experimenting with flame size or intensity may be necessary to gain proficiency. On first attempts it is not unusual to burn holes through the metal. These are sometimes incorporated in finished work as creative accidents. A compressed air/natural gas torch seems to perform best for the texturing of silver alloys and 14-karat gold. Adjust the torch to give an oxidizing heat and hold the flame just above the metal until a faint shimmering of the surface occurs. Just as the shimmer appears, move the torch forward slowly and in its trail

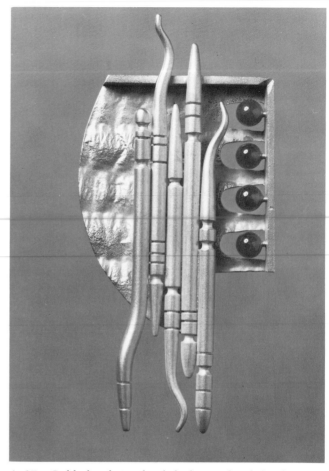

4–27   Gold-plated pin of nickel-silver with jade beads; torch-textured, constructed, and sandblasted. Collection of Bill Rickard. Photograph by Peter Krumhardt.

4–28   Belt buckle of copper and nickel silver; torch-textured, constructed, and sandblasted.

4–29   Belt buckle of brass and nickel silver; torch-textured and constructed. Collection of David Nicholas.

4–30   Torch-textured NuGold.

the cooling metal will contract into a network of ridges. A herringbone texture may be created by moving the torch across the metal in a linear path with subsequent passes opposite one another. Shallow crater or dotlike patterns can be formed by holding the flame in one spot until a shimmer appears and quickly lifting the torch. After gaining familiarity with the surface's reactions, experiment by angling the torch and adjusting the flame's intensity.

4-28

4-29

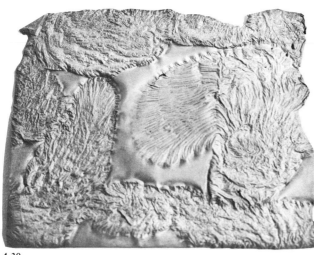

4-30

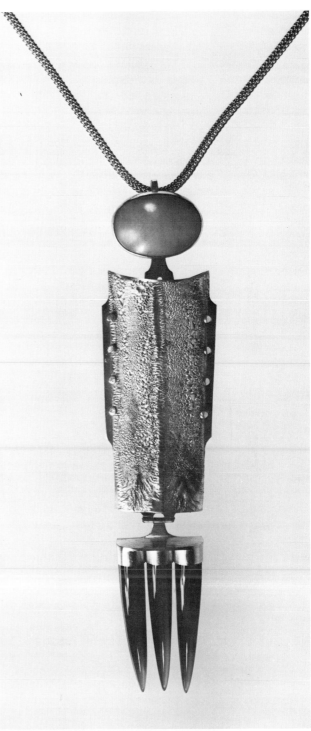

4–31 *Pendant of sterling silver, nickel silver, and brass with amber and carnelian; torch-textured and constructed.*

Other metals can also be torch-textured. Sterling silver is less controllable than 820, but with care can be textured. Prepare and apply the torch to sterling as outlined for the 820 alloy. Most of the copper alloys can be textured to some degree and require no preparation. Nu-Gold and like alloys work especially well. For those wishing a silver color, but not the expense of silver, nickel silver (alloy 752) is a good substitute. Nickel silver tends to remain at the shimmer state for a longer period than silver or the other copper alloys. This characteristic gives the worker greater flexibility in terms of torch movement, angling, and rate of travel over the metal. While a texture composed of striations or ridges can easily be created on nickel silver, a very rich surface of tiny craters and perforations may also be achieved (figure 4–32). Natural gas/compressed oxygen and oxygen/acetylene torches seem to work best on nickel silver. Oxygen/acetylene is especially effective in developing a highly perforated, cratered effect.

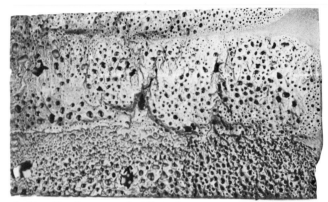

4–32   *Torch-textured nickel silver.*

GRANULATION

Granulation and eutectic bonding methods have been used since early Egyptian times. Interest in granulation has risen and fallen through history with its peak achieved by the Etruscans. Because of the tedious nature of the process, few contemporary jewelers have successfully incorporated granulated surfaces in their work. Those jewelers who persevere and succeed with this process produce striking examples for others to strive for.

The process was named for its adornment of metal surfaces with small granules of metal. Today, granulation implies the practice of attaching tiny metal balls or chips to a surface without the addition of solder. Joining of the two metals occurs through a process of eutectic bonding just at the points where the granules touch the parent metal.

The practice of granulation in western cultures declined over the years until it became a lost art. At least part of the reason was the growing use of silver and gold metallic solders and the general impact of increasing technology. Apparently, western jewelry makers did not have time to spend on the tedious work. In 1933 an Englishman, Henry Littledale, applied for a patent for *Improvements in Hard Soldering* and *Mixtures and Hard Soldering Processes.* In his application Littledale

4–33   **John Marshall.** *Brooch of fine silver and gold; repoussé, chasing, and granulation. The granulated and chased surfaces contrast beautifully with the gracefully curved, polished elements. Courtesy of the artist.*

4–34   **John Paul Miller.** *Granulated and constructed pendant of gold. The surface texture resulting from many tiny granulated pieces is amplified by selective polishing and oxidation. Courtesy of the artist.*
4–35   **Ira Sherman.** *Ring of 14-karat gold with iolite; cast and granulated. Courtesy of the artist. Photograph by Connie Brauer.*

4-34

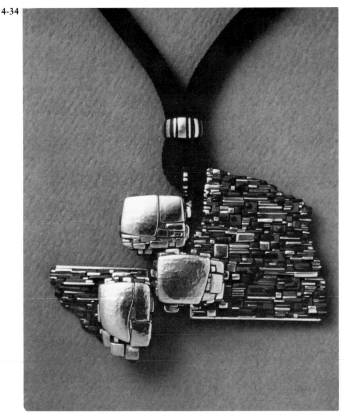

4-35

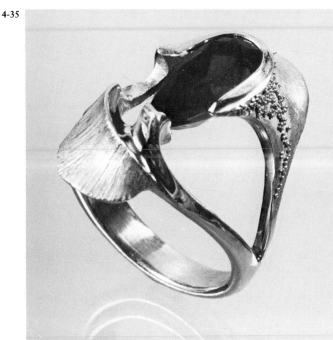

pointed to the major drawbacks encountered with standard techniques in soldering delicate jewelry pieces: solder flooding or spilling, solder or small pieces being displaced by boiling flux, and the difficult task of cleaning and finishing delicate areas flooded with solder. Littledale proposed to break down the needed elements to their basic chemical compounds and use these just at the point of contact between the joining pieces. Instead of the usual metal solders, he reduced these to metallic salts or oxides. Littledale stated, "When metallic oxides are heated in the presence of carbon, they are reduced to the metallic state. When properly compounded, the metals thus obtained fuse together and form an alloy and at this stage become a metallic solder, and the fusing takes place at a temperature below that of the fusing point of the individual metals." Appendix 2 lists some of the metallic salts and oxides that Littledale used in his research. These were usually mixed to a paste consistency with water and the individual decorative pieces covered. The parent metal was covered with an animal-base glue and the applied pieces set on and held in place by the glue. Upon heating, the glue carbonized and the oxides became a solder, fusing the pieces. Littledale's formal research has stood the test of time and remains one of the clearest pictures of the basic process. Several recent studies reaffirm his general findings.

In our work, silver and gold are the metals most commonly granulated. With some research and practice, other metals will also work. Fine silver and the higher-karat gold work best. Unpredictability with sterling and low-karat golds makes them less desirable for granulation. The following process uses fine silver.

1 The parent metal receiving granules should be completely finished and cleaned with denatured alcohol. On preconstructed work, it is best to construct the piece with IT solder in order to alleviate the possibility of solder reflowing during the process of granulation. After considerable practice, patience, and a bit of luck, the entire work can be assembled using eutectic fusion. Eutectic soldering need not incorporate just granules or tiny spheres. Practically any size or shape will bond given sufficient contact area with the parent metal.

2 Preparation of the spheres traditionally used in granulation is quite simple. Bits of metal are cut to size, melted, and allowed to draw into molten balls and cooled. For work needing only a few granules,

the spheres can be made on a charcoal block using the torch. In any case, bits of silver wire can be measured, cut, and melted as a trial to find the desired sizes. Once the size of the wire is determined, the needed number is cut and melted on the charcoal.

3 In order to make a large number of spheres, several lengths of wire can be snipped at once. Hand shears or the table shear can be set up with an adjustable stop so that predetermined sizes are cut each time. An adjustable device similar in concept to that of a tube jig can be adapted to the shear.

4 A ceramic or graphite crucible is used to contain the bits of wire while melting. Snips of wire are arranged in the crucible on layers of powdered charcoal. The layers should be approximately ½ inch thick. Care must be taken so that the snips do not touch one another, otherwise the pieces will melt and flow together.

5 Place the crucible in a kiln preheated to approximately 1,800° F. Allow it to remain for half an hour. A gas/air melt furnace is also an excellent heat source and will accomplish the melt in about five minutes. To check if the melt has occurred, a small amount of charcoal can be removed. If not molten, continue heating. With the melt complete, let the crucible cool for a few minutes and then pour the contents into a pan of water and detergent. Agitate the water by hand and let the charcoal float to the surface. Pour off the charcoal and rinse the granules.

6 If making spheres of varying sizes, they can be separated to size by pouring them through a graduated series of wire screens. A sieve apparatus can be fashioned with squared wooden strips and screens of diminishing sizes arranged top to bottom (figure 4–36). One pour and a few shakes will permit the granules to drop to a level corresponding to individual sizes.

7 Keep in mind that various formulas can be used to bond silver granules. Considering the finished appearance and bonding strength, the following formula is offered:

    6 parts distilled water
    1 part hide glue
    1 part borax
    2 parts antimony trioxide or copper chloride

Some jewelers forgo the metallic salts and simply copper plate the granules. My experience has been that the plating method is unpredictable and often results in textured surfaces.

8 With the base metal prepared, granules can be

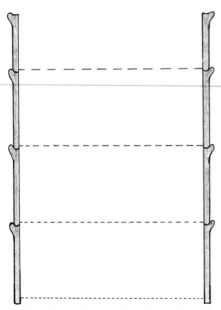

4–36 *Stacked sieve for the graduated separation of granules.*

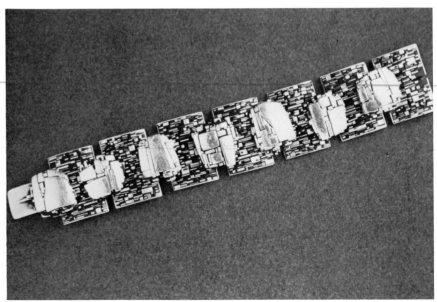

4–37 **John Paul Miller.** *Granulated and constructed bracelet of gold. Courtesy of the artist.*

placed in the desired arrangement. Lay the granules on a few layers of paper towel and dab several brushfuls of the solution over the granules. Excess liquid will be absorbed by the towels. Use fine-tipped tweezers to set the granules in place. Placing the workpiece on the heating surface before setting the granules on the piece alleviates the need to move the workpiece and possibly dislodge the granules.

9 The torch should have the capacity to produce a reducing flame of sufficient size to cover the entire granular surface and to bring the workpiece to fusing temperature. As the piece is heated, observation of the metal's color is critical. Failure to recognize the moment of fusion can cause overheating, orange peel, reticulated surfaces, or melting. While the piece comes to a red heat, granules will be dark and their contact points glowing. In an instant these points will appear to flash. This occurrence is difficult to describe but can be equated in appearance to that of the flashing of a solder joint. Remove the torch as soon as fusion occurs.

10 Granules are relatively delicate and may be broken off if mishandled. Care should be taken in finishing to avoid their breakage. Usually, pickling and a gentle scrub with a soft brush is adequate. Lubricate the brush with soap and water. For a high polish, use a soft cotton buff and rouge.

PHOTOETCHING

Photoetching allows jewelers to duplicate detailed positive or negative photographic images onto metal. The metal is coated with a light-sensitive resist, a high-contrast negative is placed over the metal, and the negative is exposed by ultraviolet light. The coated metal is then processed in a developer, removing part of the resist. The actual etch may take place in the traditional bath or by electrochemical means. As in any photographic process, there is great latitude for experimentation. Several practice pieces should be printed, varying exposure times, contrasts, and developing times. Appendix 4 lists suppliers from whom the appropriate chemicals may be purchased. In ordering, specify a positive or negative resist solution.

In practice, one must take precautions with the chemicals and the fumes generated. Always wear gloves,

4–38 **Betsy Douglas,** Star Pin. *Sterling silver and copper with quartz, pearls, photograph, and Plexiglas; construction, marriage of metals, and photoetching. Courtesy of the artist. Photograph by Lynn Hudson.*

glasses, and an apron. Be sure the darkroom and work areas are well vented.

The following general outline is provided to give the beginner a point of departure for photoetching copperplate. A complete listing of recommended supplies is given in Appendix 4.

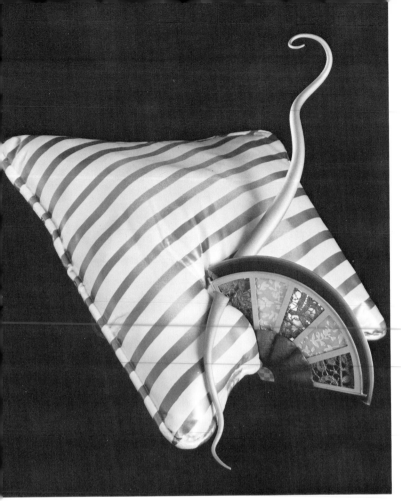

4–39 **Kate Wagle,** Slice. *Copper, silver, brass, bronze, titanium, fiberglass, and auto lacquers. The artist uses photo-etching to pierce intricate patterns through thin sheets of brass into which she fuses sheets of silver. The process results in a marriage of metals well suited to manipulation and forming. Courtesy of the artist.*

4–40 **Brigid O'Hanrahan.** *Constructed bracelet of silver and photoprinted niobium. Courtesy of the artist.*

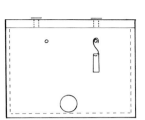
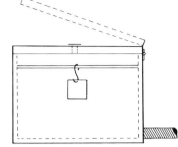

4–41 *Drying box.*

1 Cut a piece of 16-gauge copper sheet slightly larger than the eventual image. Drill a small hole in the center of two opposite edges. Clean the plate with a slurry of fine pumice powder and water until water runs freely and does not ball on the metal's surface. Allow the metal to air dry. Cleanliness of the metal is essential to the adhesion of the resist solution. Any remaining pumice will retard adhesion. Attach two short wire hooks through the drilled holes.

2 Working now in a darkroom under a safelight, pour enough resist into a shallow glass tray to completely cover the metal plate; ½ to 1 inch should be adequate. Using the wire hooks as handles, dip the plate at a slight angle through the solution until a smooth, bub-ble-free surface appears on the cleaned side. If bub-bles persist, they can be brushed away lightly with a clean, soft brush. Hang the plate above the tray to allow the excess resist to drip off. The plate must now dry thoroughly. This process will vary with the re-sist's viscosity and the brand used. Some craftworkers simply allow the resist to air dry in the darkroom, others make up a vented, light-tight box with an inlet hose for attaching an electric hair dryer. In either case, the resist manufacturer's instructions should be followed as closely as possible.

3 Figure 4–42 illustrates the construction details of a light box used for exposure. With some experimenta-tion, sensitized plates can be explosed in sunlight, with a slide projector, or with tungsten lights. Where high quality and routine success are expected, a light box is generally preferred. Figure 4–43 shows the relationship of the plate and negative to the light source. Place the negative and plate over the glass. Be sure the negative's emulsion side faces up, against the clean side of the metal; close the box. Turn on the

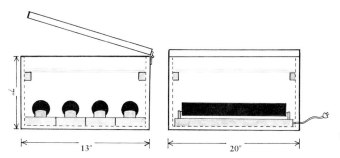

4-42   *Light box.*

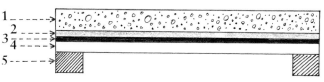

4-43   *Negative position relative to the light source: (1) foam backing; (2) metal plate, clean side down; (3) negative, emulsion side up; (4) glass; (5) support; (6) light.*

black lights and begin timing the exposure. Exposure times may vary considerably with each processing. Experiments can be made on small samples and the results recorded for given time brackets. Eventually set times can be accurately determined for a given negative. Again, follow the manufacturer's instructions for the specific resist, light sources, and distance.

4 After exposure in the light box, develop the plate for 30 seconds to a minute in normal light. To develop, submerge the plate in a glass tray containing 1 to 1½ inches of resist developer solution. The plate should be slightly agitated during this process. Moving the plate or tray gently side to side is adequate. Rinse the plate in cold water and then immerse it in a tray of resist dye for 10 to 20 seconds; rinse. If the image is unsatisfactory, the plate should be recleaned and steps 1 through 4 repeated.

5 Return the plate to the drying box for 30 to 45 minutes at a temperature not exceeding 250°F. Cover the back of the plate with contact paper in preparation for the acid etch. A glass tray is used to contain the etching solution. **As always, the acid vapors must be well vented, and remember to pour the acid into water (not the reverse).** The plate is now etched in the standard manner to the depth desired. Bath agitation will assist for optimum results, but is not absolutely necessary. After etching, the piece should be rinsed and the remaining resist removed by burning away with the torch or by soaking in a solvent.

The following are two commonly used etching solutions:

> 4 parts nitric acid
> 6 parts water or
> 400 grams ferric chloride crystals
> 1,000 milliliters water

4-44   **Anni Ayers,** Dylan. *Photoetched and constructed pin of sterling, 14-karat gold, and rutelite crystal. The artist's mastery of the photoetching technique permits her a broad range of subject matter. Here the vivid image of a pop star is used effectively as the foreground. Courtesy of the artist.*

ELECTROFORMING AND ELECTROPLATING

The following technical outline and accompanying photographs were provided by Professor Lee B. Peck, Northern Illinois University at DeKalb. All photographs for these sections are by Gordon Means, unless otherwise noted.

In electroforming and electroplating, a coat of metal is deposited on a metallic or nonmetallic matrix through electrolysis. The electrodeposition of metal on a given surface dates back to the early 1800s. Industrial research and its commercial application has produced a vast body of information, and new discoveries in the area are continually being made. While the information is readily available, it is highly technical and often difficult to understand. The contemporary artist/jeweler using these processes has had to adapt them for use on a smaller and less mechanized scale. The potential uses of electroforming and electroplating are endless, limited only by the worker's imagination. Because these processes are relatively new to us, experimentation is often necessary and is encouraged.

In electroforming, the buildup of a metallic surface over a matrix form is such that the resulting structure is self-supporting. After the electrodeposition of metal is accomplished, the matrix form may be removed. It is also possible to create an object by electroforming heavily into an open-faced cavity. In this approach, the coating of metal occurs from the back of the matrix. Objects can also be formed hollow and light in weight that incorporate many other materials such as plastic, glass, stones, ceramic, and wood. In most instances these forms would be impossible to create using the more traditional techniques of casting or direct metal fabrication. An additional advantage is that pliable or more easily worked materials than metal, such as wax, styrofoam, papier mâché, and clay, may be electroformed and so "transformed" into metal. Electroforming as a textural or joining device is also used in conjunction with casting, fabrication, or on an already-electroformed piece.

In electroplating, a thin layer of metal is deposited over a rigid and permanent object, which remains in place. Electroplating is used primarily as a surface treatment either for decorative patterning or the overall refinement or upgrading of a surface, as in gold-plated jewelry.

4–45 Harold O'Connor. *Constructed brooch of sterling silver and electroformed copper. Courtesy of the artist.*

Electrodeposition: How It Works

Electrodeposition is the term used to describe the flow and deposition of positively charged metal ions from a metal source (the anode) through a solution (the electrolyte) onto a negatively charged matrix form (the cathode) (figure 4–46).

The source of power or electrical current most often used is the electroplating rectifier, a unit that changes alternating current from an ordinary electrical outlet to direct current. The system is controlled by a rheostat mounted on the rectifier, enabling the user to vary the voltage output. A range of 1 to 15 volts and 20 to 25 amps is usually sufficient for forming most jewelry and small objects. Rectifiers are the most reliable source of power. While they may cost more to purchase initially, they will save time and money in the long run (figure 4–47).

A less expensive source of current is the automotive battery charger, which reduces the 110 volts from a common AC outlet down to usable levels of DC current. If a battery charger is chosen, it will be necessary to install an ammeter just off the negative terminal in order to monitor the amount of current passing through the system. The current is then controlled by a rheostat attached to the positive terminal of the charger.

4–47 *Electroplating rectifier, sulfuric acid, cupric sulfate, and copper anodes.*

4–46 *Electroplating/forming system.*

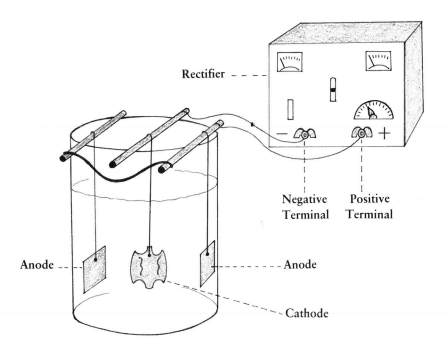

Rectifier

Negative Terminal

Positive Terminal

Anode

Anode

Cathode

Another source of current is the common battery. As with the battery charger, an ammeter and rheostat should be installed to monitor and control the current. While the initial cash outlay is not great, it is a costly and inefficient power source in the long run. If either a charger or battery is chosen as a power supply, the use of a voltmeter is helpful. Rectifiers come equipped with voltmeters. It is not always necessary to monitor voltage since under normal conditions the voltage remains proportional to the current in the solution. However, a voltmeter can alert you to a problem, such as a depleted electrolyte or poor or corroded electrical connections.

There are many suppliers of electroforming or plating rectifiers. Their cost is related to the amount of DC power output and number of built-in accessories. Some of the more sophisticated machines include an automatic current reversing system. It is questionable whether the process of periodically deplating actually creates a more satisfactory deposit.

Plating Tanks

Almost any noncorrosive, nonconductive container can be used as a plating tank to hold the electrolyte. However, two things must be considered in the selection of the proper tank.

1 **Size.** This will be determined somewhat by the scale of the work to be electroformed. While jewelry items are usually small in scale, it may be more efficient to form several pieces at one time, thus requiring a larger tank. Keep in mind that the objects to be formed must be fully immersed in the plating bath.

2 **The solution to be used.** Besides considering the corrosive nature of the plating solution, the temperature of some baths must be kept higher than room temperature. In these cases the plating tank must be able to withstand the heat necessary for optimal plating. A local discount department store or hardware store is a good source for purchasing several different and inexpensive types of plating tanks. In many instances an inexpensive polyethylene or polypropylene bucket or wastebasket can be used as a tank. The plating solution may be heated, if necessary, with an immersion heater. Porcelain enameled pots, Pyrex cookware, and chemistry beakers are a few examples of items that can be used as plating tanks. If the solution is placed in a stainless steel tank or in one with a porcelain finish, the bath may be heated over a direct flame.

Setting Up the Tank

Once the proper tank is selected, the following items are necessary.

1 **Bus bars.** Rigid rods of copper or brass, about ¼ inch in diameter, will serve as positive or negative carriers of current to the anode or cathode. These bus bars are positioned to rest over the full length of the tank and should be located to permit the object to be plated to be surrounded by suspended anodes. This facilitates the even distribution of metal ions. When using a polyethylene or polypropylene tank, pieces of wood or some other nonconductive material should be placed between the bus bars and the tank in order to prevent direct contact between the two, since any heat generated through the bus bars will tend to melt the top edges of the plastic tank (figure 4–48).

2 **Copper wire.** A good and inexpensive conductor of current, copper wire is used to carry a positive flow of current from the rectifier to the anodic bus bars and to also conduct the return current from the cathodic bus bars back to the negative terminal of the rectifier. The wire must be of sufficient gauge to carry the amount of amperage needed. Insulated copper wire, the kind used by electricians, can be purchased in a hardware store in the needed voltage and amp rating or gauge. Copper wire ranging from 18 to 24 gauge should be used to suspend the cathode (workpiece) and the anodes from the bus bars into the electrolyte. On large systems, the anode may be bolted to the bus bar with brass bolts. Copper alligator clips should be used to attach all copper wires from the rectifier to the bus bars for good contact. If the plating setup is to be used for an extended period of time, it is a good idea to plate the copper alligator clips and the immediate contact areas of the bus bars with 24-karat gold. This will virtually eliminate corrosion of the contacting surfaces and will assure good and reliable electrical contact.

3 **Anode.** The anode is a heavy sheet of metal that provides the source of positive metal ions to the electrolyte bath, maintaining a constant concentration of ions in the bath while metal is being deposited on the cathode (workpiece). Anodes are connected to the positive terminal of the rectifier.

In some baths, particularly in gold plating, a stainless steel anode can be used in place of pure gold. While this type of inert anode will supply current to

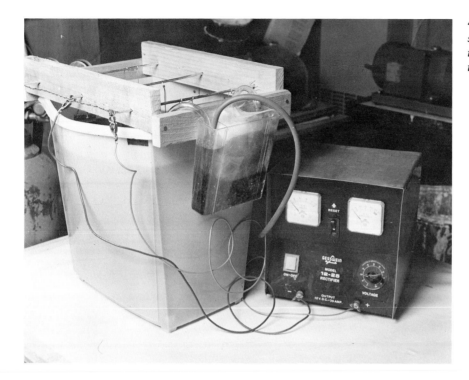

4–48 *Bus bars positioned in wood supports and resting over the plating tank. Note simple aquarium filter containing fiberglass and charcoal.*

the electrolyte, it will not supply metal ions. Metal salts, obtained from plating supply companies, are used to replenish the bath periodically. One good source for stainless steel anodes are kitchen or barbecue spatulas with the plastic handles removed. For electroforming or plating copper, a soluble copper anode is best.

Logically, the total combined surface area of the anodes should approximate that of the workpiece so that the object being plated will be adequately covered. If the surface area of the anodes is much greater than that of the cathode, unwanted textural growth can result. Also, the surface area of the anode and the rate at which it dissolves should be equal to the surface area of the cathode and the rate at which metal is deposited on it. When this occurs, it is referred to as a *balanced tank*.

Anodes should be placed evenly around the workpiece so that metal is deposited uniformly on the object. If, however, the aim is to plate only one side of a piece, the anodes should be concentrated on the side of the piece to be plated. Attach the copper wire to the anode by drilling a hole in the anode and hooking the wire into it at a point above the bath level.

4 Cathode. The piece to be formed or plated (cathode) can be either metallic or nonmetallic. The choice of a matrix material may be based on its flexibility and other properties that will allow it to be formed into an aesthetically pleasing object. The cathode is connected to the negative terminal of the rectifier.

Nonmetallic Matrices   Almost any nonmetallic material may be used as a basis for the electrodeposition of metal (figure 4–49). Some nonmetallic matrix materials will remain as part of the final piece after forming, such as ceramics, glass, stone, certain plastics, and bone, and can even contribute to the strength and durability of the finished piece. When the matrix is made of wax, it should be thoroughly boiled out in water to protect the wearer or user of the finished piece from having wax leach out onto clothing. Other matrix materials such as paper, cardboard, styrofoam, and wood may all be burned out in a kiln, in a well-ventilated area.

Some nonmetallic matrix materials are so light that they will float in the plating bath. This may cause warpage and shape distortion of the piece or, since it is buoyant, it may become separated from the cathode wire, thus interfering with the flow of current and dis-

4–49 *Common objects used as electroforming matrices: plastic berry basket, doilie, drinking straws, waxed cardboard milk carton, wax wires, pearl-tipped pins, seashells, grommets, marbles, beads, plastic tabs.*

rupting the total process. One solution to the buoyancy problem is to attach a nonconductive, noncorrosive weight to the bottom of the workpiece. This could be done by attaching a plastic-coated wire or monofilament nylon fish line to the bottom of the cathode, and hanging the weight from that line or wire. This will keep the work submerged in the bath.

If the matrix is porous (paper, cardboard, etc.) it may also distort through absorption of liquid when introduced into the plating bath. To prevent this, a coating of lacquer or urethane should be brushed or sprayed on the matrix until it is sealed.

When the object has been satisfactorily shaped and is ready for electroforming, the copper wire must be attached securely so that the form can be suspended from it into the bath. The cathode wire can be waxed or glued in place. It is important to attach the wire in an inconspicuous place on the piece so that when forming is completed, and the wire removed, the remains of the original connection will not detract from the looks of the finished piece. For this reason, it is a good idea to consider the placement and method of attaching the cathode wire while designing and constructing the matrix (figure 4–50).

After the cathode wire is secured to the matrix, the matrix must be made electrically conductive before plating can occur. Various conductive sprays, powders, and paints are available; silver compositions are superior to those of bronze and copper on jewelry-size forms (figure 4–51). When using the silver paint, always keep the silver in suspension by periodic shaking and stirring or the particles of silver will settle and the matrix will be covered with the nonconductive lacquer or alcohol paint base. Be sure to apply a small amount of conductive paint to the joint of the cathode wire and matrix to assure a positive electrical contact (figure 4–52).

Metallic Matrices The easiest matrix to electroform is an all-metal object. It is important to keep in mind that the metal matrix must be compatible with the electroforming bath used. For example, a steel matrix will etch in an acid copper bath, causing poor adhesion of the metal ions on the cathode. For general electroforming purposes, copper and copper alloys, silver, gold, and titanium are suitable for immersion in the acid copper bath.

After the matrix is completely shaped, traditional finishing techniques can be used on the surface to

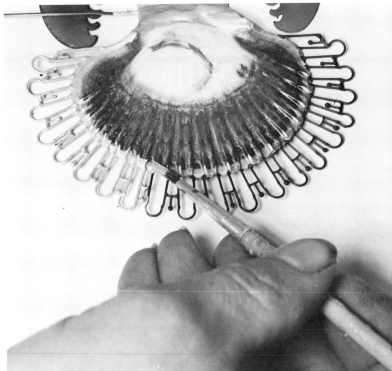

4-50
4-51

4-52

4—50 *Piece being readied for electroforming. Cast sterling bird's head on the left will be riveted on after forming is complete. The titanium wings have been selectively gold plated and heat colored and will be cemented to the wax wire and seashell tail. The cathode wire to the left will also be cemented to the shell matrix.*

4—51 *Spray bronze, silver paint, and a solvent (butyl acetate).*

4—52 *At the top of photo: the cathode wire is cemented to the back of the piece and coated with silver paint both at the joint and part way up the wire. The wax wires and edges of the shell are covered with silver paint. This will cause the copper to grow, connecting the lacy wax wires firmly to the shell in a bezel-like formation.*

achieve the look desired upon completion; for example, high polish, steel wool, pumice, hammer marks. With the matrix finished, the copper cathode wire is attached. This may be done by soldering, wrapping, or hooking the wire through an area of the matrix to make metal-to-metal contact. Again, the attachment of the wire should be in an inconspicuous spot on the piece so the joint can be hidden or blended into the surrounding area after plating is completed.

Another important consideration is the cleanliness of surfaces to be plated. If a film of dirt or grease remains on the matrix, metal ions will not adhere to the surface and will result in bare spots, irregular plating, roughness, staining, and so on. Pieces that have been soldered or annealed should be pickled to remove surface oxides or scale and then scrubbed with a solution of detergent and water. Ultrasonic cleaners also work well. The piece may then be wiped with a soft tissue dampened with acetone. This should be done in a well-ventilated area. After cleaning, do not handle the piece with oily fingers.

Selective Plating

Often the aim of electroforming over a metal matrix is to join two forms or to add texture to a piece. Electroforming can also be used to fill in an etched area or line with a contrasting metal, giving the effect of an inlay. Once the underlying metal form is created, the worker can electroform further to build up areas of texture or inlay, or electroplate to color and refine a surface, or to develop a pattern with a thin metallic deposit.

When selectively plating, a stop-out material must be applied. Stop-out materials such as wax, asphaltum, epoxy paints, lacquers, latex rubber, plastic tapes, contact paper, and even permanent felt pen markers will successfully resist plating solutions for at least a minimum amount of time needed to plate a light coat of metal. In certain instances, the bath's operating temperature will be too high to use some of these stop-outs. Be certain the stop-out and bath temperature are compatible. A commercial material, Miccropeel, is a particularly good stop-out. It is a paint-on, lacquer-based product that will peel off a smooth surface when dry (figure 4–53). Miccropeel Reducer, also commercially available, can be used to dissolve the stop-out. All lacquer or solvent solutions must always be used in a well-ventilated area.

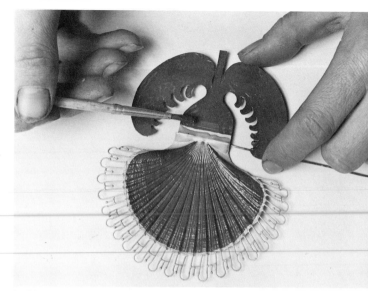

4–53 *Titanium wings being painted with stop-out lacquer to prevent copper growth on the metal surface. Note that the shell was also painted with the stop-out to keep the acid from etching and destroying the shell's surface and color.*

4–54 *The piece is placed in the tank and suspended from the cathodic bus bar.*

Plating Baths

Because it is far too costly to electroform in gold or silver, the most commonly used electroforming metal is copper. After a piece is formed in copper, a thin deposit of gold or silver can be applied, giving it the appearance of solid gold or silver. Many types of acid copper-plating solutions are currently being used. Of these, the copper sulfate or acid copper bath is the most extensively used. Besides being easily prepared, it is simple to control and maintain. If the tank is kept in constant balance, that is, the surface area and deposition ratio of anode to cathode is kept equal, only periodic replenishing of the sulfuric acid is necessary to reduce the resistivity of the bath. This formula has proven suitable for both electroforming and plating copper:

> 24 ounces copper sulfate
> 5 to 8 ounces sulfuric acid
> 1 gallon distilled water

It is possible to brighten the copper deposit and decrease its graininess by adding a small amount of pure molasses to the bath. One-tenth of an ounce per gallon of bath is sufficient.

In mixing the bath, increase the volume by increasing the component amounts proportionally, but make no substitutions. **Always add acid to water to avoid a splattering reaction, and pour slowly to minimize splashing.** Next add the copper sulfate and allow it to dissolve while stirring with a glass or plastic rod. Always prepare and operate the bath in a well-vented area.

The operating conditions of the copper sulfate bath should be as follows:

> Temperature—room temperature (not less than 60°F, 80°F optimum)
> Voltage—1 to 10 volts, depending on anode and cathode size
> Current density/amps—0 to 40 amps

Once the bath is prepared and the bus bars are in place, immerse the workpiece in the solution and suspend it from the cathodic bus bar. While submerging the piece, tilt it from side to side a few times to dislodge air bubbles that may have become trapped on the surface of the work. Make certain to hook the cathode wire to the bus bar securely to ensure positive electrical contact (figure 4–54). Next, place the anodes in the tank so that they surround the cathode evenly and then connect them securely to the anodic bus bar. Make certain the bus bars are connected by wires to the appropriate rectifier terminals.

Forming/Plating

In electroforming, begin with a small amount of current. This may be as low as one amp for a single piece of jewelry. After about two hours of plating, take the piece out to see if all areas are covering evenly. If there are bare or rough spots, the cause must be determined before an even buildup occurs. Often, a small amount of conductive paint over the unplated or rough spots is all that is necessary. Allow the paint to dry and then return the piece to the bath. A smooth, solid pink base of metal over the form is needed before any textural development should be attempted. Once the initial base is deposited, various surface effects can be achieved. When the piece is plating evenly, increase the current by ½ amp increments and observe the piece every two hours to make sure there is no burning from excessive current and that a textural growth is beginning. Burning is evidenced by surface discoloration and the deposit of sandlike grains of metal on the object that are easily rubbed away. It is possible to create a controlled granular texture by carefully taking any of the following steps:

1 position the anodes closer to the workpiece.
2 increase the amperage.
3 heat the electrolyte.
4 prolong the immersion time.
5 increase the bath agitation.

Always use these techniques in moderation, and monitor the process closely to avoid burning and excessive granular buildup.

One important aspect of electroforming to keep in mind is that metal is deposited in an unannealed state and is therefore resistant to bending, is brittle, and may easily break (figures 4–55 and 4–56).

In electroplating, generally just a thin coat of metal is applied. Attach the workpiece directly to the negative terminal wire of the rectifier and bob the piece up and down in the bath by hand to provide agitation. Use between one and two amps and continue plating for approximately five minutes.

4–56 *The finished piece.* **Lee B. Peck,** Bird Pendant. *Electroformed copper, titanium and bronze with sea shell and 24-karat gold plate. Courtesy of the artist. Photograph by Gordon Means.*

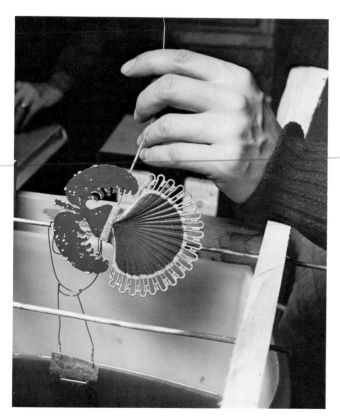

4–55 *Electroforming is completed. Note the growth that has formed on the metal parts through tiny holes in the stop-out. These nodules can be picked off easily when the stop-out is removed.*

Safety Precautions

Whenever the object is removed from the bath, either for inspection or when plating is completed, it should be rinsed in a solution of warm water and baking soda to neutralize the acid. It should then be rinsed in plain running water. The use of goggles, rubber gloves, rubber apron, and sufficient exhausting of the resulting fumes are all absolutely required throughout the forming or plating process. All manufacturer's instructions should be followed regarding the installation and operation of the related electrical components.

Commercially prepared baths for plating other metals are available in cyanide and noncyanide mixtures. All manufacturer's label instructions should be followed scrupulously and the worker should become familiar with the proper precautions relative to the specific solutions used. Those using cyanide solutions are strongly advised to have a cyanide antidote kit available. The accidental breathing or ingestion of cyanide may result in death.

Filtration

For most small systems, constant filtration of the bath may not be essential. However, periodic removal of foreign particles or impurities is recommended in order to keep the bath fully operative and plating evenly. An easy way to filter the electrolyte is by pouring it through a funnel lined with a coffee filter or chemical filter papers. Dissolving anodes release particles that may form on the cathode to create unwanted roughness. Loose fitting, synthetic cloth bags can be tied around the anodes to collect the flaking particles. Periodic rinsing of the bags to remove the sludge is necessary. Filtration can also be accomplished with an aquarium pump and filter unit. Commercial pumps and filters are available for large plating systems (figure 4–57).

Agitation

The use of a filter pump will also provide agitation to the electrolyte. This may be adequate for small tanks. If greater agitation is needed, a magnetic or electromechanical stirring unit may be installed. These can be purchased from plating suppliers (figure 4–58). For jewelers with a filtered compressed air source, low-pressure air can be used for agitation. A plastic tube can be placed in the bottom of the tank and air passed through it to bubble up around the cathode. Movement of the electrolyte prevents gaseous bubbles from form-

4–57 A commercial filter is used for filtering the bath in a large tank. Note the large anode at the top of the photograph is bolted directly to the anodic bus bar. The object at the lower right that is partially submerged is an immersion heater for heating the bath.

4–58 A motor with a propelling rod attached is mounted above a large plating tank to agitate the bath. The piece on the left has been electroformed using plastic tape as a stop-out.

ing on the workpiece and pitting its surface. Keep in mind that while agitation speeds the plating process, excess can create unwanted textural growth.

The materials and equipment mentioned throughout this section may be purchased from firms listed in Appendix 4.

COLORING TITANIUM

Thanks to modern technology and the jeweler's ever-open eye for unique materials, we now have the opportunity to employ a family of refractory metals in our work. These metals are corrosion-resistant, lightweight, and can easily be given a range of vivid colors. These qualities make these metals ideally suited for use in jewelry making and explain their current popularity.

Professor Lee B. Peck provided the following technical information and the photographic sequence for this section.

The Process
Titanium is a gray-colored refractory metal having a melting point of 3,272°F. It is often used in the plating industry for its noncorrosive properties, and in the aerospace and defense industries for its light weight and great strength. It is worked with a great deal of difficulty and is not cast or soldered using traditional jeweler's techniques. Forging titanium is difficult, but can be done. It can also be shaped by bending, or with hammers or dapping tools over a resilient backing. While it dulls saw blades and drill bits rather quickly, titanium can be pierced as well as polished, etched, sandblasted, and engraved.

The coloring of titanium occurs when a thin film of oxide forms on the surface of the metal, interfering with light waves striking that surface. The variation in the thickness of the film is what causes the apparent variation in color on the metal. This same optical effect creates the iridescent colors seen in an oil slick on water. The color of oxidized titanium is permanent unless the oxide film is disturbed by abrasive action or by grease and dirt forming over the film.

Two methods used to color titanium are heat oxidation and anodization. While the discussion in this section deals with titanium, the same coloring phenomenon also occurs on tantalum and niobium, two other refractory metals available to jewelers. The coloring techniques discussed here may also be applied to these two metals. The resulting colors will differ with each metal. Titanium is purchased by the pound in sheet and wire form, and by the foot in tube form.

Preparing the Metal's Surface for Coloring
Because the surface condition of the piece will have a bearing on the resulting colors, it is an important element to consider. While an acid-etched surface will give an intense color, a sandblasted surface will appear softer, and a polished surface will yield yet another effect. One piece might combine several surface treatments.

Titanium can be etched in the following solution: 20 percent nitric acid, 20 percent hydrofluoric acid, and 60 percent distilled water by volume. **Hydrofluoric and nitric acids can be extremely dangerous and should only be mixed and used under an effective fume hood. Always add acid to water and wear rubber gloves, safety glasses, and an apron while working.**

Before coloring, the metal must first be cleaned by washing in a solution of detergent and water, dried, and wiped with acetone. After cleaning, avoid touching the metal's surface with greasy fingers. An oily film will act as a resist during the coloring process. After the surface preparation and cleaning, the metal is ready to be colored.

Coloring by Heat Oxidation
Heat oxidation is best applied with a torch. While a kiln will provide adequate heat, the process is hard to control and viewing the workpiece difficult. Consequently, the results are more haphazard. This is, however, one way to produce an overall ground color that can then be selectively etched, sandblasted through a stencil, engraved, or plated to create a contrasting, controlled pattern.

Colors generally occur between 930°F and 1,635°F, beginning in the pale amber range and going through various shades of purple, blue, green, and finally to brown at about 1,600°F. Further heat increases the oxide film's thickness and the resulting colors are muddy.

The preferred torches for this method are oxygen/acetylene, butane/oxygen, and propane/oxygen or hydrogen. Torches will bring forth rich colors in the amber, maroon, purple, blue, and brown ranges almost immediately. A broad torch tip will produce a wide,

Susan Noland. *Forged and constructed ring of 14-karat gold with citrine. Courtesy of the artist. Photograph by Leslie Becker.*

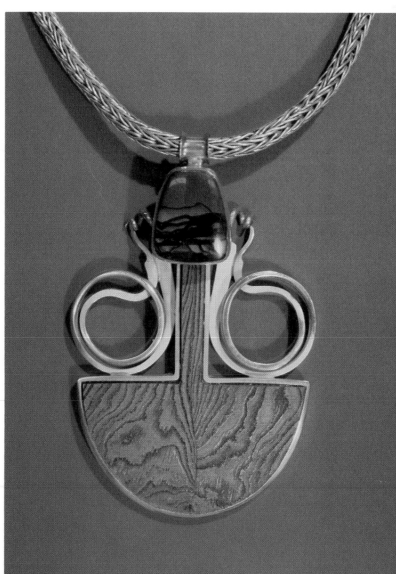

William Fiorini. *Pendant of sterling silver and Damascus steel with agate; laminated, woven, and constructed. Courtesy of the artist.*

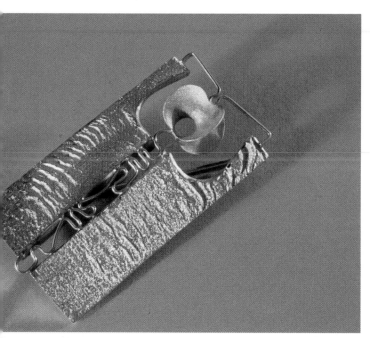

Heikki Seppä. *Reticulated and constructed pin of 14-karat gold. Courtesy of the artist.*

Carrie Adell. *Constructed interlocking ring set of gold with diamonds. Courtesy of the artist. Photographs by M. Warren.*

David Pimentel. *Set of three brooches. Fused and constructed in sterling silver, copper, brass, and bronze using marriage of metals and mokume. Courtesy of the artist.*

Jean Sampel. *Pressure set ring of 14-karat gold with quartz crystal. Courtesy of the artist. Photograph by Leslie Becker.*

Hannelore Gabriel. *Constructed combs of sterling and nickel silver with garnet and pearls. Courtesy of the artist.*

Tim McCreight. *Locket of sterling with moonstone; constructed and engraved. Courtesy of the artist.*

Hiroko and Gene Pijanowski. *Brooch and stand of silver and copper; solder inlaid and constructed. Courtesy of the artists.*

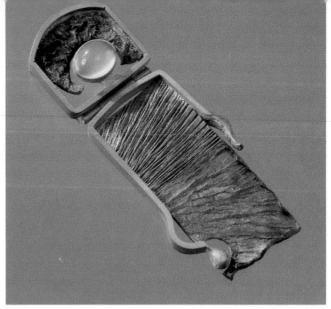

Lee B. Peck, Bird Pendant. *Cast and constructed in sterling silver and titanium, plated in 24-karat gold and oxidized. Courtesy of the artist.*

Mark Knuth. *Hammer textured and constructed pin of brass, nickel silver, and copper with moonstone. Courtesy of the artist.*

Enid Kaplan. *Constructed necklace and brooch of 14-karat gold, sterling silver, brass, copper, nickel and silk with moonstone and black pearls using marriage of metals. Courtesy of the artist. Photograph by Doug Long.*

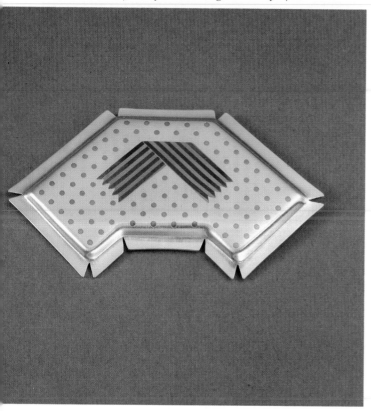

Kate Wagle, Island. *Brooch of sterling silver and brass; construction and fused photoetching. Courtesy of the artist.*

John Paul Miller. *Pendant of 18- and 24-karat gold with enamels; fused, constructed, and granulated. Courtesy of the artist.*

Randy Long, Silver Kite. *Brooch of sterling silver, copper, and Kuromido; die forming inlaying and marriage of metals. Courtesy of the artist.*

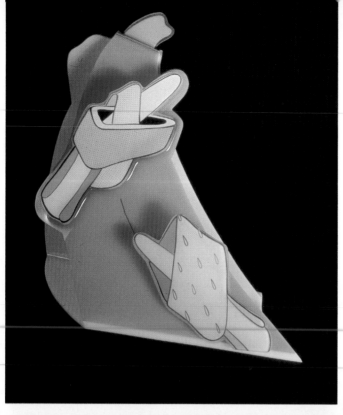

Amy Davison. *Sculpture with detachable brooches of epoxy, acrylic, and graphic film; drawn, constructed and cast. Courtesy of the artist.*

Joseph Hall. *Brooch of sterling silver, titanium, and brass; anodized and constructed. Courtesy of the artist. Photograph by Steve Young. Collection of Robert Ebendorf.*

Bob Natalini. *Constructed pendant of polyester, electronics and sterling silver. Lower elements simulated to tumble by ten sequentially flashing lights. Courtesy of the artist.*

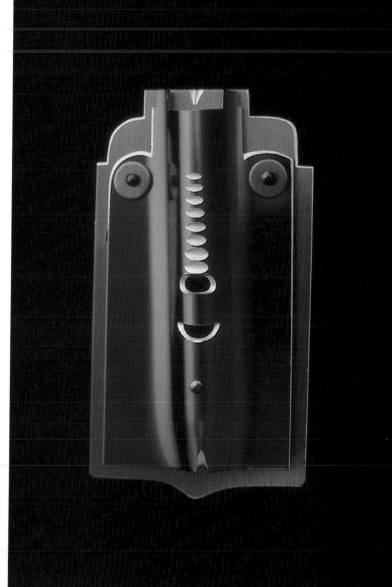

David LaPlantz. *Constructed pin of colored aluminum engraving stock. Courtesy of the artist.*

Lynda Watson-Abbott, Ribbon Wrapped Pin. *Sterling silver and felt tip marker colors. Colors are applied over a sandblasted surface and fixed with a waterproof fixative. Courtesy of the Artist.*

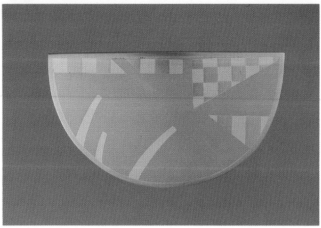

Lisa D'Agostino. *Constructed pin of copper, sterling, nickel silver, and brass using marriage of metals. Photograph by Peter Krumhardt.*

Doug Samore. *Pin of silver, brass, niobium, and tantalum; anodized and constructed. Courtesy of the artist. Photograph by Paul Milligan.*

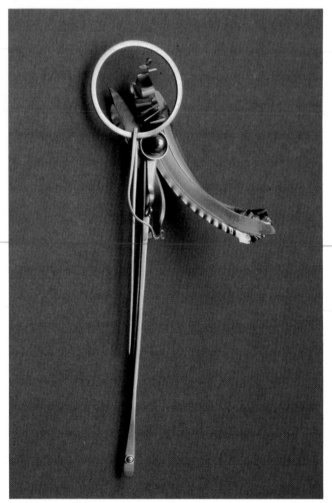

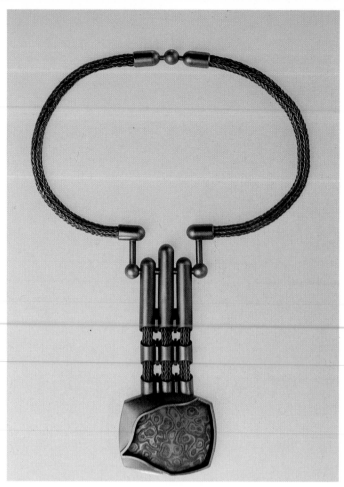

Dale Wedig. *Pendant of sterling, nickel silver, brass, and Damascus steel; constructed, woven, and sandblasted. Courtesy of the artist.*

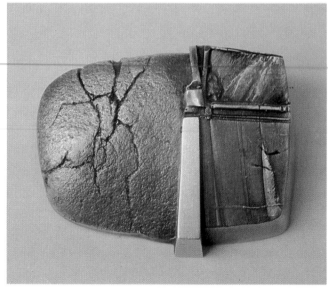

Al Gilmore. *Pin of bronze, sterling, and brass; constructed and thin shell cast. Courtesy of the artist.*

varied section of color. For intricate patterning, a fine-tipped torch with an orifice approximately the diameter of a pin can be used. This will permit a precise, easily controlled flame. When using the fine tip, it is recommended that it be used on 20- to 28-gauge metal. Thinner gauges will heat rapidly and allow the concentrated heat to create narrow heat bands.

The most effective means of applying the torch is to hold the workpiece in one corner with tweezers and direct heat to the underside. In this way, both the torch and workpiece can be moved around independently to create the desired effect. By heating from below, the emerging colors can readily be observed without interference of glare from the torch's flame. Some practice is required to learn how much heat to apply before too thick an oxide film builds up and the colors begin to degrade.

A variation on this approach is to selectively stop-out areas of the metal with a lacquer resist and to electroplate a contrasting metal onto the titanium before heating. After plating and removing the stop-out, the torch can then be applied beneath the unplated areas. Oxidation colors can be developed to complement the plated surfaces (figure 4–59).

Anodized Coloring

In anodizing titanium, an oxide film is formed on the surface of the workpiece (the anode) in an electrolyte solution. Electrical current is drawn through the solution by means of a titanium or stainless steel plate (cathode). Equipment needed for anodizing is similar to that used in the electroforming and plating process.

An electroplating rectifier with a rheostat, ammeter, voltmeter, and an output range of 0 to 150 volts is the most reliable source of electrical current. A clear glass tank, Pyrex beaker, or large wide-mouthed jar tall enough to accommodate the workpiece is adequate to contain the electrolyte bath. Other nonconductive, noncorrosive containers can be used as substitutes.

Almost any acid or alkaline electrolyte will work. An excellent formula for the anodizing bath is a 10 percent solution of ammonium sulfate in tap water. A 5 percent solution of sulfuric acid in water will work, too. Anodizing will even occur in fresh cola! **When mixing the electrolyte remember to add acid to water (not the reverse!) and to mix and use it in a well-vented area. When not in use, the bath solution should be stored in clean, noncorrosive containers.** If the solution becomes

4–59 *After selective gold plating, the titanium is heat colored from the underside with a small butane/oxygen torch.*

discolored or the anodizing action is slow, the bath should be replaced.

In anodizing, the anode is the workpiece that is to receive the oxide film. If the work is to be totally immersed in the bath, it should have a titanium or stainless steel wire firmly attached to it for positive electrical contact. This will ensure an evenly anodized film. If the piece does not need to be totally immersed, it may be attached directly to the insulated lead of the rectifier with heavy-duty alligator clips. The anode is connected to the positive terminal of the rectifier. **Always remember that the power must be off when connecting to either terminals of the rectifier.** A sheet of titanium or stainless steel will act as the cathode. It should be roughly the size of the workpiece. The cathode is connected to the negative terminal of the rectifier, also with a heavy-duty alligator clip.

After the bath has been prepared, the workpiece cleaned, and proper connections made to the rectifier, the anode and cathode are placed in the electrolyte. Place the pieces as far apart as possible in order to help the oxide film form evenly, producing more uniform and clearer colors. **Because the voltage necessary to anodize titanium extends into the potentially lethal range, the utmost care should be taken to avoid electrical shock. The work area must be kept dry and rubber gloves should be worn during the anodizing process.** When everything is in place, the power is turned on and increased in 10-volt steps allowing the voltmeter to return to zero with each 10-volt increase. The oxide film becomes thicker as voltage is increased.

Voltage	Color
3 to 5	pale yellow
10	golden
15	dark golden brown
20	purple
25	purple blue
30	Prussian blue
35	sky blue
40	gray blue
45	green blue
50	pale yellow green
55	green tinge
60	green gold
65	green with purple marks
70	rose gold
75	red purple
80	gold purple
85	dark dull purple
90	green purple
95	dark green
100	matte, streaky gray
110	pale gray

When making a piece with more than one color, it is best to stop-out the areas that are to receive lower voltage colors, and apply the highest voltage color first. After removing the stop-out resist the lower voltage colors can be applied successively, without any effect on the first colors. This can be achieved with all the colors down the line, provided all the areas to receive lower voltage colors are stopped-out when the higher voltage colors are being applied. Because the coloring comes entirely from the oxide film, the metal beneath remains gray. This is true in both the oxidation and anodization process. If unwanted color is produced, it can be etched, sanded, or polished away. After anodizing is completed, the piece should be rinsed in clean water and patted dry with soft tissue to avoid streaking. Should the oxide film become dulled from dirt or grease, it may be restored by carefully washing the piece with a solution of detergent and water. Refer to Appendix 4 for a listing of suppliers for refractory metals.

COLORING ALUMINUM

Considering the wide use of colored metals, it is surprising that very few jewelers have incorporated the technique of color anodizing in their work. In some respects, colored aluminum has as much creative potential as the currently popular refractory metals. Aluminum can be easily formed by any of the traditional metalworking techniques, and it is light in weight and relatively inexpensive. The only drawback is that the anodization and coloring process is multistep, requiring more time and equipment than other coloring techniques. Those having experience with electroplating and the related equipment should be able to set up an anodizing system with little problem. **Keep in mind that the process involves hazardous chemicals and electrical current. All manufacturer's instructions should be followed scrupulously, work areas well vented, rubber gloves, apron, and safety glasses be worn, and the area kept dry. The reader**

4–60 Joseph Wood. *Pins of anodized and colored aluminum. Courtesy of the artist.*

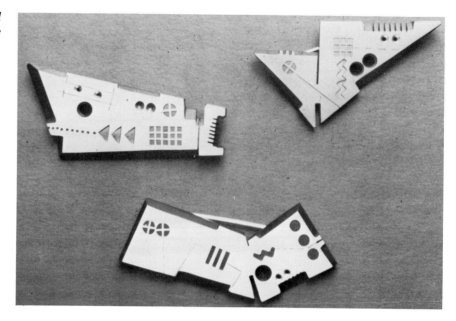

should study the section on electroforming and electroplating before proceeding.

The Process

Anodization of aluminum is the process by which an aluminum oxide film is developed electrochemically on the metal's surface. The process consists of making the work piece electrically positive (the anode) in an electrolyte bath of sulfuric acid and water. Other types of electrolytes are used industrially but are generally inferior in terms of the resulting colors. The oxidation film created on the aluminum's surface changes the physical and chemical characteristics of the metal surface causing it to become more corrosion-resistant, harder, and more abrasion-resistant and allows dye color to be absorbed into the surface.

A typical anodizing/coloring process involves surface preparation and cleaning of the metal, anodization, several rinses throughout the process, dyeing, and sealing. This, of course, is simplifying the steps and the number of chemicals and bath containers needed along the way. The accompanying schematic illustration (figure 4–61) will give the reader some idea of what is involved.

Fortunately, for our purposes the processes can be altered somewhat to fit individual needs. The following guide through the steps of anodization and coloring can be supplemented by researching related books listed in the bibliography.

1 In general, highest-purity wrought alloys bring about the clearest anodic film and thus the most vibrant colors. Colors will develop with less quality as alloys having a larger amount of constituents are used. Alloys of the 1,000, 5,000, and 6,000 series provide high-clarity oxide films and bright colors. This is not to say many other alloys will not develop interesting effects that might well fit one's work. All alloys can be anodized and colored to some degree.

2 On forms requiring welded seams, the filler material should be as close as possible to the parent metal in alloy constituents as this will have some bearing on the uniformity of the oxide coating and color of the finished piece.

3 Cast forms are perhaps the most difficult on which to apply uniform coloration. A casting's inherent porosity (resulting from the material's crystalline structure not being compressed or worked as in the case of extruded or wrought material) will likely cause spotting or result in some areas not taking the oxide film or color. Another problem occurs when alloy components become segregated in the casting process and take the oxide coat unevenly. Alloy series 535 and A-514 are those that work best for casting. A mild etch with dilute acid and neutralization in a bath of sodium bicarbonate will aid a cast form's dye-absorption qualities.

4 Surface preparation is an extremely important factor

Basic Steps of the Sulfuric Acid Anodizing and Coloring Process

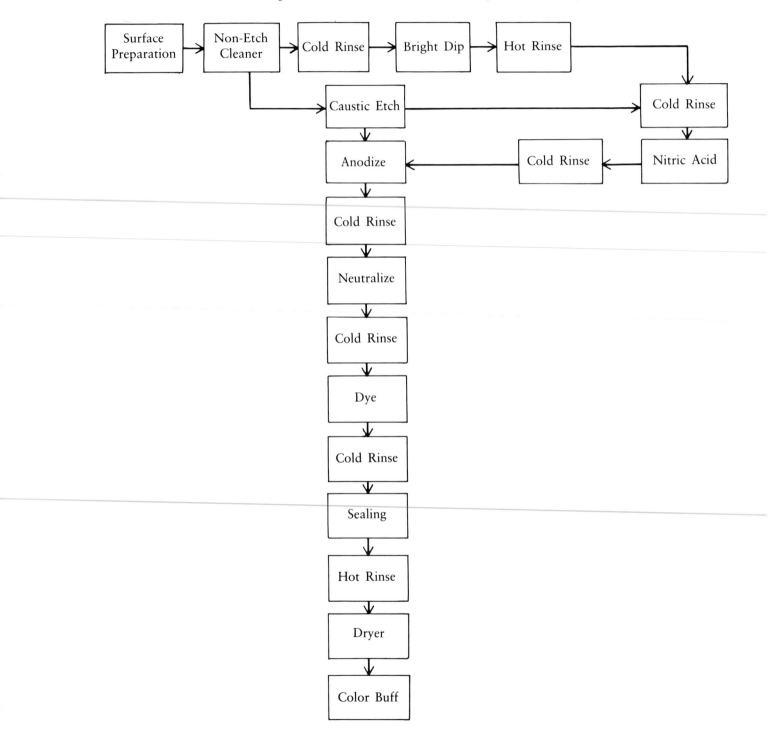

relative to the creative application of the process. The jeweler's expertise and inventiveness with other jewelry-making processes can easily come into play in creating a wide variety of effects in the finished work. For example, buffing and electrochemical brightening will develop a mirrorlike finish. Emery cloth, brushing, or coarse buffing will bring forth textural surfaces. Sandblasting over stopped-out areas allows the worker to create patterns of crisp-edge contrast. Carried further, sandblasting or etching will create relief forms. Overall matte finishes may be achieved with mild etching solutions. In any case, regardless of pretreatment, the metal must be chemically cleaned prior to being anodized. Cleaning is generally completed in a nonetching alkaline bath. Improper cleaning will cause spotty anodizing and contamination of the electrolyte bath.

5 Sulfuric acid based electrolyte bath is most commonly used in anodizing. Solutions of 15 to 25 percent by weight at 70 to 75°F are recommended. Electrical current requirements will vary depending on the bath's electrical conductivity, temperature, and the size and type of alloy being anodized, but will generally range from 10 to 20 volts. The time required for anodizing depends upon the desired oxide thickness and the color that will eventually be applied. For example, a decorative metallic gold color would require a very thin (.08 mils) oxide coating while a black color subject to the weather's wear might call for an oxide coating fifteen times as thick. Oxide coatings for decorative purposes are generally in the range of .0001 to .0007 inch think. Anodizing times are typically 10 to 30 minutes. Bath tanks may be of plastic and sheet lead may be used as the cathode. Cathode surface area should be approximately that of the workpiece. The anodized work should be suspended in the bath by aluminum or titanium hooks or wires. Bath agitation can be supplied by small-diameter plastic tubing delivering filtered compressed air. The following list gives the approximate amounts of sulfuric acid needed to make up baths of specific percentages.

15 percent—12   fluid ounces of sulfuric acid per gallon

18 percent—14.7 fluid ounces of sulfuric acid per gallon

20 percent—16.6 fluid ounces of sulfuric acid per gallon

25 percent—21.4 fluid ounces of sulfuric acid per gallon

6 As indicated by the schematic, several rinses will be required as work progresses. The number of rinses will depend on the design of the workpiece. Regardless of one's design, rinsing after anodizing is essential in order to prevent contamination of the dye bath by sulfates or aluminum constituents. Poor rinsing can cause uneven or streaked coloration. Rinsing should take place immediately after anodizing and the workpiece quickly placed in the dye bath. At this point, a warm rinse is most effective. Enclosed forms should be neutralized after a prerinse and then rerinsed in warm water. Rinse and neutralizing tanks may also be of plastic. It is best to use distilled water, but tap water will suffice unless it is excessively hard or iron content exists.

7 Colors are developed by dye absorption into the anodic film. The actual process is quite simple. A bath of water and .025 to 1 percent dyestuff is generally used. The solution is heated to 150°F in a stainless steel, glass, plastic, or fiberglass container. Immersion heaters work well. Baths can be agitated mechanically or by compressed air passed through a filter and oil trap. Oil passing into the dye bath through the air system will contaminate the solution and result in a spotted and streaked workpiece. If a metal bath tank is used, hooks or workpiece attachments must be physically isolated from the tank; otherwise, galvanic current will be generated and cause pitting of the work. Plastic hooks can be safely used to suspend the form. A 10-minute immersion time is usually adequate in coloring most objects.

8 Coloring is normally followed by a sealing process wherein the workpiece is taken immediately from the dye bath, given a thorough cold-water rinse, and then immersed in the sealing bath. The sealing bath tank should be of stainless steel or other inert material capable of withstanding temperatures in the 200°F range. Sealing baths should be constantly filtered through activated carbon. Sealing consists of immersing the workpiece in a hot water solution for approximately 10 minutes. This closes the microscopic pores in the anodic coat, thus preventing further staining as well as leaching out of color. A typical sealing solution is composed of water with .5 percent nickel acetate and .5 percent boric acid. The nickel acetate/

boric acid solution prevents leaching and keeps smutty deposits from developing on the workpiece. In lieu of adding nickel acetate and boric acid, commercial sealing salts are available. After sealing, the work is rinsed in water at 150°F and then dried. Appendix 4 lists a major supplier of sealing salts and dyes.

Suppliers of anodizing materials are usually helpful in providing in-depth information regarding the process, optimum components, and maintenance of baths. For those wishing to explore this technique, suppliers can be contacted for additional information.

Multicolor Anodizing

In addition to the one-color anodizing process, multicolor anodizing offers many possibilities. Considerable research will be needed before actually proceeding in these areas. The following five methods are feasible.

1 A multiple anodizing entailing a normal process of anodizing, coloring, and sealing; application of resist to particular areas; stripping of the entire oxide film from unprotected areas; and repeating this entire process for each additional color.

2 A single anodizing in which an anodic film of sufficient thickness to absorb the color required for the darkest shade is first applied. The workpiece is dyed but left unsealed, a resist is applied in specific areas, and the uncovered dye bleached out with a solution that leaves the oxide film intact. This process is repeated for each subsequent shade. To finish, the resist is removed with a solvent and the entire workpiece sealed. In some instances, where a dark shade is to be dyed after a pastel, a modification omits the bleaching step and the supplementary dye is applied directly over the preceding color.

3 Special combined ink resist enables specific patterns to be applied on an anodic coating in several colors. A ground color may then be added by conventional dyeing, as the ink resist serves as a stop-out for the printed areas.

4 Preanodized, photosensitized aluminum is commercially available and used in the printing industry. Images in black can be produced by photographic means and the background colored by the immersion dye method.

5 A combination of any of these along with sandblasting, etching, or selective electroplating.

CHAPTER FIVE

Forging

5–1 Jon Havener. *Forged and constructed pin of sterling silver. Side elements were laterally bent while forging. Courtesy of the artist.*

HAMMER WORK

Forging is a forming process by which metal, usually standard sizes of rod and wire, is hammered into new forms. Few techniques so completely demonstrate direct personal effort as does forging. By controlled blows of the hammer, a redistribution of the original mass occurs, creating new shapes not easily achieved by other means. With experience, the number of form possibilities is unlimited. Compression and movement of the metal is attained by the force of the hammer's face penetrating the metal's structure as the metal is supported over an anvil (figure 5–2) or a metalworking stake. The hammer and the supporting surface act much like the rollers of a rolling mill. Rather than a smooth rolling, squeezing action along the total width of the structure, only selected areas are worked, thereby permitting the craftsperson to create the desired form.

For most jewelry-making purposes, nonferrous metals (silver, gold, and copper-based materials) are forged cold. The direction of the movement of the metal is dependent on the shape of the hammer's face and the angle at which it is used. Two common forging hammers are the cross-peen hammer and a slightly rounded flat-faced hammer (figure 5–3). The cross peen acts much like a wedge as it penetrates the metal's structure, compressing and stretching the mass perpendicular to the peen face with little or no stretch perpendicular to the handle (figure 5–4). The fact that stretch only occurs fore and aft allows the worker to direct blows at specific points, widening, elongating, swelling, or thickening as needed. The cross peen is ideal for precise control and economy of materials. A slightly rounded flat-faced hammer causes the metal's mass to stretch in all direc-

5–2   *Anvil of heat-treated cast steel.*

5–3   *Cross-peen and flat-faced forging hammers.*

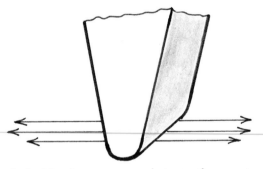

5–4   *Metal's movement relative to the cross peen.*

tions. This hammer works well for smoothing out other hammer marks or to widen and elongate with each blow. Since the metal moves in all directions, some degree of control is lost (figure 5–5).

Another important factor is the depth to which the hammer penetrates the surface. At times, the worker must exert substantial force to move the metal; at other times delicate blows must be delivered. Generally, this variation is needed when working from thick to thin as the form evolves and refinement nears. Uniform compression and stretching occurs as the hammer's face strikes parallel to the workpiece's surface. A twist or tilt of the hammer allows the face to angle causing greater compression on one side. Deliberate, controlled angling of the hammer is an effective method of creating curved forms. This technique is sometimes used to forge rod or wire into neck pieces. Again, facility with the hammer comes only with experience.

After each pass of the cross peen, many jewelers routinely rework the hammered surface with a planishing hammer. Its slightly domed face is used to smooth the characteristically bumpy surface left by the wedge effect of the cross peen. In planishing, the forging marks or series of high and low points are compacted to a uniform level. A few minutes of careful planishing will shorten finishing time considerably. To forge a uniform thickness or cross section, it is a good practice to work both sides of the metal or, in the case of tapering rod, all four sides. This is necessary because metal compression

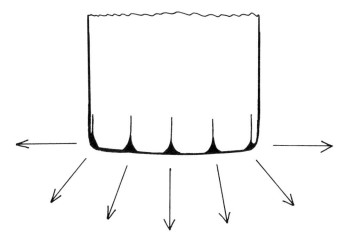

5–5 *Metal moves in all directions when struck with a rounded flat-faced hammer.*

5–6 **Barbara Mail,** The Black Sheep as Father of the Bride. *Fibula of sterling silver, 14-karat gold, ivory, amethyst, crystal, optical lens, and dried flower petals; carved, forged, and constructed. Courtesy of the artist.*

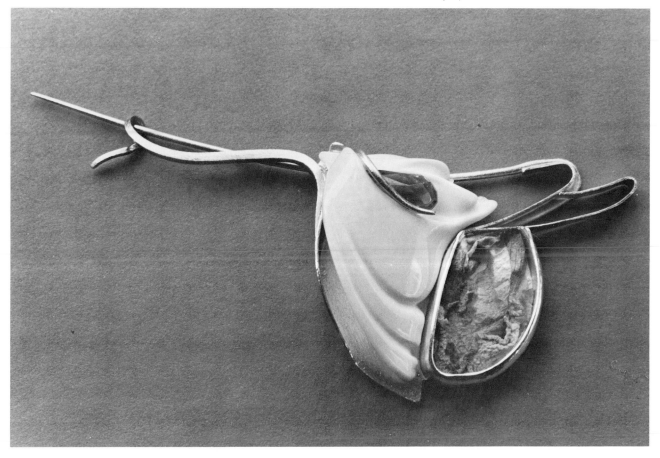

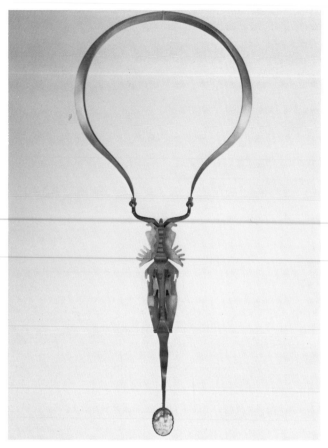

or spread is less on the anvil side. This practice also prevents projecting edges from folding over and perhaps closing entirely (figure 5–8). If projecting edges develop they should be planished back (figure 5–9). If edges develop to the point that they cannot be flattened, the surface should be filed smooth. As work progresses, close attention must be given to the increasing hardness of the metal, making it brittle and less malleable. When this occurs, the piece must be annealed to return it to a workable state. A practical indicator of the need for annealing is the resistance felt to the hammer as the form takes shape. The ability to sense resistance and subtle changes in hardness comes through practice. If the finished piece is to remain work hardened, as for example a pin stem or springing element, the work should not be annealed after the final forging pass. All metals react differently to forging; some are more malleable and require annealing less often. Figures 5–10 through 5–20 illustrate the forging of a spoon-like form. Figure 5–21 shows its final use in a pendant.

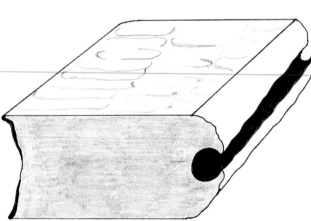

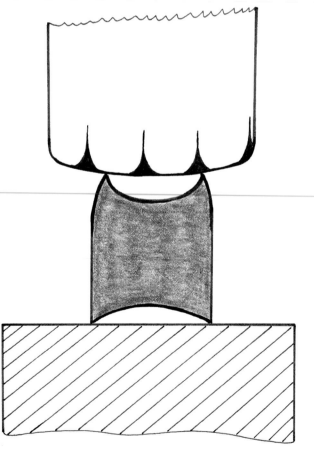

5–7 **Mark Knuth.** *Pendant of copper and brass with agate created through marriage of metals, forging, and construction. Courtesy of the artist.*

5–8 *Section showing how projecting edges develop and eventually close if not corrected.*

5–9 *Edges are corrected by planishing back.*

5–10 *Double spoon shape made of 6-gauge copper.*
5–11 *Round-faced forming hammer is used to stretch and dome one spoon end.*
5–12 *Spoon end roughly domed.*

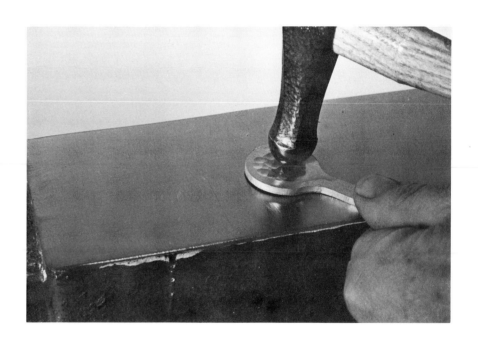

5-13

5-14

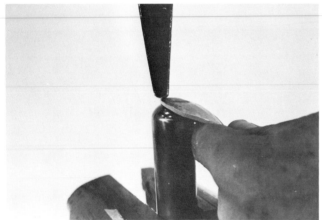

5-15

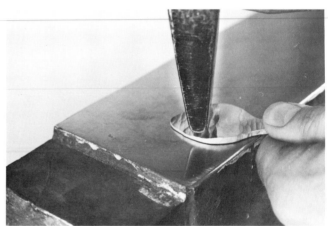

5-16

5-17

5–13 Spoon is further formed and refined with a planishing hammer over a small steel stake.

5–14 The midsection is thinned or "drawn out" with the cross peen over the tip of the anvil's horn.

5–15 Selected areas of the spoon's edge are thinned with the cross peen.

5–16 The other end is forged and drawn out into a tonguelike form.

5–17 The size of the roughly forged spoon relative to the original cardboard pattern. This comparison gives some idea of the yield or the extent to which this shape in 6-gauge material can be forged. The bowl was further stretched prior to finishing. The tongue end was left relatively thick.

5–18 The forming hammer is used to sink the bowl end into a stump recess.

5–19 The spoon's bowl was pushed inward at red heat with a spoon stake over a solder pad.

5–20 Forged and planished spoon. The final finish was then achieved by filing, emerying, and buffing.

5-18

5-19

5-20

5–21 *Final use of the forged spoon shape: pendant of sterling silver and copper with moonstone. Gold-plated, woven, forged, and constructed.*

An important and often overlooked factor in forming metal is the need to retain enough material for compression during planishing and removal in filing and buffing. With accurate hammer work, very little material need be removed in the final stages of refinement. Even so, neglecting to leave enough material for finishing ends in thin, flimsy, or poorly fitted work.

While it is most common to forge rod or wire, thick sheet or plate can be used. Rough shapes may be precut and their final forms defined with the hammer (figure 5–22). Regardless of the materials used, work need not be large. Controlled, accurate hammer work may be applied to create or work harden small articles like pin stems, dangles, clips, chain links, and other decorative elements.

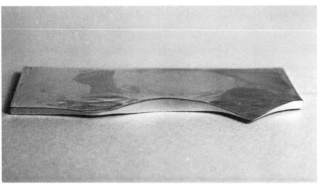

5–22 *Forged plate demonstrating thinning and upsetting.*

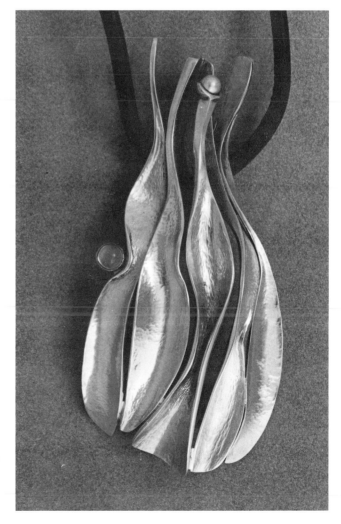

5–23 **Jon Havener.** *Pendant of sterling silver with pearl and moonstone. This forged and constructed piece depicts a creative use of tool marks framed by highly refined thick and thin edges. Courtesy of the artist.*

TAPERING

Drawing out or forging a tapered rod is generally faster and more economical than shaping with a file. The basic process is the same regardless of the size of the form, whether it is a large tapering neckpiece or a delicate hanging element. Start with a square rod and keep it square until the desired taper has been forged. Begin at the thickest section of the rod and hammer outward to its end. Hammer blows are struck with less force as the taper evolves. Each new pass of the hammer is started closer to the thinnest end of the rod (figure 5–24). Each of the rod's four sides is worked equally. Care must be taken that the hammer be struck precisely at right angles across the rod's axis. This assures a straight, even taper and prevents the rod's cross section from developing a parallelogram shape (figure 5–25). In the event a parallelogram does develop, the two extreme projecting edges can possibly be forged back (figure 5–26). In some instances it is more expedient to hammer down all edges, rounding the rod and resquaring. This step is taken with a relatively flat, round-faced hammer. Several practice pieces will help the worker judge taper rate and the amount of elongation attainable. Experience will soon provide accurate determinations of what size material to start with and at what point to begin the taper. If in the end a round cross section is desired, planish down all projecting edges as the piece is slowly rotated across the face of the anvil.

Tapers and some linear forms may also be shaped with the rolling mill. The process is called *grade rolling*. When using the mill for this purpose, the rod is put through the rollers in steps beginning at the thin end. Figure 5–27 illustrates an exaggerated view of the process. The resulting steps are later planished down.

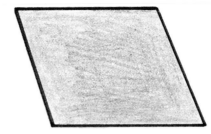

5–25   *Parallelogram.*

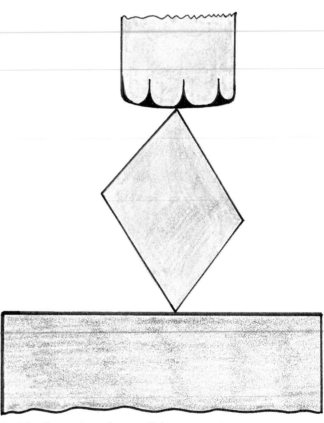

5–26   *Correction of a parallelogram section.*

5–24   *Exaggerated view depicting the development of a taper.*

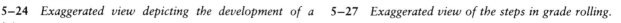

5–27   *Exaggerated view of the steps in grade rolling.*

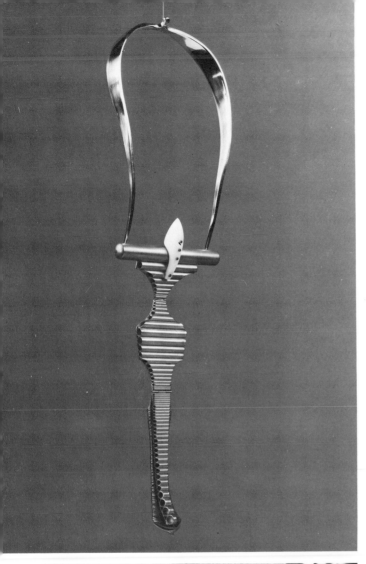

HOT FORGING

Although hot forging is more often thought of as a blacksmithing or decorative iron technique, it can save time for the jeweler, particularly when forging heavy stock. Many aspects of forging iron and nonferrous metals are quite different. Therefore, this section deals only with the materials commonly used in jewelry work: copper, brass, bronze, silver, and gold.

Metal heated to a dull red color becomes extremely plastic and is easily shaped with a hammer. With pliers, wrenches, or tongs, its form can be twisted or bent with ease. When accustomed to the character of cold metal, one soon discovers the need for restrained hammer force when working the metal hot. Ideally, forging should take place in subdued light in order to accurately distinguish the metal's color and reduce the possibility of overheating. Cracking or shattering may occur if forging is attempted at temperatures above the dull red color. For optimum efficiency, the workpiece should be forged quickly and returned to the heat source before it cools, thereby reducing the reheating time. The anvil should be close to the heat source and tools within reach to further reduce the time between heating and forging.

There are other heat sources to choose from. For occasional needs, a natural gas/compressed air torch with a large head is adequate. A bed of pumice stones surrounded on three sides by firebrick provides a heat chamber in which to place work (figure 5–29). Rather than relighting and holding the torch by hand, a simple torch stand can be constructed to direct a constant flame, freeing both hands for work (figure 5–30). Where natural gas is not available, other types of torches may be used, but usually at greater expense or less efficiency. While not practical in all shops, a coke forge is an excellent heat source.

5–28 *Neckpiece and pendant of sterling, brass, and Delrin. Hot forged, constructed, and gold plated.*
5–29 *Heat chamber constructed of soft fire brick and pumice stones.*

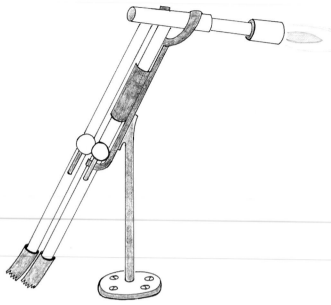

5–30 *Torch holder.*

HAMMER TEXTURING

While not usually thought of as a forging technique, the application of hammer textures may be employed in a dual role. As texture is being created, surfaces can also be thinned, upset, or thickened at the same time. In seeking hammer effects beyond the traditional planishing mark, contemporary jewelers have recently begun working with a variety of hammer shapes and sizes. Hammer faces are sometimes altered by grinding to new shapes or incised to desired textural patterns. As metal is struck, its surface is marked with texture corresponding to that applied to the hammer's face. Textures may range from subtle, uniform lines, to deep, coarse breaks along the edge of the work (see figures 5–31). Inherent in the use of hammer texturing is the option to use the same energy to shape or define the form of the object. Most workpieces can be supported over common stakes or the anvil. Coarse, broken-edge textures are best achieved over the extreme edge of the anvil's face with the hammer angles slightly outward to prevent damage to the anvil.

A reversal of this process is the embossing or hammering of sheet metal into a hard, textured surface. To explore possible effects, begin with a domed-face hardwood or plastic mallet and thin annealed sheet copper. The choice of textured material to hammer over is limited only by the imagination. A few examples are concrete, sandpaper, corroded steel, screen wire, fibers, plastics, and hardwood. Slightly different textures with similar materials can be achieved using thicker metal and steel hammers. See also chapter 9 sections on plated laminations and Damascus (pattern welded) steel.

TOOL CARE

The importance of proper tools, especially the anvil, cannot be overemphasized. Forming stakes may be suitable surfaces if an anvil is unavailable. A good anvil provides a smooth, massive, permanent fixture to work upon. The smooth, flat surface of the anvil face and the tapered horn provide shaping surfaces for most forged jewelry forms. New anvils are available through a number of tool, blacksmithing, and jewelry supply firms. Used anvils may be acquired in searches through scrap yards, farm auctions, or junk stores. The decision to

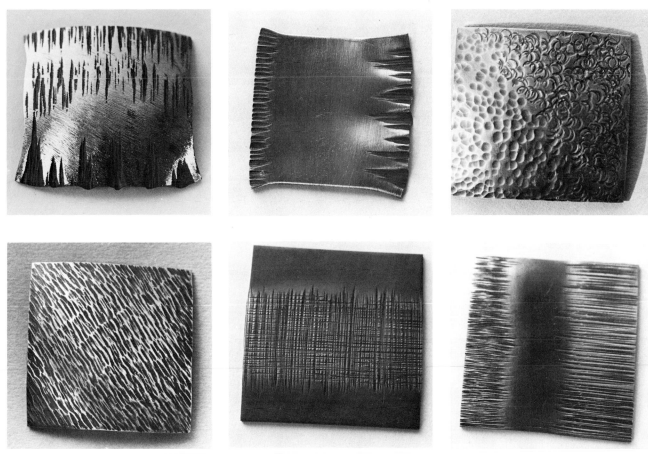

5–31 *Hammer textures created using a variety of hammer face shapes and sizes.*

purchase a used tool should be considered carefully. Time and money spent searching for and resurfacing a tool may be greater than that expended on a new, guaranteed tool. Used anvils must be examined thoroughly. Bowed or deeply pitted surfaces may be beyond repair.

Modern anvils have several inherent advantages over older anvils. Generally, today's anvils are made of select, high-quality steel and are cast in one piece. With older anvils, tempered steel faces were welded onto soft iron bodies. The resulting stresses or strains between the tempered work surface and the softer body often cause chipping of the edges or splitting of the face. One-piece anvils can be precisely heat treated so that hardness decreases gradually downward, from a hard face to a comparatively soft body, leaving no stresses in the anvil.

The heat-treatment process is made possible by the homogeneity of the anvil material throughout and by modern facilities for precise heat treating.

Placement of stakes or the anvil surface should be at a comfortable working height. For the standing, average-height worker, a comfortable working level is usually around 29 inches. This is not an ironclad rule and could of course vary with the individual. The hammer should just touch the striking surface as the worker stands erect with the arm parallel to the body (figure 5–33). While working on small, delicate pieces, some workers prefer a comfortable sitting position. Although not as effective for long periods as on work of considerable mass, sitting does allow a close, accurate view of the process. Anvil placement should be at approximately the same height while the worker sits.

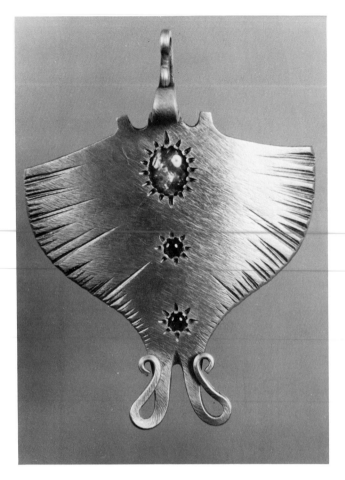

Routine maintenance and care of tools is important. Sharp edges of hammer faces should be filed down and polished smooth. The anvil's face should be flat and free of scratches and dents. In short, all surfaces in contact with the forged piece should be smooth to prevent marring the work in process. Preventive care of tool surfaces will save hours of finish work. Slight scratches in tool surfaces can be removed by hand with abrasive paper and polishing tools. Deep marks can be taken out with files and, in some instances, a belt sander. Soft cast-iron stakes can be planished to remove dents.

5–32 *Pin of copper with opal triplet and garnets. Textured with a hammer and file.*

5–33 *A check of proper anvil height.*

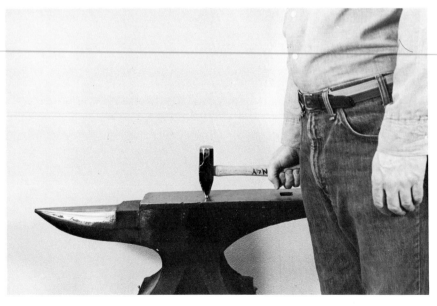

THE FORGE

Throughout our examination of jewelry techniques, we will focus on areas that might call for the use of a forge. While many jewelers will never require one, those wishing to explore metal laminations or hot forging in depth will find a forge necessary. Forge design has remained relatively unchanged for many years (figure 5–34). In its basic form, a forge is made up of a forced-air system that directs air beneath a fuel bed of coal, coke, or charcoal. Generally, air is forced in below the coals by a centrifugal blower driven by hand or an electric motor. Heat intensity is determined by the rate and volume of air flow, usually determined by the blower's speed. For our purposes, the forge's fire provides a relatively large, hot, and clean heat source. Forges are fueled by soft, low-sulfur coal, small chunks of coke, or charcoal. In some areas of the country, it may be difficult to purchase small quantities of blacksmith's coal or suitable coke. Some craftworkers forgo the expense of large quantities of coal or coke, and for occasional use purchase bagged charcoal locally.

Forges need not be large and heavy like those typically found in a blacksmith's shop. Smaller forges can be made portable to be used inside or outside the shop. Used inside, the forge must be vented, sometimes through existing ducts and hoods. In some areas, small rivet forges may be purchased secondhand at farm auctions or in scrap yards. These forges are similar in appearance and size to the typical backyard barbeque cooker. A relatively lightweight forge can be fabricated with angle iron and steel plate (figure 5–35).

Additional information on the forge can be found in chapter 9 and in the excellent books listed in the bibliography.

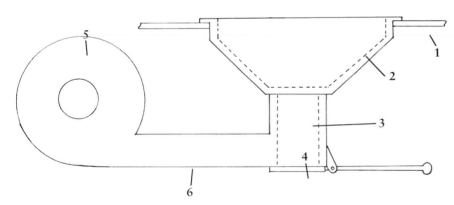

5–34 Forge details: (1) bed, (2) fire pot, (3) tuyere, (4) ash door, (5) blower, and (6) air inlet.

5–35 Lightweight, homemade forge.

CHAPTER SIX

Casting

GLOSSARY OF CASTING TERMS

Burnout. The process used to cure and heat molds and to evacuate the model.

Button. Excess metal that forms in the mold area left by the sprue former. The excess metal or button provides additional force to the liquid stream and acts as a reservoir in supplying metal to the casting as it solidifies.

Crucible. A container in which the metal is held while it is melted. Crucibles are generally made of ceramic or graphite materials.

Flask. Variously sized stainless steel cylinders designed to surround and contain the mold body.

Investment. A plasterlike silica-based material used to make molds.

Model. A permanent or disposable form used to create the mold cavity.

Mold. A hollow or negative space into which molten metal is poured or injected.

Sprue. In its solid state, the sprue suspends or supports the model inside the flask and liquid investment material. Sprues are eventually evacuated by heat. The resulting channels are the paths through which molten metal enters the mold cavity. Wax wire is the material typically used to make sprues.

Sprue base. A rubber or metal disc-like fixture used to seal the flask's bottom edge against the leakage of investment material.

Sprue former. The center, conical portion of the sprue base. The point of attachment of the wax sprues.

Casting was the second major breakthrough discovered by prehistoric metalworkers. At some point after learning to beat metal into utilitarian shapes they techniques. Before examining the casting process, however, an important question should be considered: Why cast it? There are probably as many answers as there are jewelers. Some jewelers cast every piece they make. This could be due to economics or simply because they enjoy working with the related materials and the process. Others prefer to work directly with metal and seldom do castings. A good guideline is to cast a piece if it cannot be accurately constructed or formed directly in a reasonable time. Too often objects are cast that could easily be constructed directly in sheet metal or wire. Cast forms should fit the process and related materials. The modeling and molding materials, tools, and equipment at our disposal offer an exciting range of expressive possibilities.

The techniques presented in this chapter are associated with preformed models. Generally, molds are carved directly or fashioned around a removable model. Most of the modeling materials examined here are relatively soft, easily carved, or pliable when heated.

6–1   Carrie Adell, Honeycomb Collar. *14- and 18-karat gold with citrines and diamonds; cast and constructed. This piece exemplifies the fine detailing and realism attainable with patient wax modeling. Courtesy of the artist. Photograph by Douglas Long.*

6–2   Lee B. Peck, 3 Bird Ring. *Cast in sterling silver with copper and gold plating. Courtesy of the artist. Photograph by Larry Gregory.*

realized that molten metal could be poured into the negative spaces of crude molds. Whatever was at hand served in fashioning these molds—stone, sand, clay, dung, wood. Upon solidifying, the metal formed the positive shape desired.

While the process has progressed from those first rudimentary pours to modern industrial castings weighing tons and sophisticated enough to support moon visits, jewelers generally do not need such advanced

WAX MODELS

Of all the modeling materials jewelers might choose, wax is the most varied in available forms and physical qualities. Jewelry and dental suppliers offer it in chunks, blocks, sheet, rod, and wire of literally any cross section and size.

Natural waxes are derived from many sources. The general types are compounds of animal, vegetable, and mineral materials. Basic ingredients are diverse and can range from beeswax and coal residue to tree sap. A number of excellent synthetic waxes are also being used. These are often composed of plastic substances or resins and are quite similar to natural wax compositions. While many jewelers make their own wax to obtain certain qualities, most jewelers purchase ready-to-use waxes. Commercial wax is blended with additives to give each product specific characteristics: softness, hardness, brittleness, flexibility, melting point, expansion, and so on. Manufacturers usually color their wax to identify their hardness or other properties.

Wax Modeling

The variety of waxes available makes it the ideal medium for model making. In a sense, wax working is like sculpting in clay. Models can be created by additive or subtractive techniques depending upon form requirements and the wax properties. Piercing, melting, dripping, filing, and sanding are all possible approaches.

6—4 Carrie Adell, Garland of Sterling Silver Garlic Pendants. *Cast and constructed. Courtesy of the artist. Photograph by Jo Moss.*

6—3 Susan Noland. *Cast ring of 14-karat gold with diamonds and integral prongs and channel settings. Courtesy of the artist. Photograph by Leslie Becker.*

Brittle wax can be filed, sawn, or shaped with rotary steel burrs, or bent and formed by hand after immersion in warm water. Separate elements of sheet or wax wire can be joined by applying a bit of molten wax at points that touch. Figure 6–5 shows just a small sample of the waxes available.

Regardless of the number and clarity of the words spoken or written on the working of wax, proficiency can only be gained through practice. A few basic guidelines, plus many hours of trial and error are the most effective teachers.

Wax-Working Tools

Wax modeling requires few special tools. The family dentist may be willing to give up older implements, the kind used to pack cavities or to scrape in and around teeth. Most are 5 to 6 inches long and are made with a variety of working ends, hooks, spoons, and spatula. Files and saw blades for cutting wax can be purchased from jewelry suppliers.

An excellent tool can be fashioned with coat hanger or heavy binding wire. The tool is formed by cutting a 6-inch length of wire and filing one end to a gradually tapering point. Starting about 1½ inches from one end, file to a fine point. A blunted point will not heat as quickly as the taper. The opposite end can be broadened to a spoon or spatula shape with a small forming hammer (figure 6–6). Further refinement of this end is usually a matter of just a few strokes of a file. Biology probes also work well.

Any tools beyond these few can be purchased or made as the work requires. Many jewelers will testify that, as with other techniques, countless tools are available but only a few are relied on steadily. In addition to these few hand tools, an alcohol lamp is needed to heat the ends of the tool and in some cases to apply heat directly to wax. The lamp can also be angled so that wax wire can be held by the flame and melted onto the model. Some jewelers use the lamp to melt wax into water, resulting in free-form pieces of wax.

After the basic form of the model is attained, final finishing can be achieved with fine files, emery cloth, or very careful buffing. Passing a model over the alcohol lamp will fire polish its surface. This method is a bit risky, especially on models having intricate detail or crisp edges. Fire polishing is most effective on soft waxes. The harder plasticlike materials are finished by hand or mechanical means.

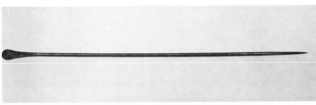

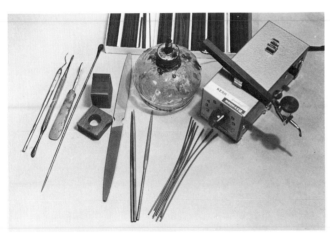

6–5   *A few of the many waxes available to the jeweler.*
6–6   *Handmade coat hanger wire wax tool.*
6–7   *Wax-working tools.*

NONWAX MODELS

6–8 Harold O'Connor. *Brooch of 18-karat gold with lapis lazuli; cast from a polyethylene model. Rich textures develop instantly through carefully heating the model over an alcohol lamp. Edges and raised areas can be smoothed and polished after the form is cast. Courtesy of the artist. Photograph by Ron Burton.*

Theoretically, any material that will burn away at a temperature lower than that at which investment begins to deteriorate may be used to make casting models—quite a range. A number of jewelers are creating exciting pieces using all types of plastic as modeling material. Plastics can be poured, carved, or bent to shape. Hobby and toy stores are a good source of ready-made plastic models that can be cut or altered to fit the creative concept. Styrofoam is also readily available in many forms and textural qualities. Styrofoam is particularly interesting to work with because of its instantaneous reaction to heat and the textures that develop. With practice, the worker can develop considerable control in forming and the placement of textured pattern. Generally, plastics and other nonwax materials do not burn out as cleanly as wax. Longer burnouts and higher temperatures may be needed for complete evacuation. The fumes or dust of any modeling material should be vented or filtered to prevent inhalation.

MEASUREMENT OF CASTING METAL

Determination of the amount of metal needed for a casting can be made after the wax model is finished. Ideally, this should be calculated with the sprues attached to the model, thus removing guesswork. Weigh the model and multiply this weight by the specific gravity of the metal being cast. A gram or Troy weight scale is generally used (figures 6–9 and 6–10). To the calculated weight, add approximately ¼ ounce or sufficient metal to fill the sprue button cavity. If the model is weighed without sprues, a bit more metal is added as compensation.

When a scale is not available, the metal's weight can be determined by volume or the water displacement method. Again, it is best to have the model's sprues attached. A narrow glass beaker is partially filled with water. Into this the model is submerged with an attached piece of binding wire (figure 6–12). The wire is needed to push the wax down, overcoming its buoyancy. The rise in water level is marked with tape or felt markers and the model removed. Metal, usually scrap or casting shot, is dropped into the beaker until water again rises to the marked level. To this is added the amount that will fill the sprue button cavity. Metal weight relative to that of nonwax models may also be determined by the water displacement method.

6–9 *Gram scale.*

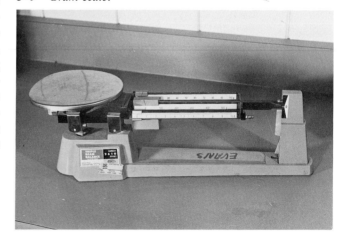

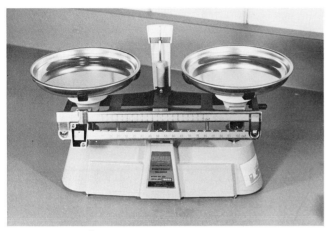

6–10   *Troy scale.*

6–11   *Graduated beaker and rubber mixing bowl.*

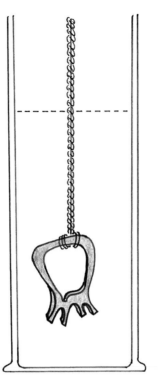

6–12   *Displacement measure.*

SPRUEING A MODEL

Sprues serve several functions. First, they give support and stabilize the model as it is being invested. Second, they provide channels through which the model is evacuated during the burnout step. Finally, these same channels are the passages through which molten metal flows into the mold.

Most jewelers used round, 6- to 12-gauge wax wires for sprues. Some use square wire of equivalent sizes. The square section is said to act as an oxide filter, the corners trapping and congealing oxides before the stream of swirling molten metal flows into the cavity. In any event, to be most effective sprues should be short, direct, and thick enough to ensure a smooth, fast flow of metal.

Models should be carefully studied to determine the optimum sprue placement. In examining the form, pretend for a moment that it is hollow and that fluid must travel, in an instant, through all its parts. Consider at how many points the fluid would have to enter in order to completely fill every recess and detail. Forms of consistent thickness and lacking intricate detail generally pose little problem. On models composed of thick and thin areas, multiple sprues should be placed around constricted areas. Like the rule for fluxing, when in doubt, sprue it.

Flat models can be placed at a slight angle to allow metal to flow smoothly, avoiding abrupt turns on entering the model cavity. Angling flat models will also help prevent the entrapment of air bubbles beneath the model. Avoid placing any portion of a model below the top edge of the sprue former or button. Molten metal would have great difficulty transversing this extreme angle (figure 6–14).

Sprues should not be attached haphazardly. Intersections between the sprue and model should make a smooth, flowing transition. Joints should not be abrupt or constricted. A smooth fillet of wax can be added around the circumference of each joint (figure 6–15). The heated end of a small spatula tool can be used to apply a bit of molten wax around the edge of the joint. The same technique is used in attaching sprues to the sprue former. On multiple-sprue models, flow is most efficient if each of the sprues joins the sprue former as near its center as possible. The practice of branching multiple sprues from one center sprue creates greater distance for the metal to flow and the additional joints cause greater turbulence in the liquid stream (figures 6–16 and 6–17). Some jewelers take the extra time to form a small, bulbous wax reservoir between the sprue former and model. Providing sprues are short and of adequate diameter, the need for a reservoir is questionable.

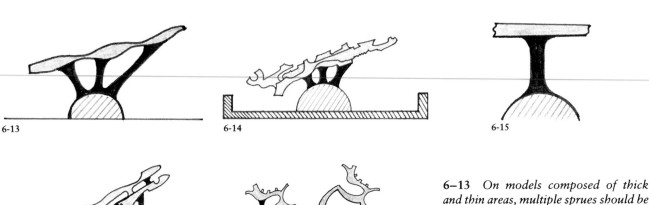

6-13   6-14   6-15

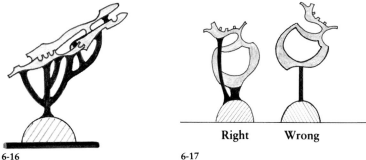

6-16   6-17

Right   Wrong

6–13 *On models composed of thick and thin areas, multiple sprues should be placed around constricted sections.*
6–14 *Sprued incorrectly. Model should not extend below the top of the former.*
6–15 *Sprue joints are made to flare.*
6–16 *Several sprues branching from a single small sprue may result in an incomplete casting.*

6–19   *Positive flask-to-base seal.*

6–18   *Assorted sizes of sprue bases and flasks.*

Before actual attachment of the model to the sprue base, trial fit the flask to the base. Select a flask that, when in place, will provide at least ¼ inch of space between the inner circumference of the flask and the model and at least ½ inch distance from the top of the model to the top edge of the flask.

Sprue bases and flasks can be purchased from jewelry and dental supply firms. Homemade bases and flasks can be made but this is discouraged. The initial expenditure for these items will be repaid in long service and the convenience of having the tools at hand. Rubber bases are available that will accept several sizes of flasks. These bases are made of pliable rubber and have several ridges around the top surface that correspond to the circumferences of various flasks. Flasks seal to the base, making plasticene or wax around the edge unnecessary (figure 6–19). Flasks are made of stainless steel and generally range in size from less than 1 inch to 4 inches in diameter and up to 6 inches in height. Jewelers usually own several sizes in order to fit the flask to the height and width of the model. In fitting, use as small a flask as possible, still maintaining the needed clearance at the top and sides (figures 6–20 through 6–23).

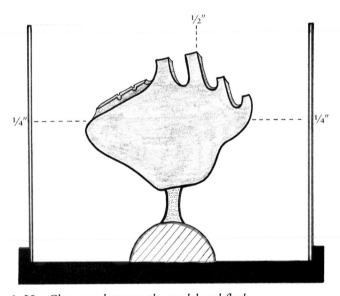

6–20   *Clearance between the model and flask.*

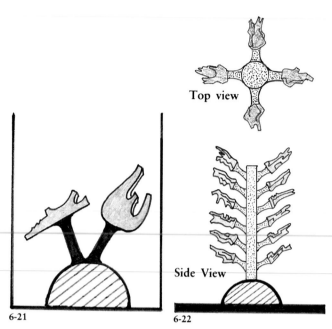

Top view

Side View

6-21

6-22

6-21   One method of sprueing several models in one flask.
6-22   Many models may be "treed" or arranged radially from a large central sprue. This technique is commonly used for production work.

6-23   Bimetal casting. The dark section to the left is precast and finished metal. The light section on the right is a model in wax attached to the metal section. Wax will be cast in a contrasting metal. The sprue to the left is for support only.

With the sprues mounted to the model, they may be joined to the base. The funnel or cone shape at the center of the base is the mounting point and entry area through which molten metal will later flow and be directed into the sprue channels. Sprue formers generally have an opening into which wax can be dripped. This provides an area to which the sprue wax can be bonded to the former. A bit of molten wax is used to join the sprues to the former. Additional wax can be used to build up and shape or refine the transition between sprues and the former. Remember, joints should be smooth and flare outward to aid the flow of the metal, avoiding the premature cooling of the metal. Minor side-to-side adjustment of the model, relative to the flask, can be made by holding the mounted model under warm water and applying a gentle pressure.

6-24   **Mark Baldridge,** Sister Blue. Bi-metal cast pendant of 14-karat yellow gold and titanium. A rather difficult process of bi-metal casting gold and titanium resulted in this graceful pendant form. Courtesy of the artist. Photograph by Bill Lane.

A small, soft brush is used to coat the model with a solution to inhibit bubble formation. These commercial products are designed to clean and relieve surface tension over the wax surface. They cause the wax surface to have an affinity for the liquid investment, thus displacing air that might otherwise cling to the surface as air bubbles. Upon casting, bubbles become solid spheres of metal. Denatured alcohol is sometimes used as a bubble inhibitor. Excess solution can be blown off and the model allowed to dry.

After the flask has been attached to the sprue base, a paper collar is taped around the top of the flask. The collar should extend an inch or two above the top of the flask (figure 6–25). Collars are temporary devices to help contain splattering investment as it is vacuumed. Short sections of bicycle inner tube may also be used as collars.

Casting investment is a plasterlike material compounded specifically for jewelry-size castings, for the model materials, and for the temperature ranges at which burnout and casting occur. The materials are extremely fine grained, giving finished castings of exact detail. Manufacturers offer many types of investment tailored to jewelry and metalsmithing needs. The basic constituents of most products are cristobalite, gypsum, and silica.

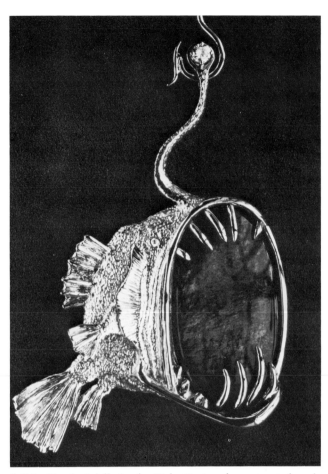

6–26 **Carrie Adell,** Angler Fish. *Cast and constructed necklace of 14-karat gold with opal and diamonds. This unique piece exemplifies the honest use of materials and technique. The artist's application of the body texture and precise modeling could only be achieved in wax and then cast. Courtesy of the artist. Photograph by the Gemological Institute of America.*

6–25 *Flask and taped on paper collar.*

PREPARATION OF INVESTMENT

Of the major steps leading to actual casting, investment preparation is perhaps the most critical. The mixing of investment and water must be precise for the hardened mold to withstand the shock of sudden temperature variations and to provide a structure through which moisture can escape. Investment must also withstand, without cracking or flaking, the rigors of steam pressure evacuating or cleansing the interior cavities of the model material.

In general, prepare investment according to these guidelines.

1 To determine precise water-to-investment proportions, the manufacturer's instructions should be consulted. Where instructions are not provided, a mixture of 4 parts water to 10 parts powder is recommended. Recommended proportions are listed in Appendix 1.

2 Measure cold tap water in a graduated beaker. Appendix 1 gives the approximate volume of water according to flask size. Pour the water into an appropriate bowl and begin adding the investment powder. Rubber bowls can be purchased from jewelry suppliers. The simplest method of ensuring that the water and powder are thoroughly blended is to stir the mixture directly by hand. While stirring slowly with one hand, gradually pour in the powder. Be sure the slurry is free of lumps as well as thoroughly blended.

3 Some jewelers forgo the weighing of investment powder and just add powder to the premeasured water until the mix reaches the consistency of heavy cream. This approach is reasonably accurate if the consistency is proven in casting and the same type of investment is used each time.

4 In the process of adding the investment powder, be sure wet hands or water do not come in contact with the investment container. Drops of water will cause the powder to form hard lumps. Moisture from any source will lessen the useful life of investment; always reseal the investment container after use.

5 The investment mixture will set in approximately 8 minutes from the moment the powder is poured into the water. This means you cannot dally around nor complete this step too quickly. Investment is compounded to be most effective if the process of mixing

6–27 *Investment vibrator. Courtesy of Kerr Manufacturing Company.*

to hardening takes the full 8 minutes. Pace yourself, with a clock if needed, to complete the investment steps in the given time. Consider what is to be done, step by step, and have the needed tools or equipment at hand.

6 Fasten the flask to the sprue base. Mix the investment and place the bowl beneath the vacuum bell. Wetting the bottom edge of the bell and the rubber gasket will help assure a positive seal. Start the pump and allow the mixture to bubble rapidly. Observe the mixture level and let it rise, settle, and continue to bubble for a few seconds. Vacuuming will take about 2 minutes. If it appears that the mixture will spill over the edge of the bowl, crack the vacuum machine vent valve for just a second and then continue vacuuming. Stop the machine and open the vent.

7 Holding the base and flask at an angle, pour the investment down the inside wall of the flask. Be sure to hold the assembly by the base or be prepared to clean up a mess. Pouring down the wall will avoid the possibility of dislodging the model. Fill to the edge of the flask and place the assembly under the vacuum bell. Again vacuum the mixture until it rises and falls. This will again take about 2 minutes. Release the vacuum and place the flask aside.

8 For those craftworkers not owning a vacuum pump, an electric variable-speed vibrating unit can be used. These are purchased from jewelry and dental suppliers (figure 6–27). The investment is first vibrated by holding the bowl in place on the vibrator top plate at high speed for 2 minutes. Then pour the investment into the flask and vibrate the flask for another 2 minutes on low speed. Vibrating the flask at high speeds may dislodge the model. The impulses of vibration dislodge entrapped air.

9 Where finances are extremely limited, a simple but less reliable method of air removal is to place the bowl or flask on a table and strike the table edge with the steady taps of a mallet.

BURNOUT PROCEDURE

After the invested flask has set for at least 30 minutes, the base can be snapped off and the paper collar removed. Scrape away any excess investment from the top edge and along the sides of the flask. Place the flask in the arm of the casting machine and the metal to be cast in the crucible. Align the crucible to the flask's sprue opening. A flask cradle of a size corresponding to the diameter of the flask is often needed to achieve the correct up and down alignment (figure 6–28). Loosen the hold down the knob near the center of the machine's arm and balance the arm assembly. Balancing must be done with the swing arm in line with the weighted arm. During this procedure, the swing arm tends to sway from side to side. This is easily remedied by placing a short piece of wire or folded strip of paper in the swing joint. Horizontal balance is attained by moving the counterweights inward or outward as the arm is gently tipped up and down until the weight equalizes at the ends of the arm. Ideally, the machine should be balanced for each casting. Through experience, some jewelers note the weight placement for various size flasks and forgo the balancing process. The weights are adjusted according to specific flask sizes.

If burnout must be delayed beyond a few hours, the flask should be wrapped in wet paper towels and covered with plastic wrap. Leaving the flask open for an extended period allows needed moisture to evaporate from the investment.

After balancing the arm, burnout is begun. It seems as

though each jeweler has his or her own method; circumstances or the equipment at hand can sometimes make it necessary to deviate from a "textbook burnout." In addition, the novice may be faced with a myriad of conflicting printed information on heat settings and burnout times. All things considered, following the burnout cycles prescribed by the investment manufacturer is recommended. One such schedule is illustrated in Appendix 1.

The process of model and sprue elimination is not a simple matter. At first glance it seems little more than just the flip of a switch: heat is applied, the wax melts out, and it is time to cast. In actuality, the process is quite complex and extremely important for the success or failure of the casting.

A look inside the flask would show us the changes that take place during the cycle. Assuming the investment is mixed properly and sufficient time has elapsed for setup, the flask is placed in the kiln. The heat is increased slowly. As the wax begins to melt, most of it drains directly down and out through the sprue openings. A portion of the wax is displaced into the walls of the mold cavity. This occurs as a result of expansion of the wax and is aided by the fact that the investment material becomes more porous when heated. If a portion of the wax was unable to leach into the mold walls, the pressure of the expanding wax could easily crack the investment. Wax has a greater coefficient of expansion than that of investment. Increasing heat will gradually eliminate most of the wax, leaving a residue of carbon. Remaining moisture in the investment continues to create steam, cleansing wax and residue from the mold

6–28 *Casting machine flask cradles.*

walls. As the temperature reaches its peak (1,300° to 1,350°F), all wax and carbon is generally eliminated. Bone whiteness surrounding the sprue opening is evidence of complete burnout. Heating beyond recommended temperatures can affect the composition of the investment components and damage the mold.

Place the flask, open end down, in the kiln. Set the flask on a ceramic trivet, steel screen, or atop several pieces of pea pumice. A slight elevation will permit free heat circulation and drainage of the model material. **Kiln areas should be adequately vented to remove the harmful fumes produced by burnout.** If the time permits and the kiln is equipped with a heat control and temperature gauge, proceed with the burnout as outlined in Appendix 1.

For those unable to purchase a kiln having a variable heat control and temperature gauge, there is a suitable alternative. A small, relatively inexpensive kiln without the controls can be purchased from jewelry suppliers. Using the following procedure, burnouts can be completed with a high degree of success.

1. Place the flask in the kiln, open end down. Turn the kiln on and leave the door open approximately 3 inches for the first hour. **Avoid touching the kiln heating coils with the flasks or tongs. This could cause electrical shock or damage to the coil.**

2. During the second hour leave the door ajar about one inch. After the second hour, open the door a crack every 10 to 15 minutes to observe the color of the flask and investment. The key indicators to look for are a reddening of the flask and changing color of the investment.

3. Using this method, there is no specific time in which the burnout will be complete. This largely depends upon the size of the kiln and size and number of flasks being heated. Once the flasks take on a noticeable red color, the burnout will go fairly quickly.

4. When the flask takes on an orange color and the investment is white, carefully lift the flask out and examine the sprue opening. The area around the opening should be white with no black or gray spots. The sprue opening should have a slight reddish glow. Always use flask tongs and protective gloves to handle hot flasks.

5. With the flask burned out, casting can begin. If several flasks are being burned out, the kiln temperature can be stabilized by leaving the door cracked open.

6–29 Lee B. Peck, Architectural Ring. *Sterling silver with copper and 24-karat gold plate, glass, and hematite; hollow casting. Courtesy of the artist. Collection of Minnesota Museum of Art.*

6–30 *Electric burnout furnace. Courtesy of Kerr Manufacturing Company.*

This should retain enough heat to keep the remaining flasks at casting temperature while proceeding with the casting. The kiln is turned off after all casting is complete.

6 Steps 2 and 3 are simply means of bypassing or venting some of the heat in the kiln. It is important that in the early stages of burnout heat be applied gradually. Leaving the door ajar allows this. The open-door approach to burnout is by no means exact or ideal, but it works reasonably well.

CASTING MACHINES

Spring-driven centrifugal casting machines are used by most jewelers. The majority of these machines are of the horizontal design (figure 6–31). Other types of centrifugal machines are available but their effectiveness relative to their cost makes them less desirable for the average jeweler. Functionally, all centrifugal machines are alike. Rotary motion imparts centrifugal force on molten metal, driving it from the crucible into the mold cavity (figure 6–32).

The arm of the machine is a two-piece assembly: the shorter arm retains the flask and crucible, the other arm is weighted and driven. The short arm is designed to pivot 90 degrees at rest and move outward, aligning with the weighted arm as the assembly spins. Pivoting the short arm prevents molten metal from spilling from the crucible upon the initial thrust of the spring drive. The molten metal is given additional thrust as the flask end swings from its angled position and is flung outward, aligning with the weighted arm. All of this occurs in a fraction of a second.

Arms are driven by an internal spring attached to a vertical shaft that is keyed to the weighted arm. After being wound, the arm is held in place by lifting a stop pin against the arm. **Machines should always be bolted down securely, ideally beneath a ventilation hood (figure 6–33). A number of the elements given off in metal fumes are harmful. Machines should also be fitted**

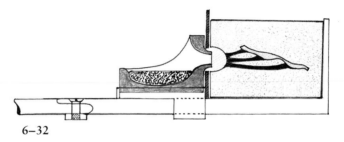

6–32

6–31 *Centrifugal casting unit. Courtesy of Kerr Manufacturing Company.*

6–32 *The centrifugal process.*

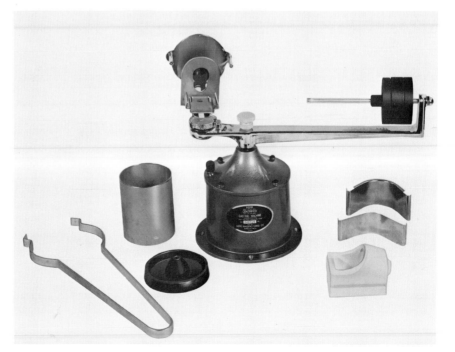

6–31

6–33 *Casting machine closed on three sides and vented at the top.*

with a cylindrical guard to contain spilled metal. A device as simple as a large washtub will provide adequate safety. Do not leave flux cans, tongs, flasks, or other objects inside or hanging on the guard. If struck by the rotating arm, objects can easily go flying along with molten metal.

To overcome possible anxiety, all beginners should make a trial run with the machine, winding the arm, setting the stop pin, and releasing the arm while lifting the torch. This should be a dry run, without the crucible, flask, or lighted torch.

CENTRIFUGAL CASTING PROCEDURE

With preparations made and the flask burned out, the actual casting process can take place.

1 The machine's arm is wound and the stop pin pulled up. Wind three turns for small flasks and four for larger flasks. Appendix 1 indicates the proper flask temperature for casting various metals. Flasks are usually heated to peak burnout temperature and then slowly cooled back to the required casting temperature.

2 If a new crucible is being used, it should be heated and flux sprinkled over the inner surface. This provides the metal a glazed surface over which to flow easily. As the flask cools back to casting temperature, light the torch and adjust it to give a reducing flame. Sprinkle a pinch of flux over the metal and begin the melt. Pure powdered borax or commercial casting flux should be used. Just before the metal becomes molten, take the flask from the kiln and place it in the swing arm with the sprue opening facing the crucible

6–34 *Metal being heated in preparation for casting. Courtesy of Kerr Manufacturing Company.*

plate. Be sure the crucible is pulled flush against the flask and the arm is angled. This step is facilitated with the help of a partner.

3 When the metal appears to be molten, quickly sprinkle on another pinch of flux while continuing to play the flame over the metal. Any scum on the molten surface should be scraped away with a carbon or steel rod. A mirrorlike shimmer will appear when the metal has melted. To assure the complete mass is liquid, the rod can be pulled through it. Take care not to overheat the metal. Rapid swirling, bubbling, or profuse fuming are indicators of this.

4 With the metal completely molten and the torch still over the surface, pull the weighted arm back to allow the stop pin to drop and release the arm. The moment the arm is released, lift the torch straight up. Coordination of the arm's release and torch removal is important. This seems to be the most anxious moment for beginners who sometimes remove the torch, hesitate, and then release the arm. Hesitation allows the metal to begin cooling and may cause an incomplete casting.

5 Let the arm spin until it stops of its own accord, allowing the metal to slowly cool. Set the flask aside for 5 or 10 minutes and then set it in a pail of water. The hot investment will crumble away, leaving an exact duplicate of the model, sprues, and former.

Refinement is just a matter of cutting the sprues free, brushing away clinging investment, pickling, and applying any of the previously discussed finishing techniques.

VACUUM CASTING

Another widely used casting technique is the vacuum-assisted gravity method. Preliminary steps to the actual pouring of the metal are essentially the same as outlined for centrifugal casting. Figure 6–36 illustrates an invested model in preparation for vacuum casting.

Before mixing investment, check to assure that one end of the flask is smooth. Rubbing the flask edge over a sheet of emery cloth will remove minor roughness. The smooth end will eventually seal to the machine's rubber gasket. Leave a space of ¼ to ½ inch between the investment level and the top of the flask. Note in figure 6–38 how coat hanger or heavy binding wire is shaped and fitted to the flask. The wires are pulled out after the investment sets to form channels in which a vacuum is created.

The actual casting process is relatively simple. After the model has burned out, the flask is placed with the sprue opening up over a silicone rubber gasket on the

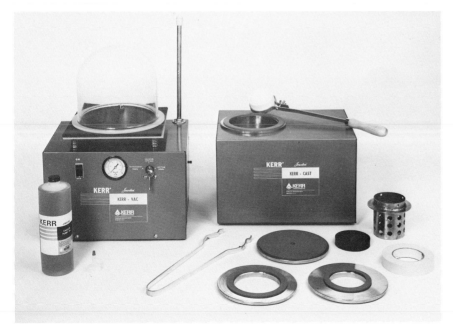

6–35 Vacuum casting unit. Courtesy of Kerr Manufacturing Company.

6–36 *Model prepared for vacuum casting.*
6–37 *Vacuum casting process.*
6–38 *A means of forming additional vacuum channels.*

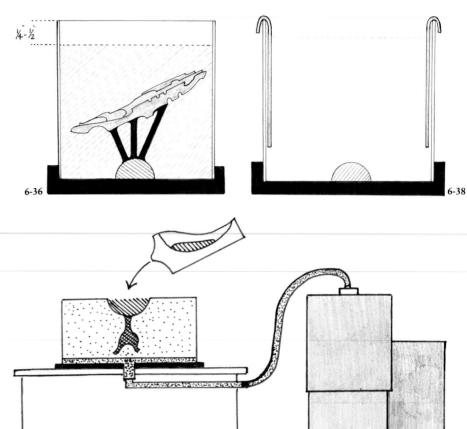

6-36

6-38

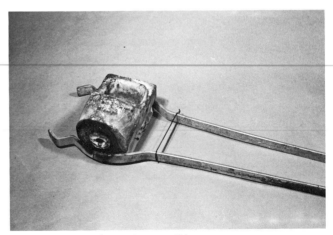

6-37

vacuum table. As a vacuum is created in the flask, molten metal is poured into the sprue opening and drawn into the mold.

Tongs and crucibles designed for pouring can be purchased from jewelry suppliers. A crucible used with the centrifugal machine can be adapted for pouring by securing flask tongs as a handle (figure 6–39). When the flask is placed on the rubber gasket and the machine turned on, the vacuum gauge should immediately start rising; if not, a downward pressure with the tongs will help the vacuum catch. As the casting is poured, the stream of metal should be a continuous even flow. Continue playing the flame over the crucible while pouring. Release the vacuum and set the flask aside. Quench the flask in 5 to 10 minutes.

6–39 *Tongs and pouring crucible.*

STEAM CASTING

Steam casting is best suited for small, relatively simple jewelry pieces. Little more than a kiln is needed to complete the process. Investment and burnout are identical to the methods used for centrifugal casting with one exception: sprues should be of 14-gauge material. This is important. Diameters larger than 14 gauge will allow premature leakage of metal into the mold as metal is being heated. Sprues of less than 14 gauge will choke off metal flow and result in an incomplete casting.

The steam device is made of a 5-inch jar lid, a nail, and wooden handle (figure 6–40). A 1-inch by 6-inch wooden dowel serves as the handle. The jar lid is filled with layers of wet newspaper that are held firmly over the sprue opening to generate steam pressure.

After burnout set the hot flask, sprue opening up, on a firebrick. Have the steam device saturated with water. Place the metal into the sprue-former cavity and immediately begin the melt. Sprinkle in a pinch of flux. Hold the steam device firmly over the flask as soon as the metal is molten. The heated flask causes the saturated paper to create steam, forcing the metal into the mold. Hold the device in place for a few seconds and then allow the flask to cool as previously outlined. This process is generally not feasible for large work or on pieces composed of thick and thin sections. Sprue systems have limited capacity for forcing in adequate metal.

ADDITIONAL CASTING TECHNIQUES

As pointed out earlier, casting is a far-ranging subject. For those wishing to study casting in depth, overviews of several additional topics worthy of future exploration are offered here. Several texts in the bibliography provide additional insights on these subjects.

Sling Casting

This technique uses the human arm and a sling device to create the centrifugal force needed to propel molten metal into the mold cavity. The model is sprued as outlined in the section on steam casting and the burned out flask is placed in the sling. Metal is heated in the former cavity of the flask. Once the metal is molten, the sling is rotated several times in an arc with the arm fully extended. Figure 6–41 shows the construction details of a sling.

Direct-Gravity Methods

Tufa Stone   Tufa is a soft, light, and porous natural stone that has been used primarily by southwest Native Americans. The stone is soft enough to be cut into sections with a saw. Two pieces are mated face-to-face by first filing and then rubbing the faces together. Remaining steps are essentially the same as those for casting with cuttlebone. Blocks of charcoal, plaster of paris, or casting investment can be used in the same manner.

Clay   In some areas of the world, craftspeople continue the ancient technique of casting into clay. The results are impressive considering the simplicity of the processes employed. A model with attached sprue is usually made of pure beeswax. Moist clay is pressed around the model and then allowed to air harden. At this point, the covered model appears to be just a lump of clay with a wax rod through one end. After hardening, the clay is placed in a charcoal fire. A bellows or

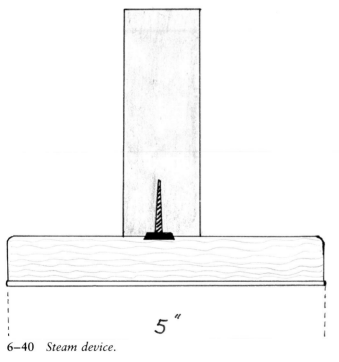

6–40   *Steam device.*

5″

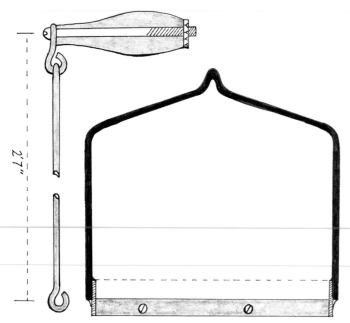

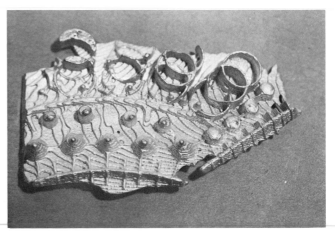

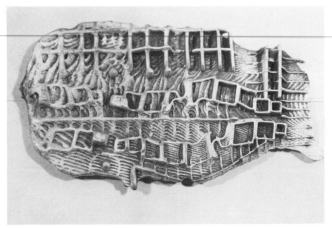

6–41 *Sling device. Transite-covered plywood base corresponding to the flask's diameter, ⅛-inch steel rod stock, S hooks, wood handle, and steel base rim.*

hand-cranked blower is used to fan the flames until the wax is eliminated. Metal is heated in the same fire and, when molten, poured into the clay mold.

Cuttlebone Considering its most common uses, cuttlebone is an unlikely casting medium. Domestically it is used to feed parakeets and canaries. In powdered form it is used as a polishing agent. It is perhaps the most unusual material we might work with.

Cuttlebone is the chalky inner shell of the cuttlefish, a ten-legged, squidlike mollusk. The interior of the bone is easily carved or scraped. Other objects can be pressed into its soft surface, leaving a negative of the pressed object. Jewelry cast in cuttlebone has a characteristic surface texture composed of wavy striations. In casting, the bone is burned and cannot be reused.

The two halves are prepared for casting by rubbing the soft faces together to flatten and create a sealing surface (figure 6–43). One or both halves may be incised or carved out to receive the metal. If the finished piece is to have a flat back, only one side is carved. A border of smooth surface should be left around the mold area to provide a sealing edge with the other half. From the top edge of the mold area, cut a wide, cone-shaped sprue cavity radiating outward to the top of the cuttlebone

6–42 *Cuttlebone castings.*

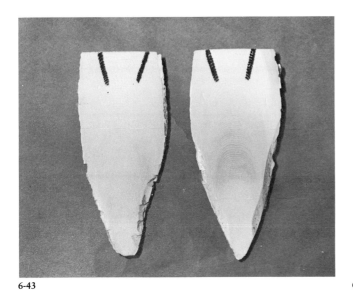

6-43

6-44

6–43 *Cuttlebone halves prepared for incising the mold.*
6–44 *Cuttlebone prepared and bound together.*

(figure 6–44). The two halves can be held together with binding wire and then placed upright between several chunks of firebrick or charcoal. Metal is poured into the sprue cavity. After solidification of the metal, the cuttlebone is dropped into water.

Large cuttlebones can be purchased from jewelry suppliers and small ones from local pet stores.

6–45 *Gold plated pin of brass and ivory cast in cuttlebone. Collection of Rachel Crow.*
6–46 **Ann Grundler.** *Neckpiece and pendant of sterling silver with lapis; cuttlebone casting and construction. Courtesy of the artist.*

6-45

6-46

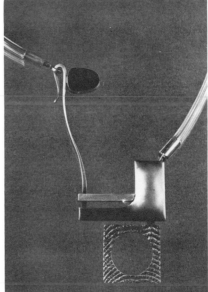

RUBBER MOLDS

For the production of duplicate cast objects, a two-piece flexible mold is used. Jewelers generally use vulcanized rubber to form a mold around an object of the shape they wish to reproduce. The original piece is centered on a metal sprue pin within an aliminum frame. Sheets of latex are cut and packed in the frame and then clamped between the vulcanizer's heating plates. The force and heat of the plates compress and vulcanize the sheets into one homogeneous mass encasing the model. The model material must be capable of withstanding a temperature of approximately 350°F. After cooling the mold is taken out of the frame and carefully cut through its centerline and the original piece removed. The result is a two-piece mold (figure 6–50).

6–47   *Rubber molds and flexible-mold rubber. Courtesy of Kerr Manufacturing Company.*

6-48

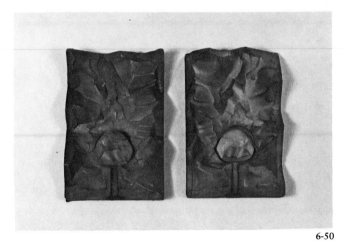

6-50

6-49

6–48   Rubber mold frames.
6–49   Rubber mold vulcanizer. Courtesy of Kerr Manufacturing Company.
6–50   Parted rubber mold.

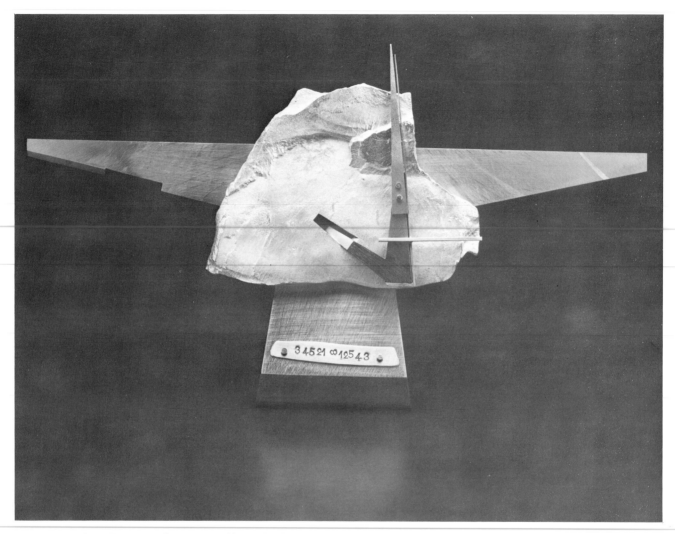

6–51 Joseph Hall. *Cast and constructed brooch of titanium, 14-karat yellow gold, and shibuichi. The center section cast is from a mold taken from a rock surface. Courtesy of the artist. Photograph by Steve Young.*

6–52 *Wax injector. Courtesy of Kerr Manufacturing Company.*

With the halves reset, molten wax is injected or poured in its cavity to produce any number of duplicates of the original. By gently flexing and parting the mold, the wax model will release. For many jewelers, the infrequent need for a vulcanized mold probably would not justify the purchase of a wax injector and vulcanizer. A number of commercial casting firms offer the service of mold making and wax injection for a reasonable cost.

Liquid, rubberlike substances can also be used to make molds. Suppliers offer one type that upon curing is transparent. This feature allows the craftworker to make a precise cut along the centerline of the model. Some of the liquid mold compounds cure at room temperature, giving the jeweler a broader choice of model materials to work with. Simple molds can be made of products as common as silicone bathtub caulking.

6-52

MODEL DUPLICATION AND LIGHTWEIGHT, THIN-WALLED CASTINGS

This process allows the jeweler to make a model of the intended object in almost any material and to then reproduce a plastic shell replica of the object to be used as a pattern for investment casting.

The following technical information and photographic series was provided by Al Gilmore, Arizona State University at Tempe.

1 A model of the object is prepared. In this instance modeling clay is preferred for its plasticity and ability to receive impressed textural details. Found objects, plastic or wood, may also be used. If porous materials are used, soak them in water to eliminate air prior to the duplication step. The model should be constructed on a backing plate.
2 Place a flask over the model to contain the duplicating compound. A steel casting flask or an aluminum rubber-mold frame works well. The duplicating material is commercially known as Duplicating Hydrocolloid and is normally used in dental laboratories for precise reproduction of denture models and the production of plastic dental plates. Chop up the Hydrocolloid and heat it to a boiling, viscous liquid. After all chunks are completely molten and boiling, remove

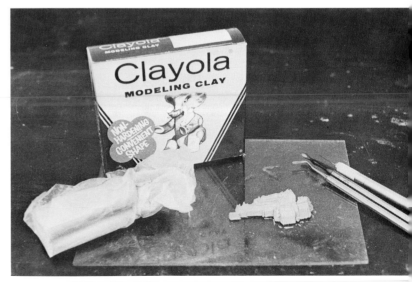

6–53 *Preparing the model.*

6–54   *Melting the hydrocolloid.*
6–55   *Pouring the hydrocolloid.*

the material from the heat source, allow it to cool to 120°F, and pour the material over the model. Place the plate and flask in a refrigerator until the Hydrocolloid is gelled. After gelling, the model and impression are separated to reveal a highly detailed impression. If the form is complex, the gelled mold can be cut from the model in an interlocking manner similar to the method used to halve a vulcanized mold. The impression may be retained indefinitely in a container of water until needed. After the plastic pattern is created, the Hydrocolloid impression can be chopped up and remelted many times.

3 Denture repair acrylic, a two-part resin and liquid, is used to form the plastic pattern. Place the Hydrocolloid impression in warm water (100°F) for approximately 10 minutes to aid the setting of the acrylic pattern. After warming, the impression is thoroughly dried with compressed air. Mix the acrylic components in a glass dish to a thin consistency then immediately pour the acrylic into the Hydrocolloid impression. As the acrylic is poured, the impression is tilted or rolled around to facilitate the coating of the impression's surfaces. The plastic pattern will set in just a few minutes and can be removed in 20 minutes.

4 The shell replica of the original is ready to be sprued. Flashing on the pattern should be removed and any defects corrected with inlay wax. Thin areas may be waxed to the desired thickness, and bulky areas ground down with a rotary steel burr. Spring calipers are helpful in determining the shell thickness. In casting gold or silver, a wall thickness of .5 mm works

6–56 Making the pattern.

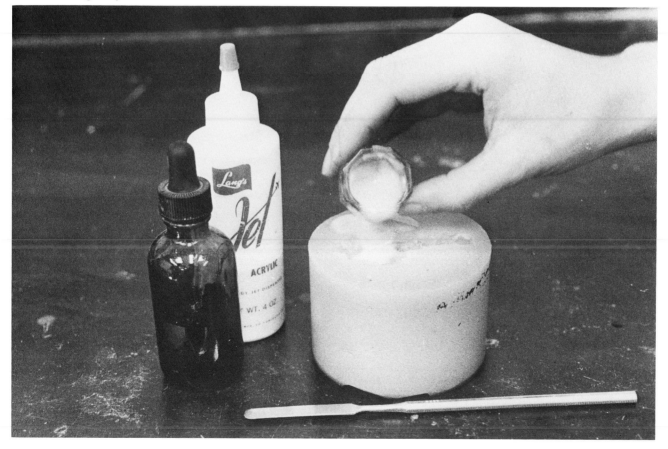

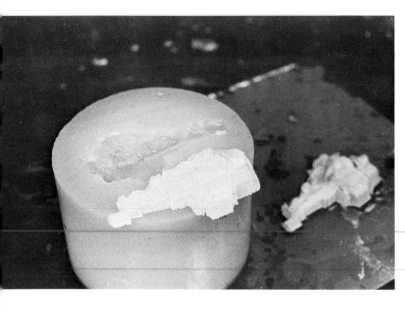

well. Patterns are sprued and invested in the conventional manner. Burnout is extended an additional hour at the 1,150°F point.

5 The casting is desprued with separating discs to avoid bending the piece. Conventional methods are used in finishing and coloring the form. Cast acrylic and epoxy elements can also be produced using this basic process. The materials used in this process may be obtained from the suppliers listed in Appendix 4.

6–57 *Model, hydrocolloid mold, and plastic pattern.*
6–58 *Sprueing the pattern.*

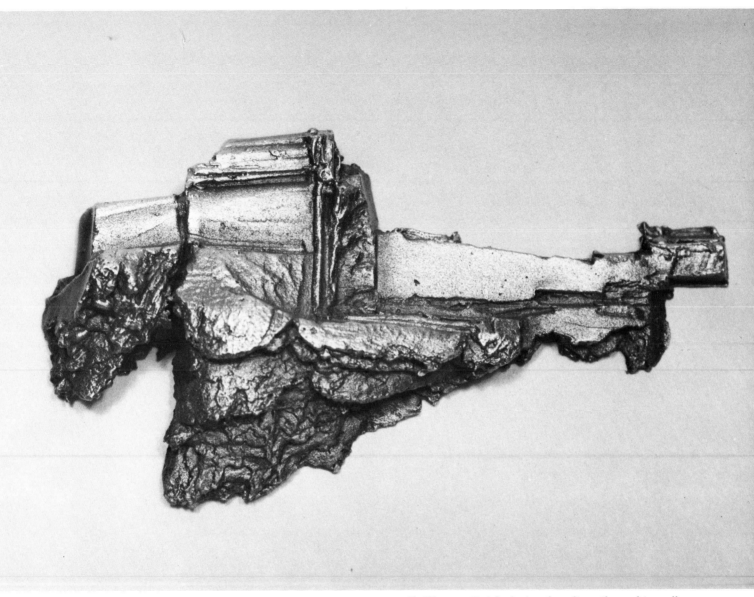

6–59   Al Gilmore. *Finished pin of sterling silver; thin-wall casting. Courtesy of the artist.*

CHAPTER SEVEN

Fastening Devices

Jewelers are hard-pressed to create new fastenings that are functionally more effective than those currently in use. The challenge is to examine the basic function of each mechanism, possibly refine it, and integrate its workings into contemporary jewelry. Fastenings should avoid unnecessary complexity, yet be substantial enough to give years of service. In addition to these mechanical concerns, fastenings should be visually suited to the joining elements. Too often linkages and fastenings are second thoughts, as if the design was conceived and executed with no concern of how the parts might be attached or how they would be made wearable. Unfortunately, this approach leads to fastenings that appear to be stuck on out of mechanical need. A poorly conceived handmade catch is not as effective as its well-made commercial counterpart. Purists may not agree, but I do not hesitate to use commercial findings on certain forms. For example, on a simple brooch where the design emphasis is clearly the front of the piece, a properly attached catch and pin stem are quite adequate. This chapter, however, focuses on the construction of handmade fastenings.

7-3 *S-hook and chain cap swivel joints. Though simple in concept, this type of hook functions well. Swivels give the chain the extra flexibility sometimes needed.*

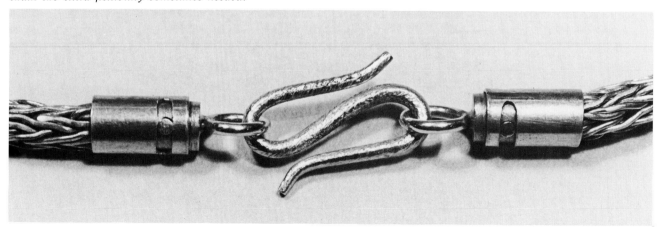

7–2 Mark Knuth. *Hollow bracelet of nickel silver, copper, and epoxy resin; gold plated and constructed. Opened to show the hinge and catch.*

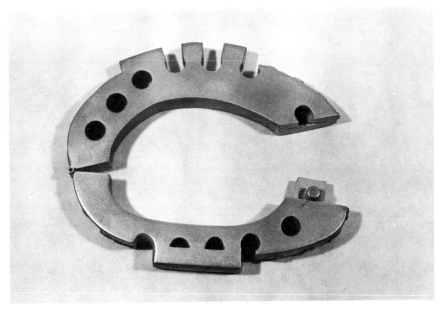

7–1 Ann Grundler. *Constructed pendant of sterling, steel, brass, copper, wood, and plastic. The artist uses a flared hook fastener to simplify attachment at the pendant. This solution is mechanically sound and visually effective. Courtesy of the artist.*

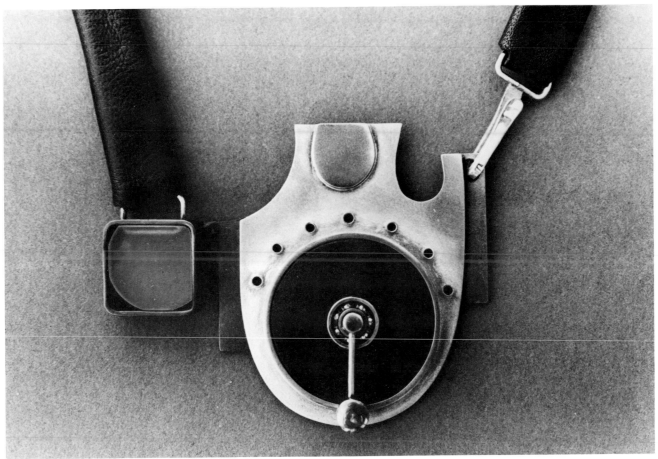

A PORTFOLIO OF FASTENERS, CATCHES, AND FINDINGS

The following illustrations show a range of fastenings that can be easily constructed by anyone having basic technical skills. Most of the illustrations do not spell out in what manner and on what jewelry forms particular fastenings should be applied or connected. The jeweler should call on his or her inventiveness in using these fastenings.

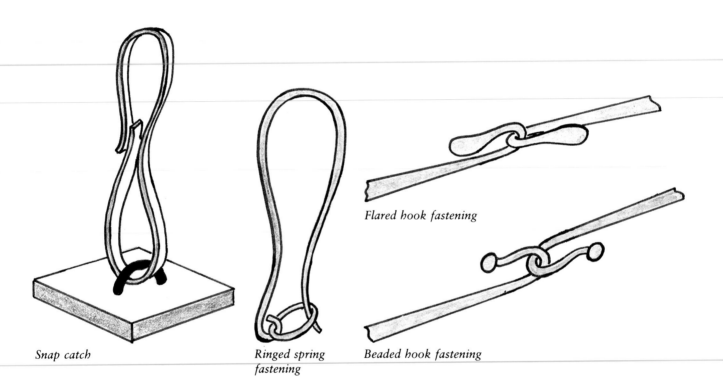

Snap catch

Ringed spring fastening

Flared hook fastening

Beaded hook fastening

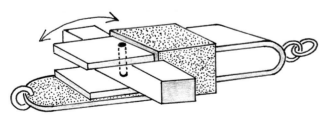

Swivel is pinned to the slide. Slide accessory.

Swivel catch

Drilled and wire beaded

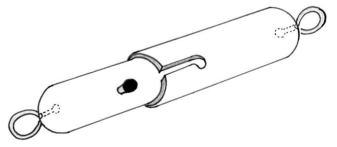

Chain end swivel barrel clasp

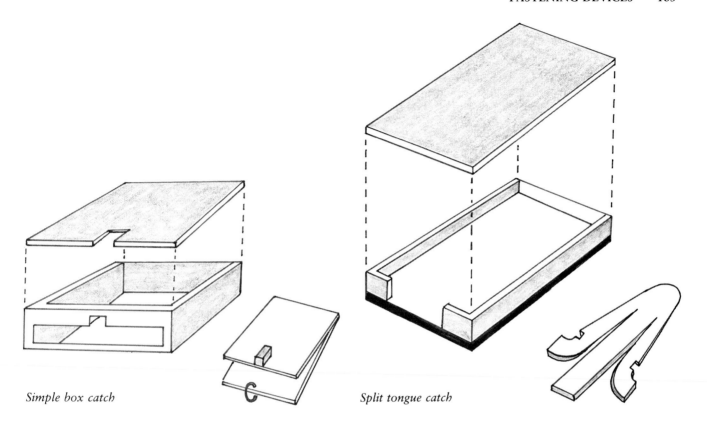

Simple box catch

Split tongue catch

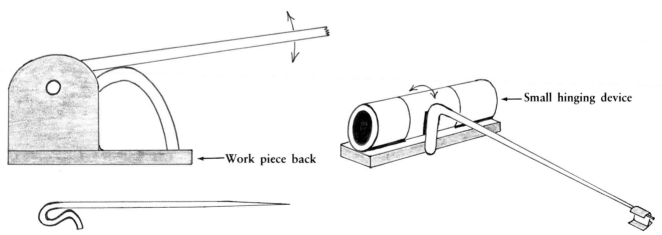

Work piece back

Small hinging device

Pin stem and joint

Pin assembly. Catch and joint soldered to the back of the work piece.

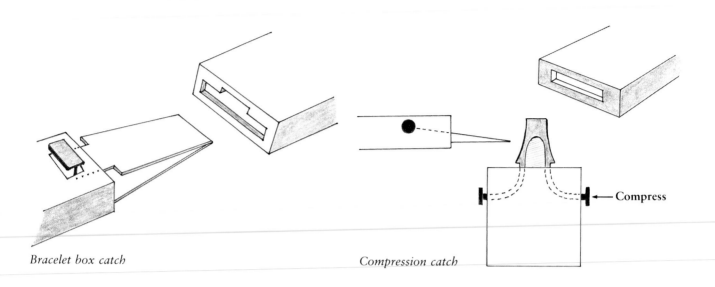

Bracelet box catch

Compression catch

← Compress

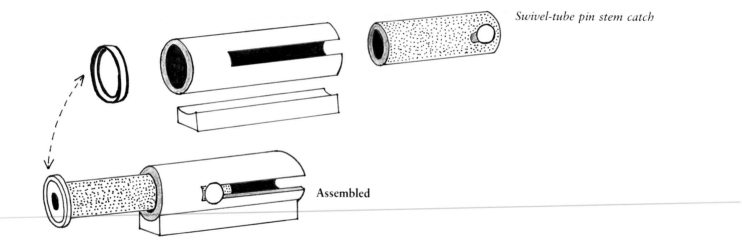

Swivel-tube pin stem catch

Assembled

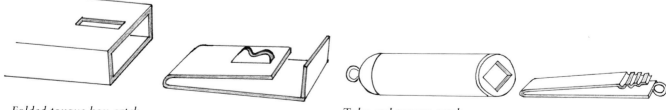

Folded tongue box catch

Tube and tongue catch

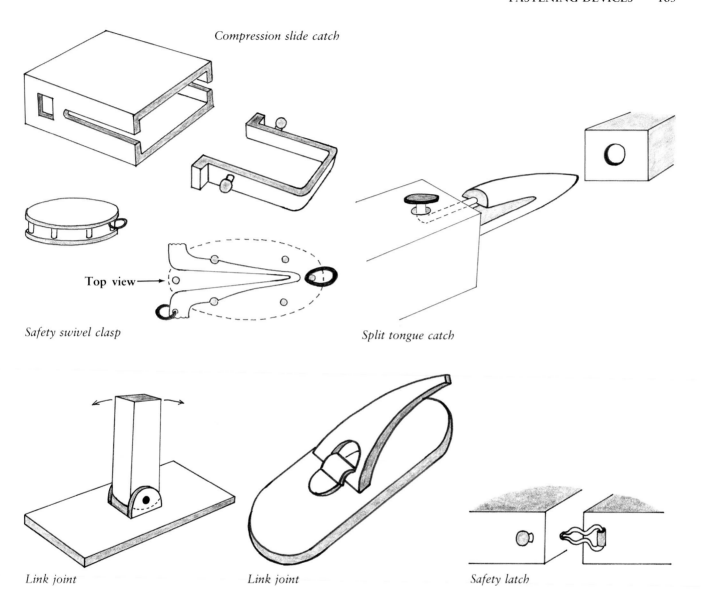

Compression slide catch

Top view →

Safety swivel clasp

Split tongue catch

Link joint

Link joint

Safety latch

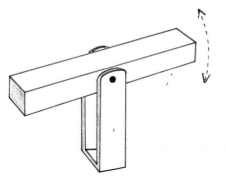

Link joint

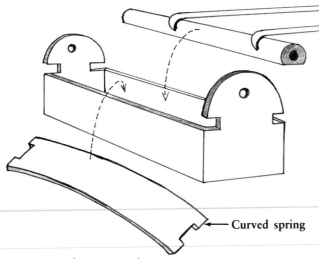

Sprung pin/barrette mechanism

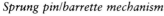

—— Curved spring

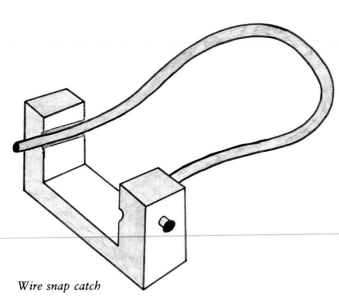

Wire snap catch

RIVETS

The basic function of a rivet is to fit through a material to provide a mechanical fastening. In its simplest form, it need be nothing more than a shank with one or both of its ends upset (figure 7–5). Rivets are generally used where the heat needed for soldering would present a problem. To many jewelers, a rivet offers more than an alternate to solder or chemical adhesive; it may also function as a decorative element. Where only one or two may be needed, additional rivets can be set for aesthetic purposes.

Rivet is soldered to the bottom piece.

7–5   *Rivet with one end soldered in place.*

For our work, there are no specific rules regarding the dimensions of a rivet's diameter or length. Visual considerations, common sense, and a basic understanding of the stresses that might be placed on a piece are the governing factors needed to judge rivet size. If a rivet's shank is too long or too thin, chances are it will bend while being set. On the other hand, if it is too short, its end cannot provide the mass needed for upsetting. From a purely functional standpoint, all that is needed is that the head of the shank extend slightly beyond the workpiece surface (figure 7–8). [We generally extend the head beyond that for added security or aesthetic considerations.] For illustrative purposes, the following guidelines use a 14-gauge wire rivet through two pieces of 18-gauge sheet metal.

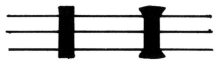

7–8   *Rivet before and after setting.*

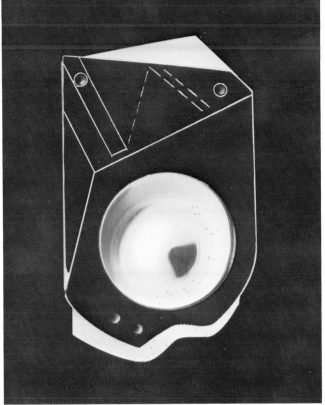

7–6 David LaPlantz. *Constructed and riveted pin of colored aluminum with a scored and engraved surface. In some instances, the nature of the materials will prohibit the use of heat. Rivets may be used in lieu of solder and, as in this example, become a pleasing decorative accent. Courtesy of the artist.*

7–7 *Pin of sterling silver and brass with agate. Gold plated, constructed, and tube riveted. Photograph by Peter Krumhardt.*

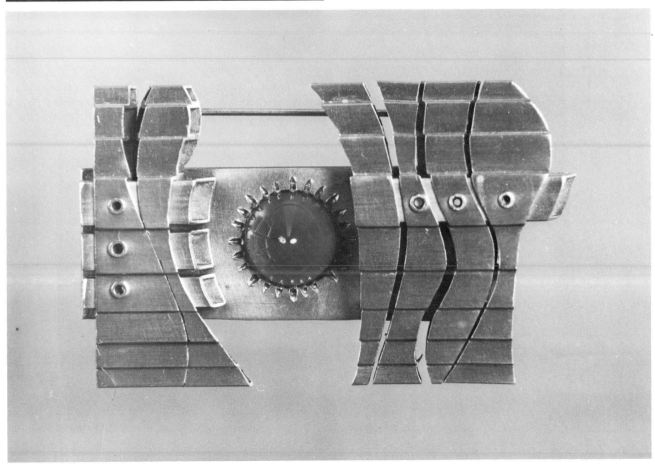

1 Mark one of the sheets at the rivet point. Center punch the mark and drill a hole with a number 52 (.063) drill bit. File or emery away any burr left by the bit.

2 Trial fit the two sheets together and mark the bottom sheet through the first hole. Center punch, drill, and remove any burrs. It is essential to use a drill bit corresponding exactly to the rivet's diameter and to have the drilled holes in perfect alignment top to bottom. Holes too large or misaligned can easily result in bent rivets.

3 Anneal the wire and file one end flat. With the saw frame and a fine blade, carefully cut the wire at a point equal to the rivet length. The saw cut should be parallel to the flat end. If not, correct the end with a file. Figure 7–9 illustrates the importance of cutting the ends correctly. Given the dimensions of our example, the rivet length should correspond to approximately the sheet thicknesses (2 times 18 gauge) plus the rivet's diameter. Remember, this is not an iron-clad rule but the choice in this instance. With practice,

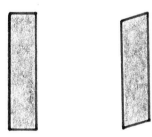

7–9 *Correctly and incorrectly cut rivets. Angled ends will cause the rivet or head to bend.*

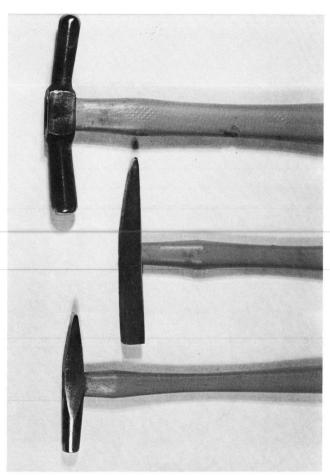

7–11 *Hammers commonly used to set rivets.*

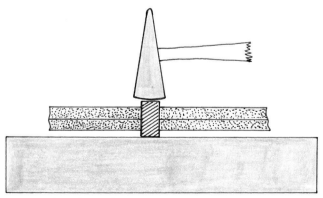

7–10 *The relationship of rivet and sheet metal to the hammer and anvil surface.*

this determination will be quite easy and often just a matter of eyeballing.

4 Figure 7–10 illustrates the proper relationship of the rivet and sheet metal to the anvil and hammer face. Equal portions of the rivet should extend above and below the sheet metal. To upset or compress the ends, one end is placed squarely on an anvil or steel block and the other struck with a hammer (figure 7–12). This step is best accomplished with the work at eye level in order to ensure that only the rivet touches the anvil and its position is vertical, otherwise the work will be marred or the rivet bent. The work can be turned over to equalize the upset on each end. Figure 7–13 shows the angle at which the hammer is directed to form a mushroomlike rivet head. The curved face of a planishing hammer can be used to form the

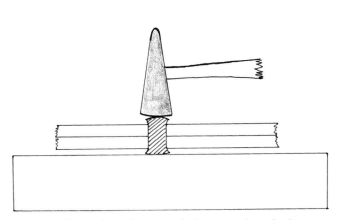

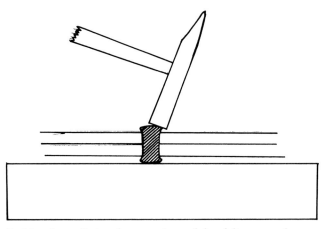

7–12   *Relationship of rivet and sheet metal to the hammer and anvil surface.*

7–13   *Setting a mushroomhead rivet.*

7–14   *A small rivet hammer is used for delicate work.*

7–15   **Harold O'Connor.** *Constructed pendant of 18-karat gold and glass bead. Small handmade screws and nuts function well as fasteners. Courtesy of the artist.*

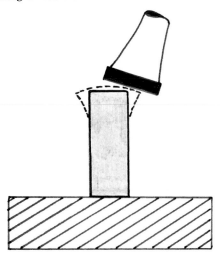

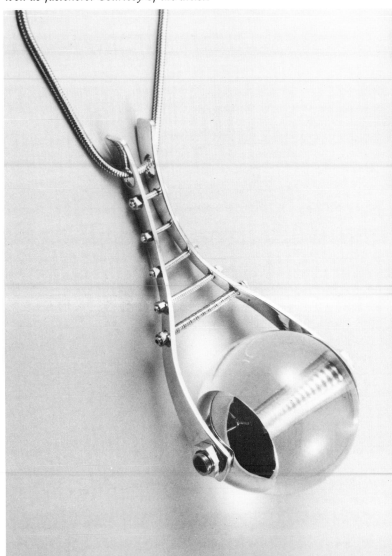

head. For delicate work, a small rivet hammer can be used (figure 7–14).

5   After the rivet is set securely, additional forming of the head is generally dependent on the metalsmith's inventiveness and the desired visual effects. Heads can be shaped and decorated in many ways. Uniform domed shapes can be formed by radially spaced blows with the rivet set, nail set, heading tool, or an appropriately shaped repoussé tool. Other shapes may be formed with a file. An effective alternative to a rivet is the use of small nuts and bolts. These may be purchased from hobby shops and craft stores.

6   Figures 7–17, 7–18, and 7–19 illustrate several other rivet techniques.

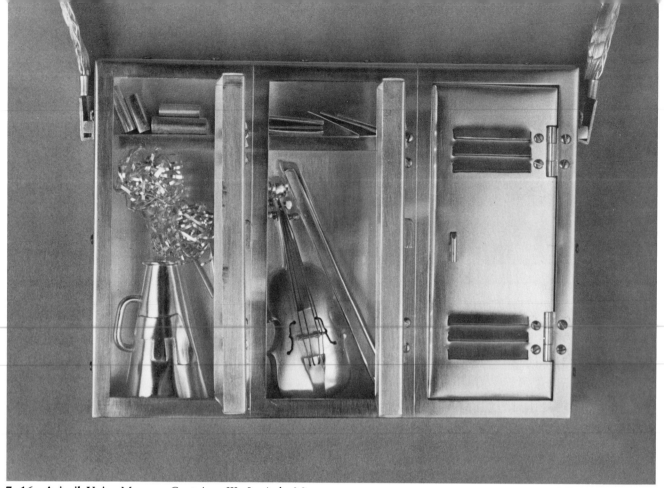

7-16 Avigail Upin, Memory Container III: Lucinda Matlock. *Woven and constructed pendant of sterling, fine silver, and steel screws. Courtesy of the artist.*

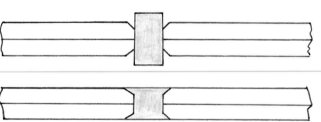

7-17 *Beveled edges cut to set a flush or hidden rivet.*

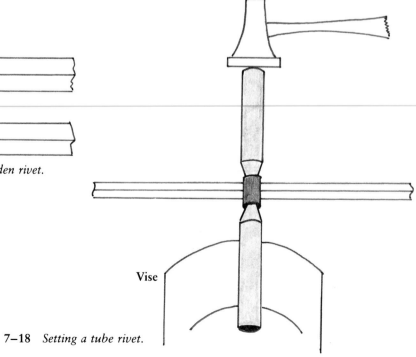

Vise

7-18 *Setting a tube rivet.*

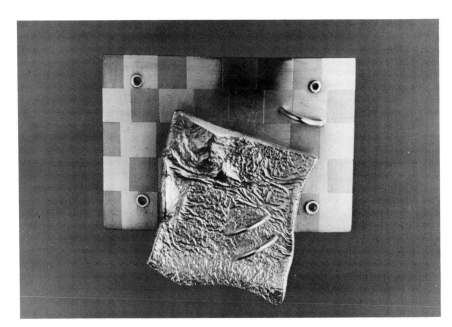

7–19 **Lisa D'Agostino.** *Pin of sterling and copper; inlaid, torch textured, and constructed with tube rivets. Courtesy of the artist. Photograph by Peter Krumhardt.*

HINGES

Articulation is often an important consideration in jewelry design. Both function and aesthetics are the major components underlying this consideration in determining the most suitable mechanism to join the various elements that might have to pivot or swing. Hinge devices clearly offer an excellent answer to the question of function. Aesthetically, the same solution may be proper, depending upon how creatively its application is approached. While the primary emphasis here will be placed on the hinging of jewelry pieces, the basic processes are applicable to other metal forms. Once familiar with the basics and construction of a simple hinge, the novice can experiment and explore the challenges of creatively integrating hinging devices in jewelry work.

Hinges are generally composed of several lengths of tubing with a pin or rod extending through them that serves as a joint or pivot point. Alternate tubes are soldered to the two pieces being joined. Figure 7–20 illustrates the soldering sequence of three- and five-element hinges. The following step-by-step description details the assembly of a simple five-element hinge used to join two pieces of flat sheet metal. Given these few points, the remaining techniques in this section will be easy to master.

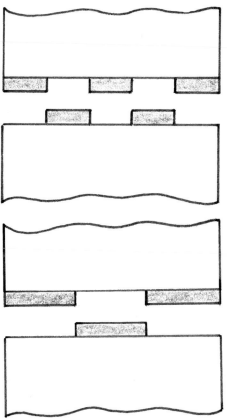

7–20 *Sequence in which a three and five element hinge is soldered.*

7–21 *Joining edges are filed straight.*
7–22 *Tubes cut to the appropriate lengths.*

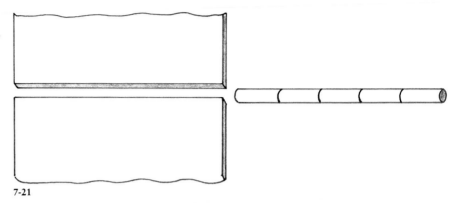

7-21

7-22

7–23 *Tube cutting jigs.*

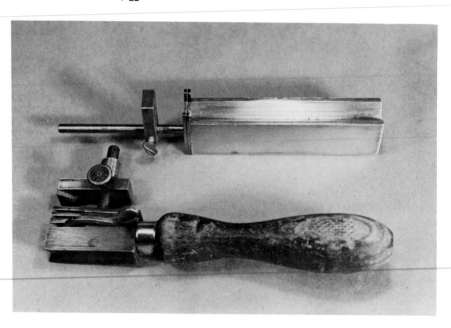

1 File the two joint edges straight and flat as if preparing a butt joint (figure 7–21). With strength and aesthetic considerations in mind, select the size tubing to be used.

2 Considering the length of the joint, measure the tubing in order to attain five equal pieces whose combined lengths correspond to the length of the joint. Cut the tube sections to the appropriate length with a fine blade (figure 7–22). A tube-cutting jig can be used to hold the tubing in alignment while cutting (figure 7–23). The jig can also be used to hold the sections while filing the ends square. Remove any burrs that might result from sawing or filing.

3 File the edges of the joining pieces at an angle corresponding closely to that of the tube sides (figure 7–24). On large pieces where thicker metal might be joined, the edges should be filed concave to correspond precisely to the shape of the tube (figure 7–25). This provides a stronger solder joint. With a file, slightly undercut the bottom edge of each section's ends (figure 7–26). File only that portion of the edge that might be subject to solder flow. An undercut

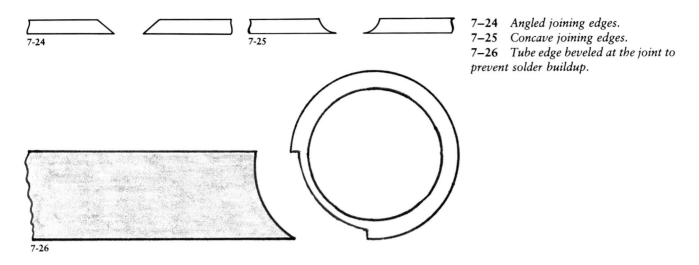

7–24   *Angled joining edges.*
7–25   *Concave joining edges.*
7–26   *Tube edge beveled at the joint to prevent solder buildup.*

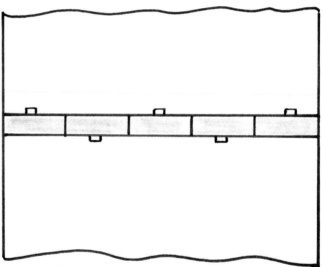

7–27   *Solder position.*

prevents a possible solder buildup along this area, which would make final fitting difficult.

4 Maintenance of the correct relationship of the tube sections to the workpiece is perhaps the hinge maker's biggest stumbling block. In this instance, a flat soldering surface and a steel aligning pin will help ease the task. Prepare a steel pin slightly longer than the hinge and of a diameter corresponding to that of the inner diameter of the hinge. Binding wire, nails, coat hangers, or old drill bits can be used. The alignment pin must be straight. Heat the pin and allow it to air cool. Repeat this several times until the pin is well oxidized. The oxidized surface will resist solder that might inadvertently spill over. Slide the tubes into their correct sequence over the steel pin and set the hinge alongside the workpiece on a clean, flat firebrick or block of charcoal. Be sure all elements are sitting flat and flush against each respective unit.

5 At this point the hinge sections will only be tack-soldered in place. Set a tiny piece of solder by each tube (figure 7–27). Do not saturate the entire joint with flux. Add just a bit at the points to be tacked. Direct the soldering flame on one section at a time. Remove the heat just as solder begins to flow. Keep in mind that the objective here is to tack the pieces in place and not to have solder flow completely through the joint. A complete flow can result in bonding adjacent tubes.

6 After tacking, let the piece air cool and remove the pin. It may be necessary to use pliers to pull the pin free. Removal is sometimes made easier by first soak-

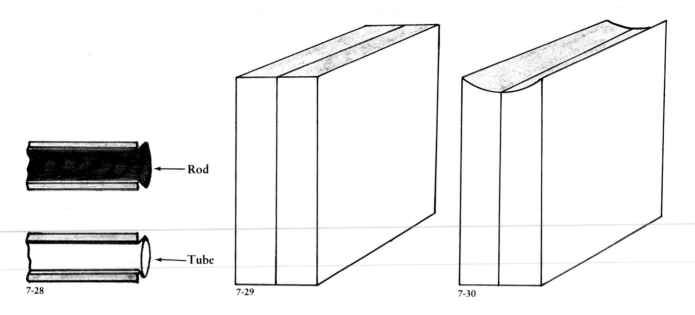

Rod

Tube

7-28

7-29

7-30

7–28   *Hinge pin of tubing or rod.*
7–29   *Hinge plates glued back to back.*
7–30   *Glued plates grooved.*

ing the work in hot water. The piece can now be pickled.

7 Replace the pin through one side. Flux each tube, add another bit of solder, and flow each joint separately. Reuse of the steel pin assures alignment as the individual joints reflow. Repeat this step on the opposite side. Remove the pin and pickle the work.

8 There are several methods of joining the two halves. Two possibilities are presented (figure 7–28). The pin should fit snugly, be visually integrated, and be removable if repairs are needed. Finish by filing and emerying excess metal from the pin and tube ends.

Rather than placing the hinge elements directly against the workpiece, the hinge may be constructed as a separate unit and then soldered or riveted to the jewelry. This type hinging is commonly used by silversmiths and generally constructed of thick sheet and heavy tubing. For our purposes, commercial tubing suffices. Preparation of the joining edges is as follows:

1 Using two pieces of 10- to 16-gauge sheet metal, file the joining edges straight and flat. Glue the two pieces back to back (figure 7–29). Five-minute epoxy works well and will separate when heated.

2 Place the metal between two pieces of wood in the jaws of a vise. The wood will protect the metal from being marred by the jaws. With the pieces secured, file a groove along the top edges (figure 7–30). The con-

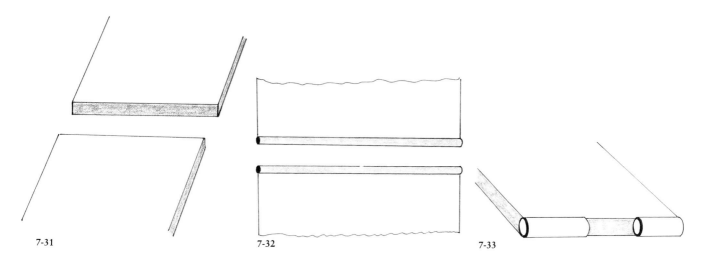

7-31   7-32   7-33

7–31   *Joining edges prepared to accept tubes.*
7–32   *Single length of tubing soldered to each half.*
7–33   *Center third cut away.*

cave groove should correspond to the curve of the tubing being used.

3 In order to maintain a uniform groove, a round parallel file should be used. Tapered files will usually cause an uneven or tapered groove. When filing, occasionally check the groove against the tubing. After forming the groove, remove the plates from the vise and heat the pieces to separate them and burn off the remaining epoxy.

4 The individual tube sections may now be prepared and attached as outlined earlier in steps 4 through 8. Joining of the finished hinge may be made by soldering or riveting it into or against the jewelry piece.

Construction of a simple three-knuckle hinge on flat sheet metal can be relatively easy. The method discussed here is admittedly a little wasteful of materials, but it eliminates the need for an alignment pin.

1 File the joining sheet metal edges as shown in figure 7–31 and solder a single piece of tubing along the entire length of each edge (figure 7–32). Solder over a clean, flat firebrick or pad.

2 Carefully cut away the center third of one tube with a fine saw blade. Square up the cutaway edges and solder joint with a flat needle file (figure 7–33).

3 Set the hinge sides together and scribe marks from the cut section onto the uncut tube. The outer thirds of the uncut tube can carefully be cut away. Cut along

7–34 *Instead of using tubes, discs are slotted and soldered to alternate sides. A hinge pin and tube spacers may be used to align this hinge.*

7–35 *To add visual interest in the hinged area, saw cuts can be made to remove material across the front of each soldered section.*

7–36 *Saw cuts give the illusion of multiple sections within each element of a hinge; i.e., a hinge composed of five tube sections will appear to be composed of twenty smaller elements when saw cuts are made into the finished hinge. This illustration shows one tube section.*

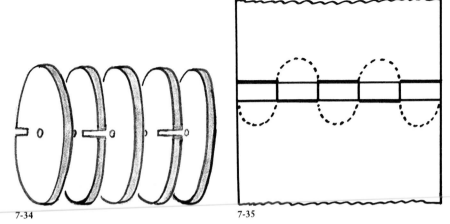

7-34

7-35

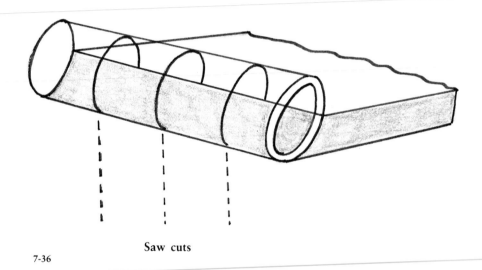

Saw cuts

7-36

the inside of the marks and finish by squaring the edges with the file. It is important to slightly undercut the second tube and carefully trial fit the pieces as filing progresses. Continue filing and trial fitting until the two sides slide together. Install the pivot pin and finish as discussed earlier.

Considering the time and effort involved in creating hinges, they should be used as effectively as possible.

With planning they will appear as integrated elements in the total work, not as afterthoughts. An understanding of the fundamental construction techniques allows the jeweler to embellish an otherwise plain mechanism. Figures 7–34, 7–35, and 7–36 illustrate several possibilities.

CHAPTER EIGHT

Inlays

Through the years, the jeweler's interest in contrast, both in color and texture, has led to the development of a number of decorative inlay techniques. Marriage of metals, niello, solder inlay, Khundun inlay, wire inlay, damascene, and plated inlay are only a few such techniques, but they provide us with the means to achieve almost any pattern or surface quality needed. From a technical standpoint, most of the inlays discussed in this chapter have one thing in common: the work is tedious and exacting. Fitting of the various elements must be precise if the work is to be visually effective.

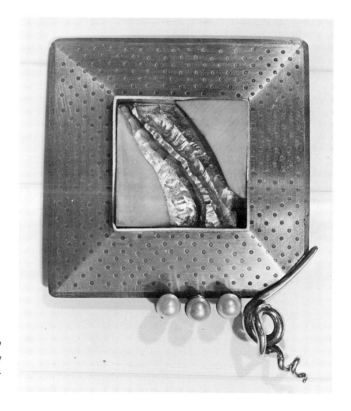

8-1 **William Fiorini.** *Pin of sterling silver and copper with pearls and ivory; forged, constructed, and inlaid. Dots of inlay add interest to a surface that might otherwise be stark. Courtesy of the artist.*

MARRIAGE OF METALS

Marriage of metals is probably the most commonly used inlay technique in contemporary jewelry. The popularity stems from its dramatic puzzlelike effect and from the fact that, compared with other means of achieving the same effect, it is relatively simple. Technically, the fitting and inlay of positive elements into negative spaces literally creates a metal jigsaw puzzle. Jewelers seeking a method to achieve crisp-edged graphic images will be drawn to marriage of metals.

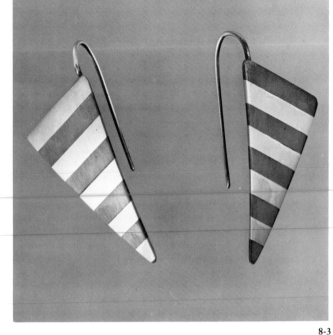

8–3 **Lisa D'Agostino.** *Constructed earrings of nickel and sterling silver; married metals. Photograph by Peter Krumhardt.*

8–2 **Lynda LaRoche,** Intrados. *Constructed brooch of sterling silver and 14-karat gold. Married metals effectively give balance and echo the use of smooth planes and hard edges. Courtesy of the artist.*

8-3

8-2

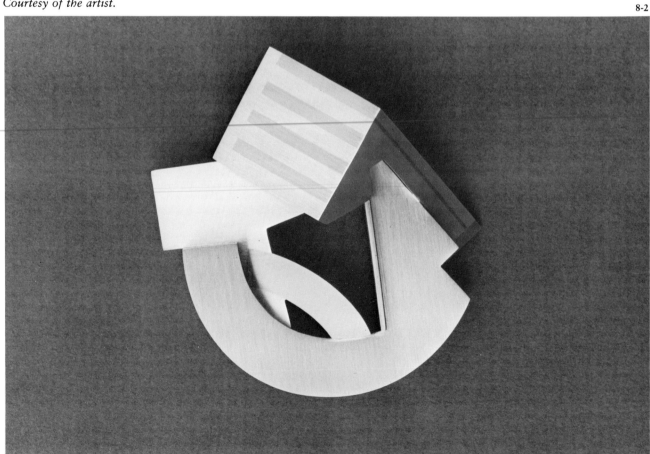

8–4 Lisa D'Agostino. *Constructed pin of copper, sterling, and nickel silver using marriage of metals. Photograph by Peter Krumhardt. Collection of Diane Itter.*

8–5 Lisa D'Agostino. *Constructed pin of sterling, nickel silver, brass, and copper using marriage of metals. Photograph by Peter Krumhardt.*

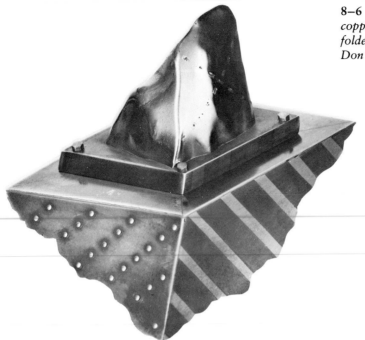

8–6 Richard Helzer, Avebury Stone Brooch 03#. *Sterling, copper, fine silver, and gold; marriage of metals, scored, folded, and constructed. Courtesy of the artist. Photograph by Don Pilotte.*

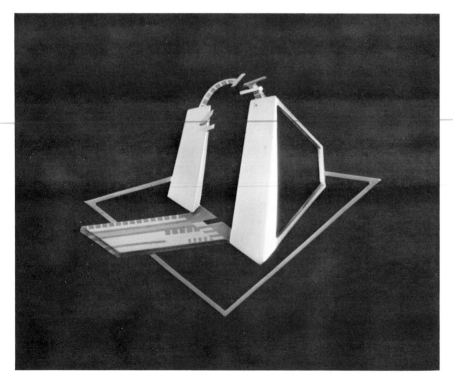

8–7 Ann Owens-Stone, Edifice Series, Brooch #3. *Sterling, nickel silver, and 14-karat gold; marriage of metals and construction. Courtesy of the artist.*

1 The value of planning will become apparent as the work progresses. Think ahead, consider what sequence to use in placing individual pieces, and cut each one with accuracy. For purposes of illustration, the larger piece or surrounding metal will be referred to as the "base" and pieces being inset as the "inlay."

2 Any combination of the copper-, silver-, or gold-based metals can be used. I prefer to use sheet metal of at least 18-gauge. Thinner material bends easily and often ends up looking flimsy. Keep in mind that filing, emerying, and buffing will further thin the metal.

3 With the jeweler's saw, cut out an inlay shape. Refine the edges with a needle file. Keep all edges crisp and true. Rounded surfaces will not butt evenly to the base and will result in a broad solder seam.

4 Lay the inlay piece over a base sheet at the point of inlay. Hold the piece down firmly or fasten the pieces with 5-minute epoxy glue. Carefully scribe a line around the edge of the cutout onto the base. A thin sewing needle makes an excellent marking tool. Pencils and regular scribe tools are too broad and will not scribe flush to the inlay edge.

5 Remove the cutout shape. Drill a small hole through the base piece just inside the scribed line and carefully saw along the inner edge of the scribed line. Refine the saw cut edges with needle files.

6 The inlay should now fit into the base piece. If some areas are too large to fit, file them further and check the fit. Continue checking and filing until the inlay will set in.

7 Figure 8–8 illustrates an exaggerated view of an initial fit. Note that the fit is not exact. Gaps will eventually be closed.

8 Lay the fitted pieces on a flat soldering surface and apply flux to the entire joint. Use hard solder to tack the pieces together at just the points that make full contact (figure 8–9). Use very small snippets of solder and remove the heat at the instant of flow. Do not attempt to close the gaps with solder. Pickle, rinse, and dry the workpiece. Inevitably, some solder will spill over around the joint but generally this is not a problem. Excess will later be filed away.

9 Next, gently planish each gap closed. The gaps are closed one at a time and tack-soldered until, eventually, the entire seam is joined. Over an anvil or flat steel stake, use the slightly domed face of the plan-

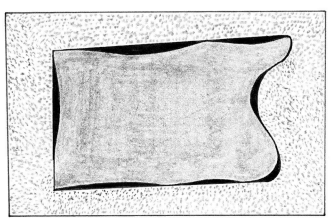

8–8 *Exaggerated view of the initial inlay fit. Dark area depicts gaps.*

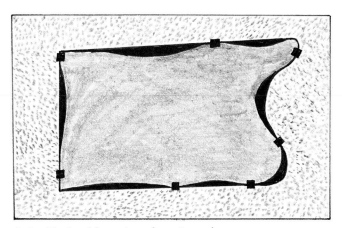

8–9 *Tack solder at just the points of contact.*

ishing hammer to stretch the metal on either side of the opening. In some instances gaps will close by planishing just on one side of the seam. Experience will reveal the best method of planishing in each situation. If possible, avoid hammering over areas of spilled solder. The hammer's impact forces solder into the underlying metal and only makes it more difficult to remove.

10 More often than not, the completed piece will end up slightly domed from being worked with the planishing hammer. File and emery the piece while still curved. Few things are more difficult than attempting to file or refine a flat surface. After the piece is completely filed and emeried it may then be flattened.

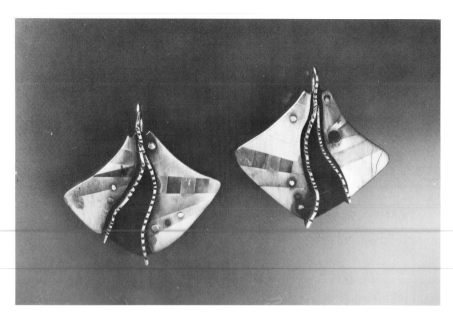

8–10 Enid Kaplan. *Constructed earrings of 14-karat yellow and white gold, sterling, copper, and brass; married metals. Courtesy of the artist. Photograph by Doug Long.*

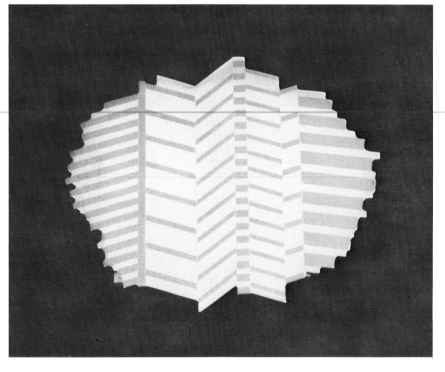

8–11 Randy Long, Kimono Fragment #1. *Brooch of sterling and nickel silver; married metals. By juxtaposing married sections of stripes and using irregular edges, the artist has created a dramatic work void of appliqué or embellishment. Courtesy of the artist.*

11 To add shapes within this basic inlay, proceed with steps 3 to 9.

12 On inlays extending to the edge of the base, it is generally easier to fit and solder the inlay pieces into an oversized base. The extra surrounding material forms a border and tends to retain the inlay while fitting and will keep seams closed during the planishing of open seams. After the inlay is completed, the excess bordering material is cut away flush with the edge of the inlay (figure 8–12). This approach requires extra material but is less frustrating than other means.

13 Marriage of metals can be finished by leaving a fine emery surface or by buffing. On some metal combinations, high polishes tend to leave color contrasts so subtle they are difficult to distinguish. A mild solution of liver of sulfur and water will bring forth the contrast.

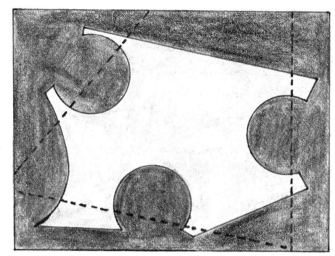

8–12 *Excess border is cut away.*

LINE INLAY (DAMASCENE)

The name *damascene* was borrowed from the Syrian city of Damascus where this technique was popularized centuries ago. Damascene has been practiced at various times by cultures around the globe; Spanish, Japanese, and Indian craftworkers still produce a considerable number of objects incorporating damascene inlay. Some feel that this type inlay is the truest form, and without question is the most difficult to master.

Today's jewelers refer to damascene as line or wire inlay. For our purposes, future references will be termed "line inlay." Line is a universal term and one better fitting contemporary work. As a jeweler becomes proficient in simple line inlay using wire, all sorts of shapes may be inlaid with wire and sheet metal. The focus here is on the simpler wire form.

The major element in the creation of inlay involves cutting a shallow, flat-bottomed groove into a base metal (figure 8–14). Another cut is angled into each of the inner sidewalls of the original groove (figure 8–15).

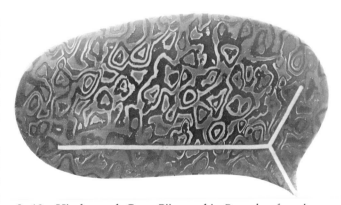

8–13 **Hiroko and Gene Pijanowski.** *Brooch of mokume gane composed of copper, Kuromido, and fine silver with line inlay of 24-karat yellow gold. Courtesy of the artists.*

8–14 *Flat-bottomed groove.*   8–15 *Groove with angled walls.*

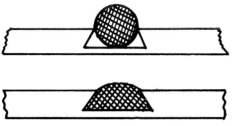

8-16 *Wire set in and expanded into the prepared groove.*

Wire is set into the groove and forced downward, filling the undercuts and groove. The wire's expansion into the undercut creates a permanent mechanical lock (figure 8–16). While the tools and their application may differ from culture to culture, the end effect is generally the same. Commercial gravers, die-maker chisels, and small handmade steel chisels can be used to incise inlay grooves. Tools can be applied by hand or with the assistance of a chasing hammer.

Any attempt to master a task through words and pictures alone is impossible. Cutting inlay grooves successfully depends on two basic factors: correct tool preparation and the manual dexterity of the worker. The reader is encouraged to pay particular attention to each detail outlined in this section regarding the angles and shapes to which gravers are sharpened and the manner in which they are held. Then, practice.

1 In studying the grooves depicted in figures 8–14 and 8–15, consider how a tool must be shaped in order to perform the task. Think about the tool's width and length, and the angle at which it is held. Consideration of these questions will provide insight as to the tool's capability.
2 The depth and width of the groove relative to the diameter of the wire must also be considered. Wire that is too small will not fill the recesses; wire that is too large is wasteful of time and material.
3 Do a series of small practice pieces using annealed copper wire in hard brass. These lines need not be more than an inch long. As the graver or chisel begins its cut, first concentrate on making shallow, uniform cuts. With experience, cuts may gradually be placed deeper. If the cutting tool is prepared properly, it will almost guide itself through a straight cut. A thin film of kerosene or cutting oil on the cutting edge of the tool will lubricate and ease the cutting action and help

maintain the tool's sharpness. Hammer blows should be delivered in a steady rhythm.

For the inlay of 24-gauge round wire, the primary groove's cut is made with a number 6 onglette graver prepared in the following manner.

1 Figures 8–18 and 8–19 illustrate the bottom view of two graver heels. These views depict the surface of the graver, which lies flush against the metal as it is cut. Think of it as a view from beneath. In figure 8–18 the heel is formed relatively short in order to cut curved lines. The side edges of the heel are cut away rather drastically compared to the example in figure 8–19. This shape allows the heel to move freely through curves with little interference between the heel edges and inner walls of the groove. The longer heel in figure 8–19 is shaped to permit the groove walls to assist in stabilizing the tool as it travels through a straight cut.

8-17 Hiroko and Gene Pijanowski. *Constructed brooch of mokume-gane and fine silver. Laminated and line inlaid. In this beautifully executed piece the crisp silver inlaid lines form a dominant pattern over the subtle striations of the ground lamination. Courtesy of the artists.*

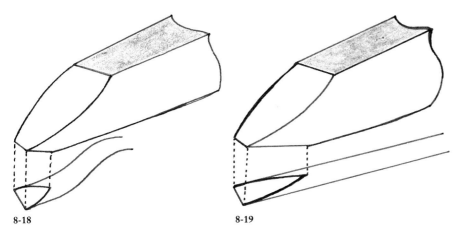

8-18

8-19

8–18 *Graver heel prepared to cut curved grooves.*
8–19 *Graver heel prepared to cut straight grooves.*

2 On a fine grinding wheel grind the face of the graver to a 45- to 50-degree angle. While grinding, keep the face cool by dipping the graver tip into a container of water. Overheating the face will alter its temper and cause the tool to chip or quickly dull. Check the face angle with a protractor.

3 An oiled Arkansas stone and a stoning fixture are used for stoning. Apply just enough light oil to flood the surface of the stone; the oil prevents impregnation of the stone by metal particles. Be sure the stone and fixture sit on a flat surface and that the stone's face is parallel to the supporting surface. A precision-steel surface or a piece of heavy plate glass works well as a support surface (figure 8–20).

4 With the graver secured in the stoning fixture, stone the heel to give the tool a 10-degree lift. Figure 8–21 shows an exaggerated view of the lift angle. Stone the heel until the width of the cutting edge is about $3/64$ inch (figure 8–22).

5 The width of the face of the graver must be reduced to create the shape of the heel (figure 8–19). In doing this, the cutting edge is also reduced to about $1/32$ of an inch. In figure 8–23 the shaded area shows that portion of the graver that is stoned to attain this final dimension. This is achieved by laying the graver on its side and moving it across the stone by hand.

8–20 *Graver fixture and stone supported on plate glass.*

8–21 *Graver prepared with a 10-degree lift angle.*

8–22 *Preliminary stoning of the heel to a width of ³⁄₆₄ inch at the cutting edge.*

8–23 *Final stoning to a width of ¹⁄₃₂ inch.*

The groove's undercuts are formed with a number 1 onglette prepared like the number 6 with the exception of the dimensions. Figure 8–24 shows the comparative dimensions and shapes of the cutting ends.

To permit the use of a chasing hammer to propel the graver, the graver's handle must be modified. Drill a ¼-inch hole through the back of the handle to the point where the handle end or tang of the graver would fit. Measure the depth of the hole (approximately ¾ inch) and insert a piece of ¼-inch round brass rod (figure 8–26). A few drops of epoxy glue will retain the plug. File away excess brass to make the rod flush with the handle. The plug will transmit the hammer's force without damage to the handle.

A practice inlay is begun by fixing a piece of hard 16-gauge brass to a flat block of hardwood. Flat-head sheet-metal screws can be used. The screws are threaded into the wood alongside the brass so that their heads act as clamps when screwed completely down (figure 8–27). Use at least two screws on each side of the brass. Place the wooden block in a table-mounted machinist's vise. With a straightedge and scribe, mark off a line approximately 1½ inches long. This will provide a cutting guide.

Tool grip need not be rigid or tiring. The grip should only be firm enough to comfortably control the tool. The position of the graver's axis relative to the workpiece and the worker is generally a matter of personal preference. Some sit; others stand. Comfort and visibility of the graver's cutting edge seem to be the most important considerations, as long as the cutting is done accurately.

Using the number 6 onglette, start the cut with the cutting edge placed squarely on the scribed line with the handle end lifted slightly. Remember the heel of the graver is angled 10 degrees to the axis of the graver so the starting lift should only be a little above that. The initial lift of the handle end should be just enough to force the cutting edge down into the metal. Once that is

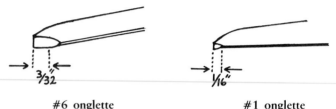

| #6 onglette | #1 onglette |

8–24 *Comparative dimensions of the number 6 and number 1 onglette gravers.*

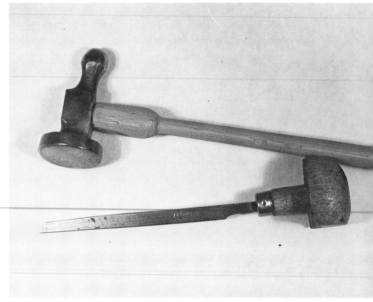

8–25 *Chasing hammer and graver.*

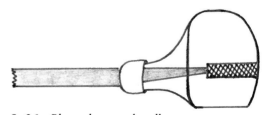

8–26 *Plugged graver handle.*

8-27 *Screw heads used as clamps.*

8-28 *Graver handle is lowered to finish a cut.*

8-29 *Graver angled to make undercuts.*

achieved, the handle is lowered to permit the heel to rest flush with or parallel to the bottom of the cut. Light, rapid strokes of a medium-weight chasing hammer are used to begin the cut and should continue as the handle end is moved down and cutting progresses. Try to visualize an x-ray side view of what should occur relative to the bottom of the groove, the tool angle, and the cutting edge. Lowering the handle further will steer the cutting edge upward and out of the metal (figure 8–28).

Continue practicing short, straight lines. Many can be cut into a small piece of metal. When satisfied with the results using the number 6 onglette, begin practice with the number 1 on the undercuts. The tip of the number 1 is slanted into the groove's bottom corner (figure 8–29). A little caution is necessary to prevent the graver's side from riding the opposite top edge of the groove, otherwise the graver face will cut into the top edge. The process of undercutting is essentially the same as that of cutting the original groove with the exception of slanting the graver. With the experience of straight-line cuts, gravers can be prepared and shaped as illustrated in figure 8–18 for practice cutting curved grooves. In either case, occasionally inspect the graver's cutting edge and sharpen as needed. Frequent dressing on number 600 emery paper will maintain sharpness and ease cutting considerably. Sharpness can be tested by setting the cutting edge against the thumbnail. If it does not catch, resharpen.

Anneal and clean a short length of 24-gauge round copper wire. The wire may extend beyond the ends of the groove and later be cut away. With the chasing ham-

mer and a slightly domed chasing punch, drive the wire into the groove. Start at either end and use medium blows against the chasing tool to drive the wire into the groove. Allow the tool's face to overlap its previous impact point. Do not allow the punch to miss segments of the wire. Uneven compression of the wire will result in raised and insecure portions of the inlay (figure 8–30). Wire remaining above the base surface can be filed off or cut away with a flat graver. The graver may also be used to cut away any excess wire extending over the base at the ends of the groove. Once the wire has been inset and leveled, the workpiece should not be heated to temperatures in the annealing range. The property of work hardness helps retain the inlay; if heated, the metals may loosen. If the jeweler is experienced with the graver and hammer, inlay channels may be cut by hand. The section on engraving (page 89) gives additional information relative to the hand process.

Another method of cutting the inlay groove is with the use of small handmade chisels. These can be formed with masonry nails, drill rod stock, or almost any thin tool-steel rod stock. The cutting ends are prepared and used as outlined for gravers. The chisel's cutting edge should be tempered to a straw yellow and the hammer end annealed.

8-30 *Wire improperly inlaid.*

8–31   *Inlaid wire.*

8–33   *Constructed ring of sterling silver and niello. Photograph by Peter Krumhardt.*

The inlay's finish is a matter of personal preference. To bring forth maximum contrast, the piece can be emeried, buffed, and oxidized. If buffed, care must be taken. Because of the different degrees of hardness of the metals, some undercutting may appear. Emery well and apply a gentle pressure to the buff.

8–32   **Glen Gardner.** *Brooch of sterling silver, copper, 24-karat gold, and niello; engraved, inlaid, and constructed. Courtesy of the artist. Photograph by Ann Hawthorn.*

NIELLO

Niello is a process of fusing a mixture of metallic sulfides into metal depressions. The darkness of the inlay contrasts boldly with the base metal. While there is a considerable difference in effect, the preparation, application, and finishing of niello are quite similar to those in enameling. After the mixture is prepared, it is ground to a powdery consistency, packed into depressions in the base metal, and then fired in a kiln. Heating makes the niello flow and fuse to the receiving metal.

The underlying metal may be prepared in any of several ways. Sheet metal can be used to construct forms with grooved, recessed, or framelike sections. Recesses can be cut directly into the metal with gravers, saw blades, acid, chisels, or steel burrs. Pierced sheet patterns may be sweat soldered onto a backing sheet and then inlaid. Recesses should be of adequate depth to securely contain the niello and assure adequate thickness for finishing.

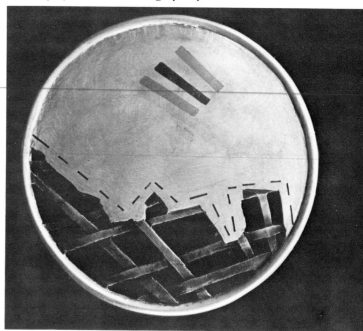

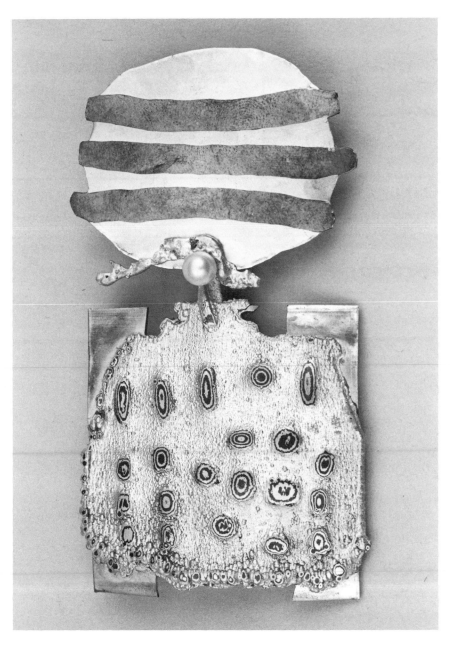

8–34 Florence Resnikoff. *Pin of silver and copper with pearl; constructed, overlaid, cast, and electroplated mokume. Courtesy of the artist. Photograph by Gary Sinick.*

A number of niello formulas are workable. History has passed on formulas used since the times of Pliny, Theophilus, and Cellini. These and more contemporary mixtures all combine a variety of nonferrous metals with sulfur. Once alloyed, subsequent remelting occurs at a much lower temperature. Niello is generally an alloy of silver, copper, lead, and sulfur.

Niello Preparation
The following steps are based on a formula of—

1½	ounces lead
1	ounce copper
3½	ounces sulfur
½	ounce silver

1 Melt the copper and silver in a ceramic crucible. Add a pinch of flux. Then add the lead to the molten mix and stir with a graphite rod. The entire process should be carried out in a well-ventilated area.
2 Pour the molten material into a crucible containing the sulfur and stir again. Reduce the heat and continue playing the flame over the crucible until the sulfur appears to be burned away. Pour the molten mixture onto a steel-surface plate or into a container of water.
3 Break the larger chunks of niello into small pieces with a hammer and then grind all of the material to a fine powder in a mortar and pestle. Grindings may be shaken through an enamelist's 80 mesh sifter to ensure a uniformity in grain size.
4 Other niello formulas are listed in Appendix 2.

Fusing the Niello

1 Pickle and thoroughly clean the workpiece with pumice powder and water. Do not touch the recessed areas with bare fingers. Coat the workpiece with a borax flux diluted with water to a milky consistency. Let the workpiece dry.
2 Pack the powdered niello into each depression. Compact the niello and mound extra material over the recess. The powder will decrease in volume upon melting and the extra should be of sufficient quantity to compensate for this.
3 Preheat the kiln to approximately 900°F. Set the workpiece on an enameling trivet and place it in the kiln. Make frequent observations of the piece and remove it as soon as the surface of the niello appears to be smooth. Quickly inspect the surface; if voids exist, refill those areas with powder and return the piece to the kiln for fusion. Do not allow the work to be heated above the fusion point. This may cause the underlying metal to be pitted by the lead in the niello. Allow the workpiece to air cool.

Finishing

Care must be taken in removing the excess niello. Keep in mind that the inlaid areas are softer than the surrounding metal and will undercut if buffed improperly. File and then emery with a strip of emery cloth backed by a flat piece of wood. If a buff finish is desired, use a broad felt wheel and light pressure.

WIRE OVERLAY/INLAY

The categorization of this technique is understandably questionable. As the wire sits atop the base plate, it is clearly an overlay. Once the wire is soldered properly and compressed into the base, it appears to be inlaid (figure 8–35). The process is relatively simple and the visual effect quite pleasing.

8–35 *Wire soldered and compressed into the base metal.*

1 Almost any shape or size wire can be used. Contrasting colors of wire and base plate are used to develop a linear pattern. A base plate of at least 18 gauge should be used. The plate will thin somewhat from compression and finishing. Ideally, the base should be of a softer metal than the wire in order for the wire to be hammered or rolled into the base.
2 Begin by annealing, cleaning, and making certain the base is flat. An irregular surface will make the soldering process difficult and possibly incomplete.
3 As with most processes, planning will help assure eventual success. In this case, consideration of the sequence in which to place the wires and solder snippets is essential. For one thing, keep in mind that wire spreads, either elongating or widening as it is compressed into the base. If adjacent pieces are placed too close they will spread into one another. Solder should be placed in areas where it can easily be cleaned away in the event of spills. For example, on curved wires solder should be placed along the outside of the curve (figure 8–36). One or two tiny pieces of solder should be sufficient if the wire touches the base throughout.
4 Use fingers or half-round jawed pliers to bend the wires to shape. Anneal and clean each piece and gently flatten them on the anvil with a rawhide mallet. On a piece of emery placed on a flat surface, carefully rub the bottom of the wire back and forth until it is clean. If round wire is used, rub until the bottom is slightly flattened (figure 8–37). This provides a broader surface area and a more secure joint against the base plate.

8–36 *Solder placed on the outside of curves.*

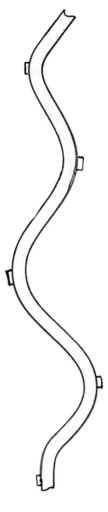

8–37 *Bottom of wire is slightly flattened.*

5 Flux the base and wires and lay them on a flat soldering surface. Place bits of solder as outlined in step 3. One piece of solder at one end of each wire may be sufficient if the pieces fit well. Apply the flame over the wire and base plate until the solder is drawn through the entire joint. Pickle and rinse the workpiece. File away all traces of solder on the base. If several wires are to be applied, do one at a time as in steps 4 and 5. Applying one wire at a time often makes the task of removing solder spills easier. Take care not to reflow the previous joints.

6 After all soldering is complete, clean the piece and file or scrape away any remaining spilled solder from the wires and base. Wires can now be hammered or rolled into the base plate. If using a hammer, go slowly and uniformly over each wire. The domed face of the planishing hammer works well. Anneal the workpiece after each pass of the hammer. A smooth inlay will require several passes of the hammer.

7 The piece can now be filed to remove hammer marks and any seam marks at the edge of the wires. If wires are securely soldered, a few strokes of the file will remove seam marks and leave a finished surface that appears to be inlaid in the traditional manner. Further refinement is a matter of emerying, buffing, and coloring.

8 This process need not be limited to round wire. Thin sheet metal shapes can also be applied.

SOLDER INLAY

Of all inlays, this is perhaps the least time-consuming. Given the proper preparation, solder inlays can be as precise and beautiful as the more traditional methods. In terms of preparation, all that is needed is a recess for the solder to flow into and fill. No undercutting is required.

1 Anneal and clean a piece of 16-gauge sheet metal. Lay or clamp the metal over an anvil or flat stake.

2 Any number of tools can be used to emboss or stamp depressions into the sheet. Formal patterns or random impressions can be applied with careful placement of the tool and accurate hammer blows to the tool. Gravers can also be used to incise lines of any depth or thickness. Experiment with chasing tools, nails, a center punch, and so on.

3 Try to keep the workpiece as flat as possible while tooling its surface. Broad depressions and dents may also fill with solder and make finishing a difficult task.

4 Flux the entire piece and flood hard solder into the recesses. A solder pick can be used to spread and smooth the solder as it flows. Use a generous amount of solder. If all recesses do not fill, add more solder and reflow. Pickle and clean the workpiece.

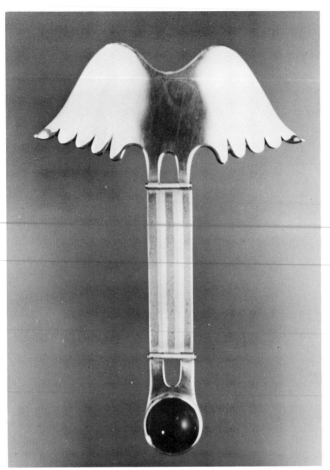

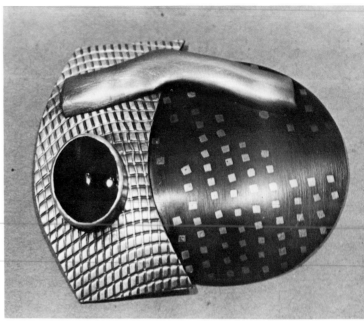

8-39 Paula Cavanaugh. *Pin of sterling silver and copper with agate. Roller embossed, solder inlaid, and constructed. The artist used the square inlay shapes to carry over the motif of the embossed silver. This unifies the work.*

8-38 *Pin of sterling silver, copper, and 14-karat gold with amethyst; overlaid and constructed. Photograph by Peter Krumhardt. Collection of Kathy Reeves.*

5 File away all excess solder until only the base plate and the solder pattern are visible. A quick dip in liver of sulfur will expose excess solder that might otherwise be hard to detect. Complete by emerying and buffing.

6 For further embossing techniques adaptable to solder inlays, refer to the sections on roller embossing (pages 84 to 86), etching (pages 87 to 88), and hammer texturing (pages 128 to 129).

KHUNDUN INLAY

Khundun inlay is seldom used in contemporary jewelry. Its name comes from India where it is still practiced to some extent. Though not known as Khundun inlay, European jewelers commonly used the technique from the fourteenth to eighteenth centuries. Renaissance jewelers often employed the inlay to embed faceted stones and enamels.

Figure 8–40 illustrates one method of using the inlay. The supporting surface below is given a tooth or stipple texture with a graver, small chisel, or pointed scribing tool. If the cavity is undercut or has angled sides, the tooth surface is not needed. To set a stone as in figure 8–41, a bit of epoxy can be used to stabilize the stone while inlaying. Pure gold or silver foil is packed in a few layers at a time with a finely pointed scribe. While packing, the angle of the scribe is varied throughout the process to create a locking effect through each series of layers. After packing, the top surface is burnished with the tip of a burnisher. The Khundum process may also be used for line inlay.

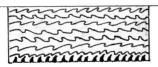

8–40   *The recess is given a tooth.*

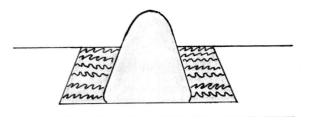

8–41   *A recess with angled sides and inlaid stone.*

CHAPTER NINE

Laminations

In this country, the use of decorative metal laminations has grown steadily in the past two decades. After exploring this technique for a dozen years I continue to be surprised and pleased with the many possibilities inherent in the process. The variety of striated patterns, lines, and colors to be uncovered is constantly intriguing. This chapter should provide the reader with the stimulus to take a bit of technical information on lamination and come up with pleasing and unusual pieces of jewelry.

9–1 *Laminated and constructed pin of sterling silver, copper, 14-karat gold, and Delrin. Collection of Stanley Nixon.*

Before going further, however, note well this warning that prefaces the printed handouts given to the students in my classes:

Lamination processes are time-consuming, frustrating, and tedious. Even when all steps are carefully and faithfully followed the results are sometimes less than desired. If you are not willing to begin with a positive attitude, not willing to expend the time and patience, not willing to be frustrated along each step, and not willing to face possible failure after all appears well and proper, don't start.

SOLDERED MOKUME

Many of today's jewelers have borrowed and modified the Japanese technique called mokume-gane, which means "woodgrain metal." In this section the process is called simply "mokume." We also modify the process by using a torch as the heat source and solder as the bonding medium. Traditionally, the process is accomplished by fusing layers of metal together in the forge. An advantage of the more recent method is that it can be carried out in any jewelry facility. The jeweler can laminate several types of metal without great concern for each metal's molecular compatibility with the others. Several colors of metal are easily obtainable from suppliers, thus avoiding the need to alloy and mill the needed stock as would also be required traditionally. While it sounds as though there is little value in tradition, that is not the case. The traditional diffusion technique of mokume-gane is discussed later in the chapter.

The following steps work well to create mokume suitable in size for most jewelry work. The process has proven routinely successful if followed precisely.

1 Metal thickness should be at least 16 gauge. Thinner metal bends easily and is more apt to warp when heated.
2 There is no set number of layers to start with. Most jewelers find 2 to 5 beginning layers are sufficient. The use of silver or gold is not necessary. Copper and brass, along with the solder layers, provide a wide range of color possibilities. A finished piece having a large number of layers may be desired but not essential. Pieces having only a few layers can be striking.

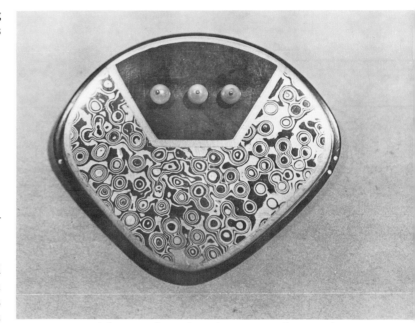

9–2 Ann Wright. *Die-formed and constructed pin of Kuromiko, silver, and mokume with pearls.*

3 For illustrative purposes, start by cutting four pieces of 16-gauge sheet metal 1¼ inch square and remove any burrs along the sawed edges. Emery one side of three of the pieces. Emery in several directions to ensure that the pieces are absolutely clean. After emerying, scrub the surfaces with a slurry of water and fine pumice powder. Rinse and do not touch the clean metal.
4 One at a time, set the cleaned pieces face up on a flat soldering surface. Flux the metal and place four 1-inch pieces of medium wire solder equally spaced on the metal. An equivalent amount of sheet solder will suffice. Use a strong flame to heat the piece; as the solder flows, spread it evenly over the entire surface with a pick. A length of coat hanger wire can be used to make a pick. File one end to a point. If some areas do not cover with solder, pickle, reflux, and add a bit more solder. After soldering and cleaning the three pieces, put each piece through the rolling mill in order to smooth the solder surface. The purpose of rolling is to make the top and bottom of each piece parallel, which will later make it possible to flatten the layers. This step is critical to

the outcome of the process and should not be overlooked. Keep in mind that rolling is not intended to decrease the thickness of the pieces, just to smooth the irregular solder surface.

5 Being careful not to remelt the solder, anneal all the pieces. Using a mallet and clean anvil surface, make each piece absolutely flat. Needless to say, this is essential. Emery and pumice the unsoldered surfaces. The bottom and top surfaces of the stack need not be cleaned. Soldered surfaces should be scrubbed well with the pumice slurry.

6 Flux all surfaces and stack the layers in the desired color sequence. Lay the stack atop a flat steel-mesh screen set on the soldering tripod. Be sure that the soldered surfaces lie against unsoldered surfaces.

7 If an acetylene or similar torch is to be used, install the largest tip. Other torches may be used, providing the flame is adequate to heat the laminant quickly. Apply a strong flame, alternating the heat top to bottom to bring the layers to soldering temperature as equally as possible. When heat is first applied, exert a gentle pressure to the center of the stack with the solder pick to stabilize the layers, which would otherwise be displaced by the boiling flux. Remove the pick when boiling ceases. Continue heating while observing the edges; as the solder begins to flow, apply a gentle pressure with the pick on the top of the center of the stack and remove the heat. Continue the downward pressure until the solder solidifies. The downward force helps drive out entrapped air and flux and may correct minor gaps between the layers.

9–3 *Electric rolling mill.*

8 Cool the laminant in water and check the edges. When you are sure all the layers are completely soldered, pickle the work. If some areas appear not to be joined, flux the edges and proceed again as in step 7; add solder to the edge as the previous solder reflows. A length of wire solder can be used and fed into the joint.

9 After the stack is completed and pickled, roll the piece through the rolling mill. Care must be taken not to overstress the lamination in rolling. Anneal the piece often and roll in one direction only. When thinned to about 8 gauge, anneal, flatten with the mallet, and saw the piece in half.

10 Double-check to assure the halves are flat. The two pieces will be soldered one on top of the other, doubling the layers. Emery and pumice the mating surfaces. Cut four 1¼-inch pieces of medium solder and evenly space them between the two pieces after fluxing their surfaces. Place the laminant on the screen and proceed as in step 7.

11 Continue the preceding steps until the desired number of layers is reached. In the final rolling, turn the piece 90 degrees after each annealing so that the resulting lamination is approximately square or rectangular. Roll the piece no thinner than 18 gauge.

12 The typical woodgrain pattern is created by exposing inner layers of the laminated stack. Dapping punches are used to bump out areas where a pattern is desired. Care must be taken when dapping to prevent excessively deep depressions. Subsequent filing and finishing may open holes where depressions extend beyond what will be the front of the piece.

9–4 *The dapping punch must be used with restraint. Excessive depth of the indentations will result in holes in the laminant when it is filed.*

13 Securing the lamination to a hardwood board while dapping the pattern will ensure the relative flatness of the finished piece. Drill a series of small holes about 1 inch apart around the extreme outer edge of the sheet and fasten it to the board with small nails or screws. Drive the nails in at a slight angle and bend them over the sheet's edge. This will hold down the edge of the metal and provide a gripping point to later remove the nails with pliers.

14 Patterns need not be just random bumps. Using a chasing tool with a rounded, oblong face, controlled linear patterns are obtainable. Within each linear area, striations will be visible. After the pattern is bumped out, the nails are removed and the bumps filed down until a uniform level is attained. Filing away the bumps reveals the layers. The piece can now be emeried, buffed and chemically colored. The mokume is ready to be used as needed.

Additional Finishing Points

1 The mokume sheet will have a slight curve when removed from the board. It is easier to file the bumps away if the piece is left curved.
2 Once the bumps are removed, it is almost impossible to completely flatten the metal. This is due to the irregular thickness of the sheet. Again, it is recommended that the sheet be left slightly curved.
3 If some layer separation appears after filing, these areas can sometimes be flooded with easy solder and refiled.
4 Have patience when coloring the finished piece. Use a mild solution of cold water and liver of sulfur. Dip the mokume for several seconds and rinse in cold water.

Strong or hot solutions bring forth colors so rapidly that interesting effects may be missed.

EDGE LAMINATION

Edge or strip laminations offer very distinct and crisp linear patterns. Metals may be combined to create a rainbow of colors. Strips of metal can be soldered side by side on edge in straight lines or with curving, wavelike effects. Once the initial lamination is assembled, it can be recut and the strips repositioned to make checkerboard patterns. Sections may also be cut off and forged, twisted, or drawn into striped wire. The possibilities are unlimited.

To begin the process, complete steps 1 through 7 in the previous section and then proceed as follows.

1 At this point, the basic lamination has been soldered and can now be rolled to the desired thickness and length. The width of the edges making up the finished pattern is in part determined by how thin the initial stack is rolled. Keep this in mind and do not roll the piece too thin.
2 Anneal, pickle, and flatten the lamination on the anvil. True and square one edge with a large file or belt sander and cut a strip approximately ³⁄₁₆-inch wide from the trued edge with the jeweler's saw (figure 9–6). Lay the cut strip aside and retrue the same edge with the sander, then again cut a ³⁄₁₆-inch strip. Repeat this step until the laminant is completely cut away. Trueing the piece prior to each saw cut provides a flat surface for soldering.
3 While in some instances a bottom plate is not necessary, using it makes the laminant less likely to crack during the rolling or forging phase. Check to see that three sides of each strip are clean and straight. This excludes the sawed side, which will face upward. Temporarily lay the strips side by side, sawn side up, to check for precise fit and to measure for the base. The plate should extend ⅛ inch on all sides of the laminant to leave a solder ledge (figure 9–7). Cut a base of 18 to 20 gauge sheet metal. Anneal, flatten, and emery the plate. Flux and assemble the strips on the plate in the desired sequence.
4 Set the plate with the strips over the solder tripod on a steel screen. This permits heating top and bottom.

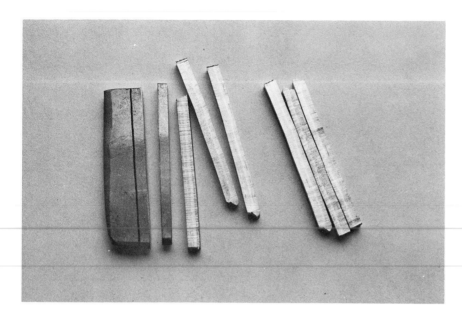

9–5 *Sections cut from the initial stack in preparation for edge lamination.*

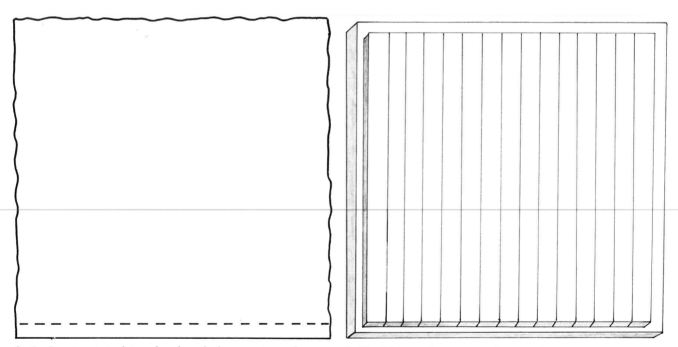

9–6 *Laminant stack trued and ready for a section to be cut.*

9–7 *Edge sections arranged over a base.*

Lay several pieces of medium solder along each solder joint and around the edges of the base plate. Use a strong flame with a tip large enough for adequate coverage of the work. Ideally, all solder will flow at once. Use the solder pick to adjust any misalignment while heating or as the solder flows. Reflowing of the laminant's original solder seams usually makes no difference because the capillary action of the solder holds the strips in place. Cool the piece in water and inspect the solder joints. If soldering is incomplete, reflux, add more solder, and reflow.

5 Pickle the work and file away excess solder from the surface of the laminant. File until only the edges of the strips appear. Using the rolling mill, the laminant can be thinned and spread in any direction. Rolling across the edges will broaden the striations and parallel to the lines will elongate the edges with little effect on their width. Do not get discouraged if solder seams split in the rolling process. This is almost inherent in the process. Even with frequent annealings, the varying compression rates of the component metals cause overstressing, resulting in splits. Pickle and clean the piece thoroughly, reflux, and add a bit of solder. In some instances, it may be necessary to close splits by carefully planishing around both sides of the opening and compressing the sides closed. Again, file away excess solder and proceed with the rolling mill. After attaining the desired dimensions, finish by emerying and buffing.

The continual reminder to file away excess solder is important. If allowed to remain, the solder would in effect be inlaid or pressed into the work surface by the rolling mill or hammer and be difficult to remove. This is true of lamination, inlay and overlay techniques.

TWISTED-WIRE LAMINATION

Like other laminations, the twisted-wire lamination offers unique design possibilities for the jeweler willing to experiment. The process of assembling the twisted wires is similar to that of edge lamination. Preparation of the twists is the only significant difference.

Choose wires of similar or contrasting metals and diameters. For example, if only copper wire is used, the silver solder will be the contrasting element defining the

9-8 *Sample edge lamination after rolling and coarse filing.*

9-9 **Ann Wright.** *Laminated and cast pins of sterling and nickel silver. Courtesy of the artist. Photograph by Peter Krumhardt.*

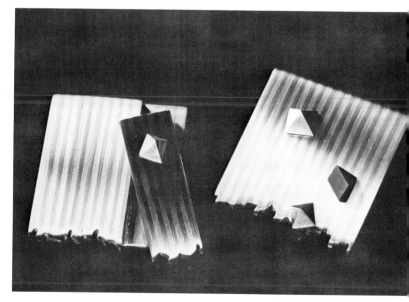

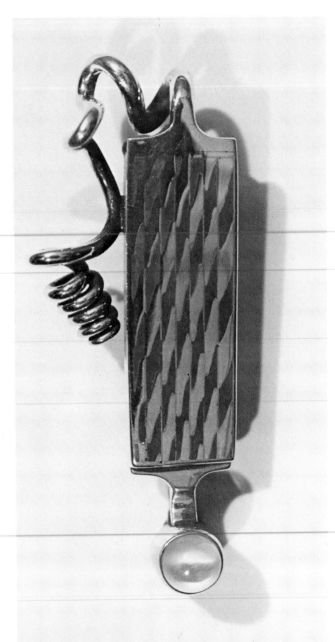

9-10 William Fiorini. *Pin of sterling silver and copper with moonstone; twisted-wire lamination and construction. Courtesy of the artist.*

9-11 *Pin of nickel silver and copper with twisted-wire lamination. Forged, constructed, and sandblasted. Photograph by Peter Krumhardt. Collection of Teri Knuth.*

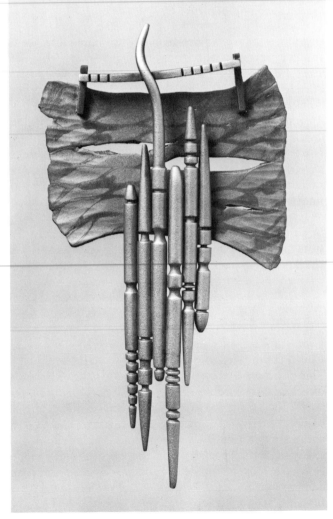

pattern of the laminant. Several types and sizes of wire can be used in each twist pattern. To begin, cut several feet of each material. Anneal, pickle, and emery each piece. Fasten one end of each piece in the side of the vise. Position the ends so that they fit together closely. Attach the opposite ends to the chuck of a hand drill. A cup hook can be fastened in the chuck and the wires looped through the hook. Be sure the wires are of equal length, otherwise the twist will be uneven. Turn the drill while at the same time gently pulling back on the wires. This prevents binding or kinking and causes the wire to twist uniformly along its length. Continue turning until the wires are tightly twisted.

In order to easily solder twisted pieces side by side, they should first be squared. The twists can be cut to the correct lengths and carefully squared and straightened on the anvil with a planishing hammer. Another method of forming them is to pull the entire length of twist through a square drawplate. Any gaps remaining due to the twist's ridges will generally fill when soldering occurs. Cut the twist to the required lengths and anneal and clean each segment with pumice powder and water. Annealing at this point alleviates the work hardness and prevents stress movement while soldering. Double-check the straightness of the pieces. Flux and lay the twists side by side on a base plate of 18- to 20-gauge sheet metal and solder with hard or medium solder. The remainder of the process is identical to soldering and finishing an edge or coil lamination.

Twists can be enhanced by the addition of square wire or strips soldered between the twisted sections. This results in a combination of solid hard edges and the checked pattern of the wires.

COILED-STRIP LAMINATION

Coiled laminations may be created in a number of ways. The basic process is the same in any case. The most direct method, and the one examined here, is the single-strip coil. This type of lamination is composed of two colors: the color of the solder and the color of a strip of contrasting metal. Those interested in going beyond this example should explore other metals and dimensions, colored solder or brazing material, and multiple strips of contrasting metals. Contrasting wire can be twisted, flattened, and then coiled.

1 Cut a strip of 20-gauge copper ¼ inch wide and 18 inches long. Anneal, emery, and flux the strip.

2 Solder a short length of ⅛-inch copper rod to the end of the strip with hard solder (figure 9–12). With round-nose pliers the end of the strip can be conformed to the shape of the rod.

3 Set the rod vertically near the center of the vise jaws. Insert the rod so that the bottom of the strip just touches the jaws (figure 9–13). With binding wire and pliers within reach, carefully begin wrapping the strip around the rod. The top edge of the vise jaws will provide support and guidance as the coil progresses. Keep the coil horizontal and as tight as possible. This is essential because slackness in the coil will make eventual soldering difficult or impossible. End the coil by bending the last ¼ inch 90 degrees, attaching a length of binding wire, and securing the wire to the rod. This step is a little cumbersome because of simultaneously having to hold the coil tight and secure the binding wire; a partner would be welcome here.

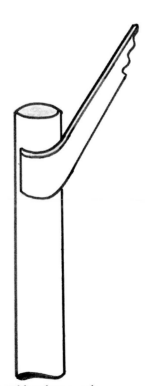

9–12 *Single strip soldered to a rod.*

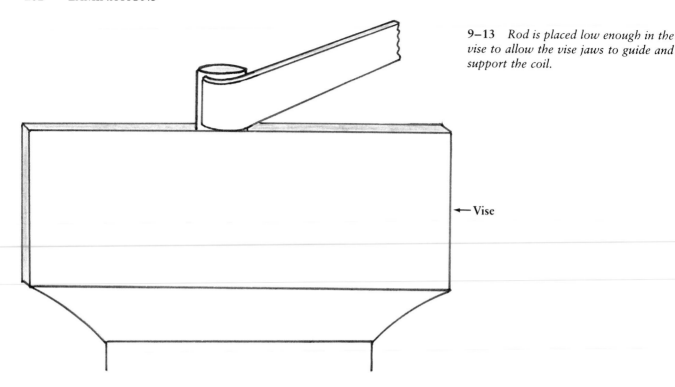

9–13 *Rod is placed low enough in the vise to allow the vise jaws to guide and support the coil.*

← Vise

4 Remove the coil from the vise and lay it rod end up on a soldering surface. Reflux and set several lengths of medium solder across the coil. Be generous with the solder. The aim is to complete soldering with a single heating. Too little solder will only cause additional work. After soldering, remove the binding wire and pickle the coil.

5 Saw off the rod flush with the laminant and file away all excess solder, top and bottom. The piece may now be rolled and finished as outlined in the section on edge lamination.

An alternative to solder-bonding coils is the process of hot quenching. Use a shallow pouring or casting crucible to contain and melt a small amount of fine or sterling silver. Flux the molten metal. As the silver approaches the melting point, play the flame alternately across the crucible and coil. Take care not to flow the solder holding the coil to the rod. The alternating heat will help equalize the temperature of the coil and the silver. When the metal is molten, use a pair of tongs or tweezers to grip the rod and quench the coil in the molten metal. Capillary action will draw silver through the coil. While the silver is still molten, remove the coil and lay it quickly on a flat surface. Finish the piece as dis-

cussed previously. The quenched coil is quite malleable and holds up well in hot forging.

DOTTED-LINE AND SNAKESKIN LAMINATION

The most interesting facet of this lamination is that within one piece, several types of distinctly different patterns can be created. I happened upon this technique while exploring the possibility of incorporating slices of wire in other forms of lamination. My aim was to first bond many small bits of wire and then distort or elongate them in the rolling process. This idea was set aside once I discovered a method of developing dotted lines and snakeskin patterns.

The dimensions given in these steps are for illustrative purposes.

1 Cut 14 inches of ³⁄₁₆-inch round brass or sterling rod. Emery the rod and drill a small hole near one end. Secure approximately ½ inch of the rod's other end horizontally in a vise.

9–14 *Snakeskin lamination. Provided by Bruce McClure.*

9–15 *Dotted-line lamination. Provided by Bruce McClure.*

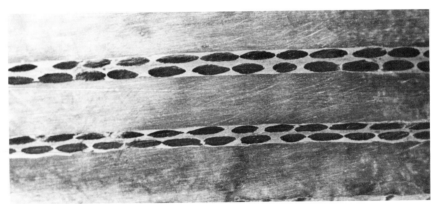

2 Anneal, pickle, and emery enough 18-gauge round copper wire to make a tight, continuous wrap around the brass rod. This will require approximately 15 feet.

3 Attach the end of the wire through the drilled hole and begin wrapping wire tightly around the rod. Take extra care to ensure the wire remains tight and that each wrap lies against the previous one. Looseness or spaces between wraps will result in incomplete soldering. Have a length of heavy binding wire ready and as the wrapping ends, bind the copper wire tightly to the rod as explained in step 3 in the section on coiled-strip lamination.

4 Flux the wrapped rod and flood medium solder through the wire surface. Use a generous amount of solder to ensure that the piece is completely covered. Remove the binding wire and pickle the rod. Cut off the excess rod and then cut the wrapped piece into four equal lengths.

5 Use a planishing hammer to form each piece roughly square. Give special attention to two opposite sides that will butt together in soldering. Make certain each piece is straight, then anneal.

6 Clean the pieces with a pumice powder slurry and brush. Flux and lay them side by side on a soft firebrick. If a backing plate is used, it is applied as outlined on page 197. To solder, lay lengths of medium wire solder along each joint and use an intense, uniform flame to cause all the solder to flow at once (figure 9–16).

7 If satisfied that the piece is completely soldered, clean the laminant and file away excess solder. File only to the surface of the copper wire.

8 Roll the laminant through the mill in the direction of the underlying rod. This places the rollers parallel to the wrapped wire and thus widens them in rolling. Considerable widening will cause the contrasting copper and silver solder to appear as a snakeskin pattern.

9 Development of the dotted-line pattern is just a matter of filing completely through the wrapped copper, exposing the lengths of rod. The lengths of the rod

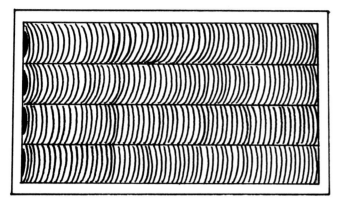

9–16 *Wire wrapped rod segments set on a base plate.*

Twisted Wire over Rod or Tubing

This pattern was also the outgrowth of early experimentation with wire as a laminant component. After working with the dot-pattern technique, it was clear that by wrapping twisted wire around rod or tubing, the result would be a v-shaped pattern.

The process is relatively simple. Follow the first four steps in the section on dotted lines, this time using twisted wires and then filing away excess solder.

Stacked Square Rod

Laminated square rods or wires are excellent materials to use in making checkerboard and related patterns. With an understanding of the basic points previously examined, the reader should have little trouble creating a variety of pieces by merely stacking short lengths of rod and soldering them as a group. From the soldered stack, thin sections can be cut, rearranged, and soldered to a backing plate. Sections may be left above the plate surface or rolled down. The finished piece should appear as inlay. Exciting results can be achieved by experimenting with metals of various colors.

will be divided by double dotted lines. Variations in dot and snakeskin shapes can be created by gently curving the lamination one way or another and filing carefully.

10 Pieces may be finished with emery cloth and buffs.

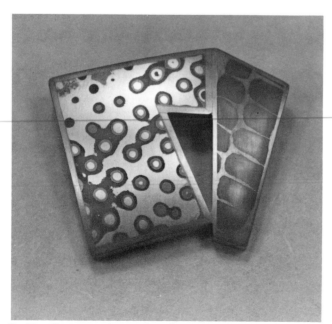

9–17 *Constructed pin of sterling silver, copper, brass, and NuGold with mokume and snakeskin laminations. Collection of Richard Daehnert.*

9–18 Bonnie Gwaltney, Marine Series Pin #9. *Sterling silver and mokume-gane of copper and Shibuichi; repoussé and construction. The artist's choice to use a mokume surface fits the concept well. The shell-like form is highly enhanced by the laminant's organic, textural patterns. Courtesy of the artist.*

9–19 *Pin of copper, Kuromido, silver, and nickel with moonstone; laminated and constructed.*

9–20 *Pin of copper, Kuromido, silver, and nickel with moonstones; laminated and constructed. Collection of Teri Knuth.*

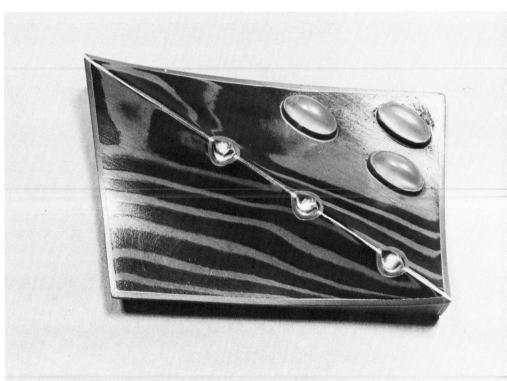

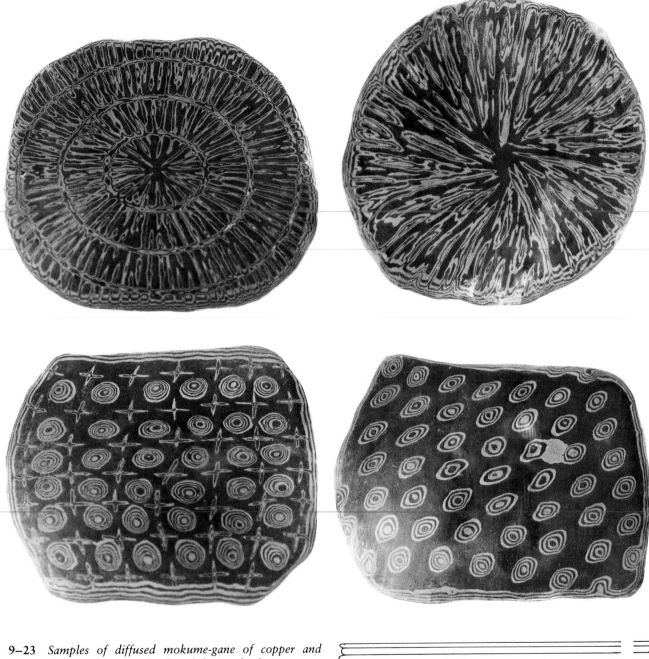

9-23 *Samples of diffused mokume-gane of copper and Kuromido. Patterns were developed during the forging stage by selective incising with drills, chisels, and steel burs. Samples provided by Dale Wedig.*

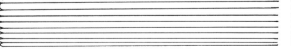

9-24 *Protruding edges cut away.*

smooth out when forged or rolled. Patterns can also be created by means of the bumping method as described in the section on soldered mokume (page 195). For this, the metal should be forged or rolled to 16 to 18 gauge (figure 9–25).

13 With the piece thinned and patterns created, the finish can be completed by filing, emerying, and buffing. Since no solder is used in the layer bonding, the mokume can be joined to other metals quite easily without fear of overheating and reflowing solder.

14 Liver of sulfur can be used to color the metals used to illustrate the preceding steps. Appendix 2 lists solutions used to color laminations composed of other alloys.

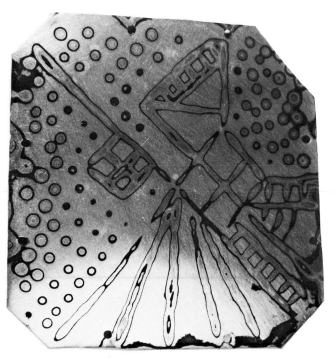

9–25 Diffused lamination thinned to 18 gauge, pattern punched from the back, and the front filed away.

DAMASCUS (PATTERN-WELDED) STEEL

Thus far we have considered only the use of nonferrous metals as lamination components. Thanks to a handful of jewelers having strayed from traditional ground, we are just beginning to see jewelry pieces incorporating iron and steel laminations. The technique requires some expertise in forging, a few blacksmith tools, and a forge. The process is, in a sense, like mokume-gane. Instead of allowing the metal to slowly diffuse under heat, iron and steel are brought up to heat in the coals of the forge, taken out at the right moment, and struck with a hammer. The impact welds the pieces together. Though theoretically uncomplicated, the process can be difficult and time-consuming.

The first evidence of patterned steel laminants dates

9–26 Dale Wedig. *Necklace and pendant of nickel silver, brass, and Damascus steel; woven, constructed, and laminated. Courtesy of the artist.*

from the second century A.D. Westerners began calling the patterned materials Damascus steel simply because that is where it was first encountered. While the technique employed today does not produce a true Damascus, for the sake of convenience many metalsmiths still use the term. Early patterned steel was produced by alloying or quenching techniques using semimolten and molten components. Damascus was used in swords, spearheads, knives, and gun barrels because of its relative strength. We cannot say for sure what was most important to early metalsmiths, the aesthetic qualities or inherent strength of Damascus steel. In either case, we are fortunate to be left with yet another exciting lamination technique.

One individual who has researched the process in depth is William Fiorini, Professor of Jewelry and Metalsmithing at the University of Wisconsin—LaCrosse. Professor Fiorini shares the following technical outline, photographs, and examples of his work.

The following preparation of tools and materials is critical to the success of making Damascus steel.

1 Traditional steel-bed, blacksmith forges are most often used as the heat source. A hand-cranked or motor-driven blower provides a positive source of air. Although gas forges can be used for welding, the heat-up time and welding environment make them second choices.

2 Low-sulfur blacksmith's coal or coke will provide a clean, high-heat fuel. Pea coke is perhaps the most suitable fuel. Its size and lack of contaminants helps maintain the reduced atmosphere required for heating and clean welding.

3 The type of flux used is important. Its function is to provide a glasslike covering over the metal, shielding out excess oxygen, absorbing some of the oxides, and in general keeping the bonding surfaces clean. Anhydrous borax is often used as a flux but its fumes are toxic. Commercial fluxes such as Borox-Ette or Crescent Weld work well and allow the material to be welded at a relatively low temperature.

4 The amount of forced air is important to the success of the lamination process. To maintain the needed reduced atmosphere, a low, continuous flow of air is best. This also permits heat to slowly and evenly saturate the workpiece. Overheating can cause sparking, scarring, or melting. It may also cause carbon migra-

9–27   William Fiorini. *Pendant of sterling silver and pattern welded steel with moonstone and shell cameo; forged and constructed. Courtesy of the artist.*

tion, a buildup of carbon in areas that might disfigure the pattern.

5 Individual layers making up the laminant pattern are steel alloys composed of varying amounts of carbon, phosphorus, and nickel. Once complete and finished, the pattern is placed in an acid solution and allowed to etch. Because of the varying alloy composition in each layer, the acid dissolves each at a different rate, leaving a distinct, contrasting pattern.

6 **Keep in mind throughout that the materials and processes are potentially hazardous. The most obvious hazard is the fire. Gloves should be worn, hair tied back or covered, safety glasses used to protect the eyes against cinders or grindings, and the excess heat, smoke, and solid particulants should be vented through a hood directly over the forge. Clothing made of synthetics should never be worn in the forge area. These materials are quite susceptible to heat and will burn rapidly. Many metalsmiths take the precaution of wearing a filter mask over the nose and mouth, safety shoes, and earplugs or muffs. Again, take care in mixing and using acids. Acids are always poured into water, never the reverse. The acid-mixing area should be well vented and protective glasses, gloves, and an apron should be worn.**

The laminant sample illustrated in figure 9–28 was developed in the following manner.

1 The initial layering is begun with six pieces:

3 pieces of wrought iron (wagon wheel), ¼ inch by 1 inch by 6 inches
2 pieces of mild steel, ¼ inch by 1 inch by 6 inches
1 piece of mild steel, ¼ inch by 1 inch by 24 inches

After cutting each piece to the proper length, grind the contacting faces to a slight bevel (figure 9–29). This configuration helps assure that when the layers are forced together in welding, flux and slag will be squeezed out. Six-inch segments are used only for illustrative purposes. In practice, shorter lengths may be used.

2 Arrange the layers alternately, mild and wrought, and spot weld the layers at each end (figure 9–30). This can be quickly accomplished with an electric welder. The extralong layer provides a convenient handle and eliminates the need for tongs. Spotting the sections at both ends prevents shifting of layers axially or from side to side. Spot welds will eventually be cut away.

3 A pea-coke fire is prepared by placing two hard firebricks on edge, end to end, on either side of the fire pot so that a deep reducing fire can be achieved. Place several pieces of balled-up newspaper and a couple handfuls of wood chips in the fire pot and light. Start the air flow as the wood begins burning and begin to fill the fire pot with pea coke until it heaps to the top of the bricks.

4 Place the stack on edge in the center of the fire. Continue the slow, even air input and occasionally turn the piece over. This should be done without removing the stack from the coals. When the laminant reaches a medium cherry heat, it is removed, given a generous

9–28 *48-layer laminated pattern welded steel.*

9–29 *Metal faces ground to a slight bevel.*

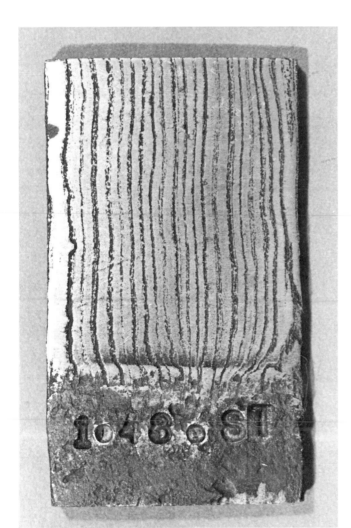

9–30 *An initial tack-welded stack.*

coating of flux on all edges, and returned to the fire. Setting the layers vertically in the coals permits flux to easily seep through the joints.

5 As the laminant reaches a high yellow heat (2,450° to 2,500°F) it is quickly removed from the fire and welding is begun. In this instance, forge welding is accomplished in three steps: first near the handle, next at the midsection, and finally the remaining third. In welding each segment, light, rapid hammer blows are delivered. At this point, the aim is simply to bond the layers and not to elongate them. After completing a segment, quickly wire brush the piece, reflux it, and return it to the fire. Again bring the workpiece to welding heat and repeat until the entire mass is welded. After it cools it may be worthwhile to grind the edges flush in order to check to see that the weld is complete.

6 With the initial layers now welded, the billet is drawn out or elongated to approximately 18 inches with the forging hammer. A number of heats will be needed and the piece should be worked at cherry-red heat. After drawing, the laminant is cut in half, the halves retacked, and the preceding steps continued to achieve 48 layers. This piece is then forged square to approximately $\frac{9}{16}$ inch and then forged into flat stock with the multiple layers showing on the wide side of the flat. The piece is flattened to approximately $\frac{3}{16}$ inch.

7 The patterned surface is now ground, emeried to 400 grit, and cleaned with alcohol. To bring forth a pattern, the piece can be etched in the solution used with the sample: 15 parts nitric acid, 15 parts hydrochloric acid, and 70 parts water for 20 minutes at a temperature just below boiling. **As always, add acid to water, not the reverse.** After rinsing and drying, the sample was given three coats of Plum Brown gun browning solution and again emeried to 400 grit to highlight the etched surface.

9–31 *48-layer wrought iron and mild steel, straight-line edge pattern.*

Thus far only the development of a straight-lined pattern has been considered. The actual welding and forging of all types of patterns are essentially the same. Variations in patterning come in layer arrangement, twisting, hammer impact, removal of material, or structure manipulation.

9–32   *48-layer wrought iron and mild steel, single-twist pattern.*
9–33   *96-layer wrought iron and mild steel, double-twist pattern.*

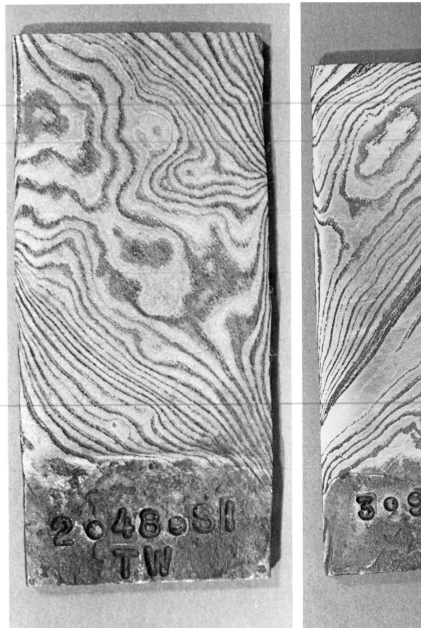

9-32   9-33

9–34 *96-layer wrought iron and mild steel, Chevron pattern.*

9–35 *624-layer wrought iron and mild steel, multiedge grain pattern. Samples and photographs for 9–31 through 9–35 by William Fiorini.*

Once the metalsmith is proficient in the basic welding procedures, sections can be rearranged by welding them side to side, end to end, at an angle, edge to side, and any number of other ways. Twisting is another means of pattern alteration. Reverse twists are created by securing a length of heated prelaminated rod in the vise and using a wrench to first twist the piece one way, then taking another heat and twisting in the opposite direction. Keep in mind that regardless of how a pattern is devel-oped, subsequent hammer blows will alter the pattern to some extent. After layers are bonded, subsurface stria-tions can be revealed by yet another method, that of material removal. Grinding burrs, chisels, gravers, or milling tools can be used to cut into the billet. After-ward the piece is reflattened. This method is quite simi-lar to the pattern development of moKume-gane. The finishing and final etch is generally the same in all instances.

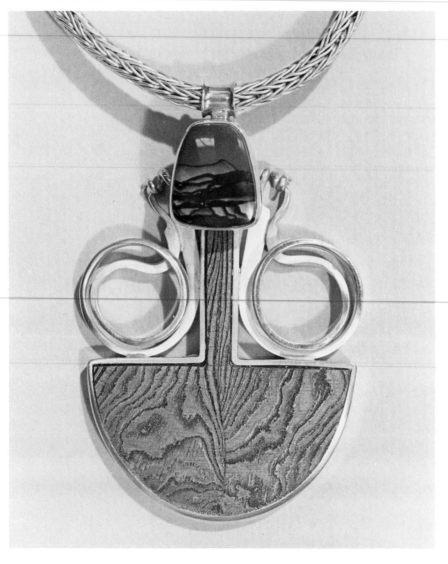

9–36 William Fiorini. *Pendant of ster-ling silver and pattern-welded steel with picture agate; forged and constructed. Courtesy of the artist.*

PLATED LAMINATION

For those who have some expertise in electroplating, exciting surfaces can be created by alternately plating layers of contrasting metals over predimpled sheet metal. After several layers are plated, the bumps can be filed down to reveal the underlying plated layers. Those interested in pursuing this technique should first study the section on electroplating.

9–37   Florence Resnikoff. *Constructed pendant of silver and copper using electroplated mokume. Courtesy of the artist. Photograph by Gary Sinick.*

CHAPTER TEN

Chain Making

In reviewing the history of jewelry it is immediately apparent that linkage systems have been important from earliest times. Historically we find pieces ranging from two simple interlocking rings to intricately twisted and interlaced lengths of woven wire. Despite the innumerable possibilities inherent in chain making, current jewelry trends have for the most part sidestepped the chain as a jewelry form in and of itself. Chain continues to be subordinate to other compositional elements. Reversal of this trend will occur when jewelers look at chain techniques as a possibility for creating major compositional elements.

Most handmade chain is composed of interlocking rings of one kind or another. Rings are generally fashioned in standard sizes of a particular gauge of wire. This practice results in chains of a uniform appearance. This chapter examines the construction of two chains, a simple interlocking-ring chain and a triple loop-in-loop. Once familiar with the basics of chain making, the reader is encouraged to explore by varying the size and type of wire, the size, shape, and number of links, and the methods for bringing together the various parts in a finished chain. Also consider ways of altering finished pieces with the drawplate and rolling mill or by twisting, tapering, and hammering.

INTERLOCKING-RING CHAIN

The following steps outline the basic procedure for making a short length of chain composed of interlocking rings of 14-gauge round wire.

1 Links are formed by wrapping a length of annealed wire around a ³/₁₆-inch round rod. One end of the wire and rod are chucked in a hand drill; as the drill is turned, one hand guides the wire around the rod. The

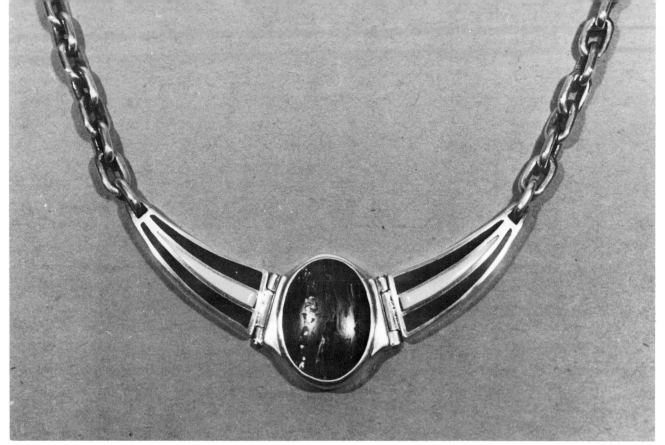

10–1 Joe Muench. *Necklace and pendant of sterling silver, ebony, ivory, and tigereye; inlaid and constructed. Chain is a visually pleasing, yet simple arrangement of elongated interlocking loops.*

wire should be kept tight while wrapping in order to form consistent rings. To ease this process, the rod and drill can be braced between the worker's body and the side of the workbench.

2 After wrapping 2 or 3 inches of the rod, the coil can be slid off the rod and cut apart with a fine saw blade. Some jewelers fit the coil around the blade, brace the coil over the bench pin, and make the cut a little at a time. Others place the coil snuggly in a vise and cut from the outside. To make a small number of rings, either method will suffice. An alternate method of creating rings is given on pg. 220.

3 Two-thirds of the rings are closed and the joints soldered. It may be necessary to use two pliers to bend and align the ends of the rings. To make the ends spring together, bend one end slightly past the other and back in place. Be careful not to distort the shape of the ring. Lay the closed rings over a smooth soldering surface, flux each one, and solder with medium solder. Rings can be arranged in rows and fluxed, and a tiny piece of solder placed on each joint. Use a tight soldering flame and move the torch carefully down each row.

4 Interlock two presoldered rings with an unsoldered ring. Close the center ring as outlined earlier. Lay the

10–2 *Chain sample: single loop through two.*

10–3 *Chain sample: single and double, over and under loops.*

three rings on the soldering surface in such a way that the previously soldered rings extend away from the new joint. Solder the third ring. This forms a linked group of three soldered rings. Continue soldering groups of three.

5 Sections of three are joined by unsoldered rings and these are soldered to make the required length of chain. In making this type of chain the greatest difficulty arises when work is overheated and causes solder to reflow or spill from a joint onto other links. Steps 1, 2, and 3 are the foundations of all soldered, multilink chains.

TRIPLE-LOOP WOVEN CHAIN

The beauty of this technique is that it allows the jeweler substantial latitude in size, shape, and color. Since individual loops are interlaced, several types of metal can be used to develop patterns or stripes. With careful planning, wire size and loop diameters can be changed to vary the finished contour of the chain. The cross section of the chain may later be modified with the rolling mill or drawplate.

The following guidelines pertain specifically to a triple loop-in-loop chain made of 22-gauge wire forming rings with a ½-inch inner diameter. Given these basic steps, one can easily create a chain arranged of single, double, or more loops.

1 In this example, each inch of finished chain will require approximately twenty-one loops or 2½ feet of wire. Determine the total amount of wire needed for a finished chain, then anneal and pickle the wire.

2 Fasten the end of a 1-foot length of ½-inch wooden dowel in a vise. Drill a tiny hole through the opposite end of the dowel. Have a roll of masking tape within reach. Loop and twist the end of the wire through the drilled hole and begin carefully wrap-

10–4 *Chain samples showing loop-in-loop variations. Top to bottom: squared, flattened or rolled, and round.*

10–5 *Wrapped wire is cut in a spiral path.*

ping the wire tightly around the dowel. Use one hand to guide the wire flush against each previous turn. It is important that the wraps be tight and uniform; otherwise, the finished rings will be unequal in size and difficult to cut. Maintain a tension on the wire while wrapping until all but 1 inch of the end of the dowel is covered. The remaining inch is used to end the wrap and provide an area to attach the masking tape. Retain tension on the wire while wrapping tape tightly around the entire length of the dowel. An extra layer of tape will ensure that the coil will not unravel when cut.

3 With a number 2/0 saw blade, carefully begin cutting through the wire. To facilitate cutting, angle the blade slightly so that as cutting progresses the blade makes a slow spiral around the length of the dowel (figure 10–5). Loosen the vise several times in the process and twist the dowel around to keep the blade over or near the top of the dowel. While sawing, try to keep the blade in the wood in order to support the thin wire in cutting. The tape acts to secure the rings as they are cut and in general provides a smoother cut through the metal.

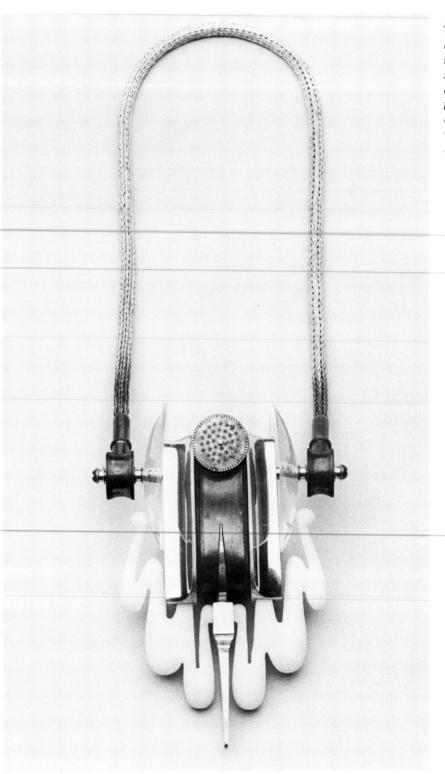

10-6 David Pimentel, Pendant #801 T.I.G. *Sterling silver, aluminum, copper, brass, Delrin, and acrylic lenses. T.I.G. welded, fused, and constructed. The scale and construction of the pendant requires a hanging device which is both flexible and visually effective. A loop-in-loop chain is an excellent solution. Courtesy of the artist. Photograph by Lynn Hudson.*

4 In addition to being a relatively easy means of forming and cutting many thin rings, the spiral cut also gives each ring overlapping ends, which are quite strong when soldered. Remove the tape and slide the rings off of the dowel. Begin fitting the ends of the rings together for soldering. The ends should easily fit together if the saw cut was smooth and the result free of burrs. Lay the rings on a clean, flat soldering pad as they are fitted. Arrange them in rows with all joints in one direction and flux each piece. Solder each ring with a tiny piece of medium or hard solder.

5 After soldering and cleaning, elongate the rings with long needle-nose or round-nose pliers. To facilitate the positioning of each ring on the pliers, a shallow groove can be filed across the back of each jaw about ¼ inch from the tip (figure 10–7). This will also ensure the uniformity of the loops. Center the solder joint between the jaws or the joint will be visible on the finished chain. Hold the ring around the plier jaws and pull outward on the handles, elongating and stretching each ring slightly. In addition to forming uniform loops, a slight stretch helps to identify weak joints before the chain is woven.

6 Lay three loops across one another in an equally spaced radial pattern. Use tiny pieces of medium solder to join the three loops at each contact point. This unit of three loops is next soldered atop a short section of ⅛-inch brass or copper rod. The rod

serves as a convenient attachment to the vise and will later be cut off.

7 Tighten the rod vertically in a vise and bend the loops straight up. The first loop of the second layer may be inserted at any point, straight through both ends of the underlying loop. Subsequent loops may be inserted clockwise or counterclockwise, as long as only one direction is followed throughout. With the second layer of three inserted, the ends are bent up. Continuing in the same rotation, the loops of the third layer are now passed through the underlying two loops. For some, this is the most difficult step to understand. From this point on, loops are passed through the previous two loops (figure 10–8). If a mistake is made and a loop is put through only one loop, the error will be obvious. Passes beneath two layers will create a chain having a relatively close and uniform weave. Continue as before. Insert loops straight across and bend up the ends as you go. A nail, scribe, or dental tool can be used to help open and align loops already in place.

8 Loops are added until the required length is reached. The chain should now be placed on the face of the anvil and gently tapped with a mallet as the chain is slowly turned. Continue this until all surfaces of the piece have been worked. Forming with the mallet is only meant to roughly round the chain and begin to make the weave uniform. Carefully anneal the

10–7 *Pliers for elongating chain loops.*

10–8 *Loops are passed through two underlying loops.*

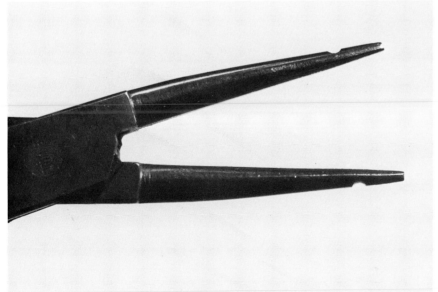

10–9   *Hardwood and nylon drawplates.*

10–10   *The starting rod is cut off and the chain capped. Sample by Mark Grgurich.*

chain. Some prefer to do this in a darkened area. Wire is easily overheated and in this case may cause solder to reflow, resulting in a frustrating situation.

9   The chain can now be drawn through a drawplate by the rod end to compact the loops and create a uniform network. Continue drawing until the desired diameter is reached. Examine the surface of the wire after each pull. Overdrawing can cause the outer surface of the wire to flatten. In the event a steel drawplate is not available, one can easily be fashioned with a piece of ¾-inch hardwood or nylon (figure 10–9).

10   After drawing, anneal and pickle the chain. Cover the chain with a thick slurry of fine pumice powder and water and gently swivel the chain back and forth. Start at one end and flex the chain inch by inch. This action tends to cause the piece to loosen and become quite flexible. Rinse and cut off the rod.

11   The basic chain is complete. Ends of the piece may be finished in any manner fitting the total design concept. Many jewelers add capped cylinders or small cone forms.

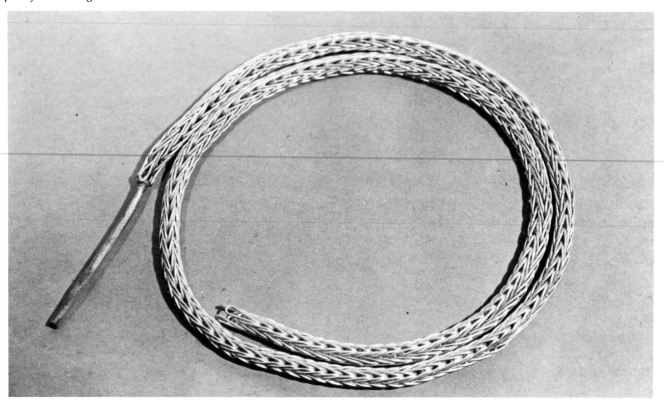

CHAIN MAIL

Because chain is flexible it can be adapted to many applications often resolved with a hinge or an awkward wire ring. A few jewelers have looked to the past for inspiration and have revived the use of chain mail, not as protective dress but as a jewelry component. Some have adapted mail strictly as a linkage device and others use it as a jewelry form in and of itself. While simple, the technique is tedious, involving multiple and intricate interlocked rings (figure 10–11). Another natural, but often overlooked place for chain, is the critical transition from one jewelry element to another. To those working on a relatively large scale, flexibility should be of prime concern. Chain and variations of are excellent solutions (figure 10–13). When, for one reason or another, the jeweler does not wish to make chain, the commercial market offers a wide selection. Jewelry suppliers provide chain of silver and gold in many configurations.

10–11 *Chain and chain mail samples.*

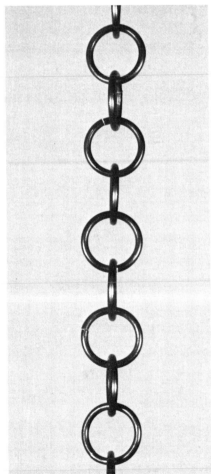
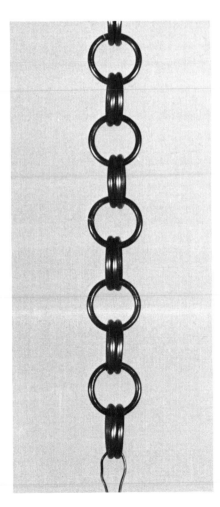
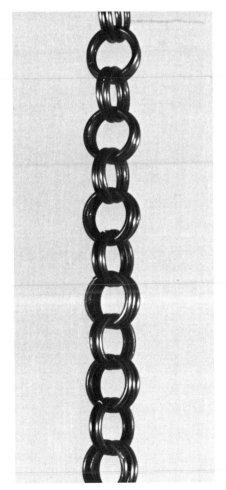

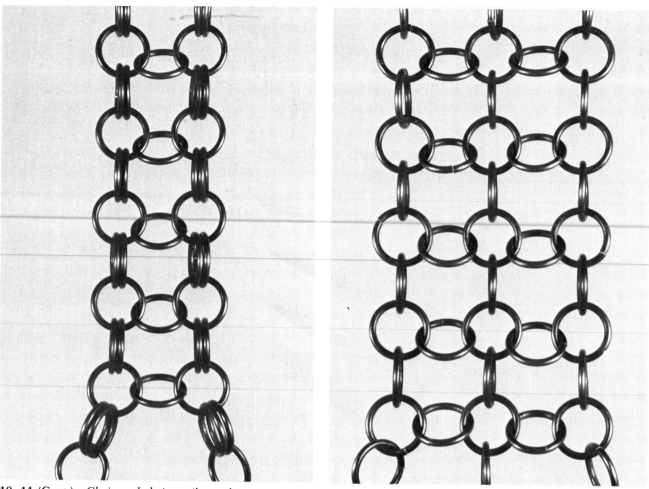

10–11 (Cont.)   *Chain and chain mail samples.*

10–12 Mark Knuth. *Pendant of copper and sterling silver; forged and constructed with chain mail and mokume lamination. A chain mail linkage system serves as a pleasing transition between the forged neckpiece and a framed mokume pendant. For this purpose, the mail links need not be soldered. Their combined strength is quite adequate to suspend the pendant. Courtesy of the artist.*

10–13 *Pendant of sterling silver, NuGold, and Delrin; woven, torch textured, and constructed. The vertical section connecting pendant and neck chain is a flattened section of loop-in-loop chain. By carefully flattening in the rolling mill, the chain retains its side-to-side flexibility.*

CHAPTER ELEVEN

Stone Settings

In earliest prehistoric times people may have tied leather thongs around their favorite rocks and hung them around their necks to drive away evil or to hasten a bountiful harvest. Magical qualities and this questionable historical sketch aside, they discovered the inherent beauty of certain stones and eventually began rubbing, cleaning, and much later cutting and polishing the stones' surfaces to further bring forth the stones' colors, patterns, textures, and brilliance. In addition to these physical qualities, stones have been attributed symbolic and monetary value.

With the advancement of metallurgy and metalworking techniques, the joining of stone and metal was inevitable. Despite the jeweler's metalworking capabilities through much of history, metal was generally fashioned as a means of displaying stones. In addition to its function as a fastener, jewelers eventually used metal's reflective quality to enhance further the qualities of the stone. Modern jewelers tend to view jewelry as an artistic expression and mix materials with little regard for the traditional hierarchy. Today our concern is to use metals and stones in ways which let them complement one another.

Rather than attempting to discuss the gamut of stones and settings, this chapter offers a detailed examination of stone settings especially suited to contemporary work. To do justice to the subject of gems and other stones, a text in itself would be required. Those who wish to seek an in-depth study of stones and lapidary techniques may refer to the books listed in the bibliography.

STONE CUTS

Stone cuts are classified in two basic forms. First is the faceted cut, generally of transparent material. Diamonds are the most obvious example. Facets or flat planes are cut and polished by precision lapidary machines. The resulting cut allows light to enter the stone and be refracted or bent at many angles to give the stone greater brilliance. Angles of the facets relative to the stone's mineral composition is critical for maximum brilliance. Needless to say, precision in cutting is essential.

The second form of cut is the cabochon. Generally, these cuts are flat-bottomed with a domed top and may be made in any number of shapes: square, rectangle, heart, teardrop, triangle, and, most popularly, round and oval. Cabochons are usually cuts of less expensive, opaque material. In cutting cabochons, light refraction is generally of little concern. Materials such as moonstone, tigereye, laboradorite, ruby, and sapphire must be oriented correctly to bring forth their unique chatoyant qualities, which appear as an eye or star reflected from underlying fibrous material.

A setting device should visually suit both the stone and the form it sets on. While a setting's primary function is to mechanically secure a stone, our challenge as artist/jewelers is to creatively integrate it with the jewelry's form and the stone. Too often, settings and stones are added as second thoughts and the visual result is a stone setting that appears to be just stuck on. This habit

11–1   *A variety of stone types and cuts.*

can be avoided by concentrating, from the beginning of the design process, on the total workpiece.

In addition to aesthetic considerations, the physical characteristics of the stone must be examined. For example, stones on the lower end of the Mohs' scale might work well in earrings or pendants but would be easily scratched or broken if set in a belt buckle or ring. The Mohs' scale indicates the relative hardness of stones (Appendix 1).

BEZEL SETTINGS

Cabochon-cut stones are most often set in bezels. Generally, a bezel is constructed of thin sheet metal and formed like a narrow collar around the bottom edge of the stone. The bezel is soldered to a base, the stone is inset, and the thin metal is pushed inward to hold the stone. A bezel can be constructed as follows.

11–2 Hannelore Gabriel. *Constructed neckpiece of sterling and moonstones. Beautifully executed neckpiece and pendant is highlighted by moonstones set in bezels that continue the use of cylindrical forms. Courtesy of the artist.*

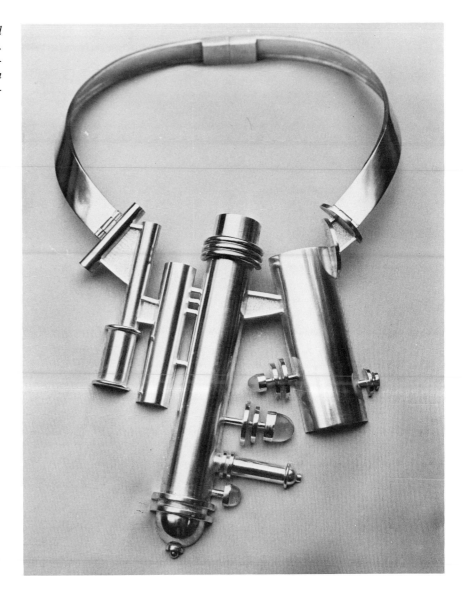

1 This example uses a strip of 24-gauge sheet metal. Any of the common nonferrous metals can be used. On silver jewelry, some workers prefer to use fine silver because of its relative softness. Fine silver also melts at a higher temperature than sterling. This may comfort the beginner. Keep in mind that 24-gauge is for illustrative purposes; no one has yet carved in stone any specific gauge sizes for bezel thickness relative to stone diameters. The jeweler's good judgment and aesthetic requirements should determine this.

2 The height of the bezel is both an aesthetic and functional consideration. If it is too high, the bezel will obstruct the stone's beauty; if it is too low it may not hold the stone. Functionally, the height is dependent on the angle at which the inward curve of the stone is cut. For stones with a rather drastic angle or sharp edge, a low bezel can be used. Cabochons cut with high domes or little angle at the sides need a higher bezel (figure 11–3).

3 After determining the strip's width (bezel height), a measurement is taken around the edge of the stone's circumference to calculate the strip's length. Lay a narrow length of paper or masking tape around the bottom edge of the stone and mark where the paper or tape overlaps. Transfer the measurement to the metal, then add a bit more length (three times the thickness of the metal is a good rule of thumb). This extra material compensates for the variation in bending the paper and the 24-gauge metal. Use a fine saw blade or shear to cut the bezel strip and file the ends square.

4 Bend the ends around a little past one another, and then move them back so they are flush. Pushing the ends past and then back creates enough tension to keep them together. It is important that the ends fit well. Since the metal is relatively thin, having to file away solder on a poorly aligned joint could result in no joint. At this point, do not be concerned with shaping the bezel. This will come later.

5 Flux and join the ends with hard solder. Equalize the heat on both sides of the joint and remove the flame the instant solder flows (figure 11–4). Pickle, clean, and file away excess solder.

6 Shape the bezel to fit the stone. In some instances shaping is a matter of carefully bending it by hand. Round, oval, or square mandrels can be used by gently tapping the bezel with a rawhide mallet. For

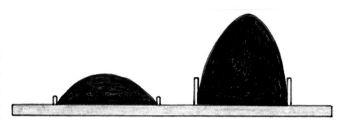

11–3 *Bezel height relative to the angle of a stone's cut. Stones having a rather sharp angle do not require a high bezel. The bezel's primary function is to mechanically fasten the stone.*

small bezels, a scribe or the round, tapered jaw of round-nose pliers, can be used as a minimandrel. In short, look around and use any appropriate tool.

7 Trial fit the stone. If necessary, stretch the bezel over a mandrel or other suitable tool. Stretching is accomplished by forcing the bezel up the mandrel with mallet blows to its edge. Reverse the bezel occasionally to avoid tapering its sides. Another method of stretching is to insert a smooth steel rod through the bezel and to roll it over the anvil face (figure 11–5). Exert equal downward force on both ends of the rod while rolling it in a short back and forth motion. (This serves as a poor person's rolling mill.) Careful planishing is yet another way of stretching. The hammer must strike flush to prevent curving the bezel. Oversized bezels are made smaller by cutting out a section and resoldering.

8 Top and bottom edges are made parallel by rubbing them over a flat file or emery cloth. After trueing, remove burrs along the edges and double-check to

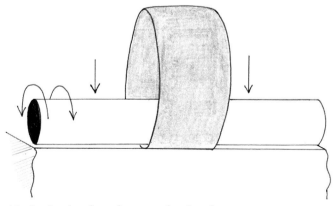

11–5 *Steel rod used to stretch a bezel.*

11–4 *Bezel ends being soldered.*

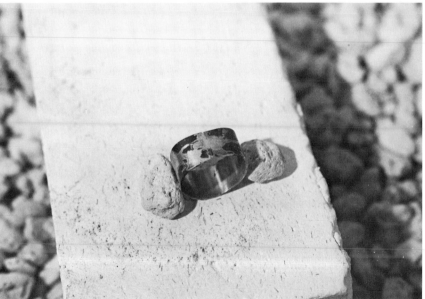

assure the stone fits easily. If the stone has to be forced in, the bezel is too small.

9 In some applications, the bezel should now be emeried and polished. After the bezel is soldered in place, it may be obstructed and difficult to emery and buff. This is a point to consider with each new creation.

10 Solder placement is important when joining the be-

zel to its backing. If the outer portion of the back plate will later be cut away flush to the bezel, solder is placed along the outside edge of the bezel. Where the surrounding plate is left intact, solder is placed inside the bezel. Equally space several small pieces of medium solder along the edge of the bezel and carefully begin applying heat. If heat can be applied to the bottom of the plate, there is little chance of melting the bezel. From the top, direct the flame in a circular motion around the outside of the bezel onto the backing. Reflective heat from the backing plate to the bezel should be adequate to raise the temperature of both pieces equally. Direct heat on the bezel can easily cause it to melt. As the solder melts, allow it to flow through the entire joint and then quickly remove the flame.

11 Many times the area lying beneath the stone can be partially cut away to leave a narrow seat or bearing below the edge of the stone (figure 11–6). This saves material, lightens the workpiece, and, in some designs, allows light to show through the stone. When it is not feasible to cut away the backing, drilling a single small hole is useful should the stone have to be removed.

12 Stones are set after the piece is entirely finished, in-cluding buffing and oxidation. This avoids the possibility of the stone being damaged by heat, tools, buffing, or chemicals. A polished burnisher is used to push the bezel over against the stone (figure 11–7). Alternately burnish short segments of opposite sides of the bezel until all gaps are closed against the stone (figure 11–8). The burnisher can also be used to smooth away marks remaining after the metal has been pushed over. A bezel pusher may also be used, especially on heavier bezels. The edges of the face of the pusher are relatively sharp; if this tool slips the stone might be damaged. To set, the face of the bezel pusher must be placed firmly on the bezel's edge and pushed inward at an angle (figure 11–9). Pushers are especially effective in tightening thin bezels when concentrated vertical pressure is needed (figure 11–10).

11–6   *Stone's backing partially cut away.*

11–7   *Burnisher force moves metal against the stone.*

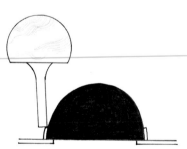

11–9   *Bezel pusher.*

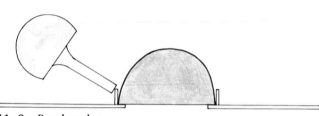

11–10   *Tightening a bezel.*

11–8   *Bezel gaps are gradually closed by applying force to opposing sides all around the bezel.*

11–11 Jean Sampel. *Constructed ring of 14-karat yellow gold with 18 bezel-set diamonds. Stones are set in a movable, caged ball. Courtesy of the artist. Photograph by Leslie Becker.*

Bezel Variations

1 Figure 11–12 illustrates a bezel containing an inner sleeve or bearing. This method can be used to set stones above a curved surface or with stones having curved bottoms. It can also be used to simply lift a stone, giving it an illusion of greater height.

2 To form a bezel and bearing over a curved shape, extra bezel height should be provided to permit filing and fitting to the supporting surface.

3 Figure 11–13 shows the preparation of the bezel's bearing for setting a faceted stone. For round stones, the bearing's inner edge is angle cut with a stone-setting burr after the bearing is soldered into the bezel. For other cuts, the angle is formed with a file prior to being soldered into the bezel.

4 The construction of a heavy bezel is essentially the same as discussed in the previous section. The differences are the thickness of the material (16 to 22 gauge) and the actual setting technique. Some jewel-

11–14 Harold O'Connor. *Constructed pendant of 18-karat gold with tourmaline and lapis lazuli set in heavy bezels. Courtesy of the artist.*

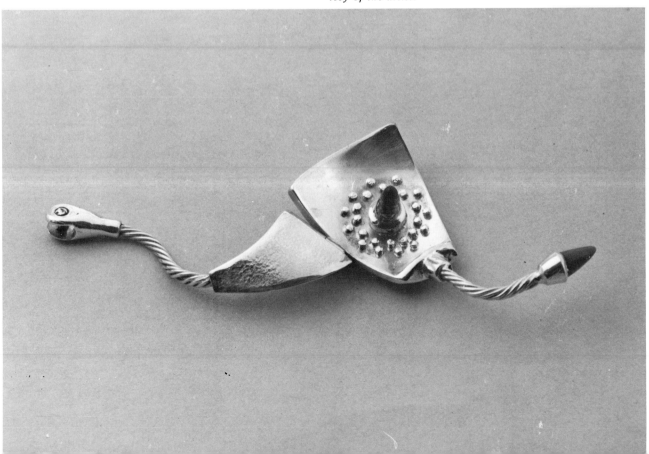

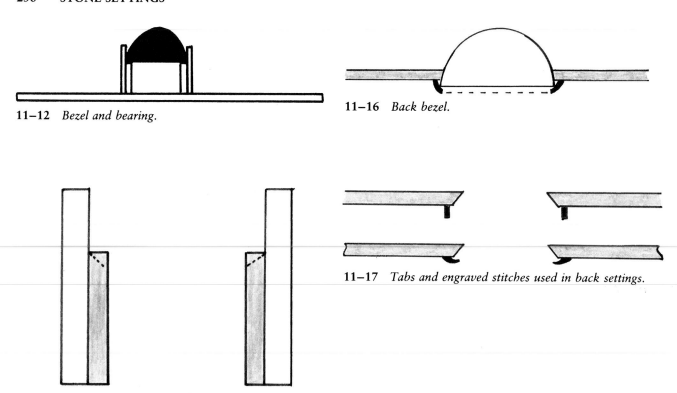

11–12 *Bezel and bearing.*

11–16 *Back bezel.*

11–13 *Bearing prepared for a faceted stone.*

11–17 *Tabs and engraved stitches used in back settings.*

ers prefer the heavier material for the visual effect of the thick edge surrounding the stone. If the bezel cannot be pushed over in the conventional manner, a flat-faced chasing punch can be used with a small chasing hammer. Needless to say, care must be taken to avoid cracking the stone. The piece must be held firmly, in a vise if possible. The final pass of the chasing tool should be applied almost straight down on the top edge of the bezel. This angle causes the edge to upset or thicken, pushing metal tightly against the stone. A miniature hammer piece attached to the flexible shaft machine is also an excellent means of forming a heavy bezel. After the stone has been set, a safe-edged flat-needle file can be used to smooth away tool marks.

5 The section on small boxes and frames (pages 78 to 80) describes the process of constructing a square or rectangular heavy bezel. Thin bezels can be shaped without scoring the corners. Bends may be made with flatnose pliers and trued on a square mandrel if needed.

6 A seldom-used variation is the back bezel. Figure 11–16 illustrates its application. The stone is inserted into a specially prepared opening from the back of the workpiece and the bezel pushed over. Engraved burrs or short metal tabs soldered to the back may also be used to retain the stone (figure 11–17).

7 Bezels may also be made of appropriately sized short sections of tubing.

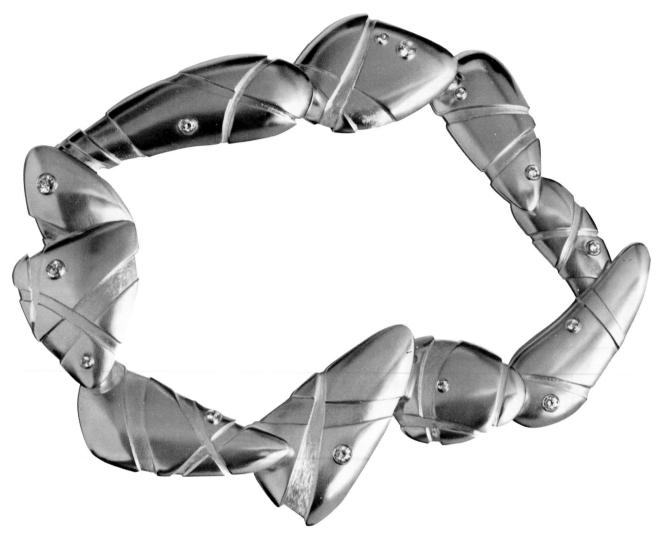

11–15   Sharon Church. *Constructed neckpiece of sterling silver with bezel set cubic zirconia. Courtesy of the artist. Photograph by Londa Salamon.*

overwork the prongs. Thin, flimsy prongs are visually weak and are apt to easily bend or break.

5 Select a stone setting burr that corresponds in size to the diameter of the stone (figure 11–23). Fasten the burr in the flexible shaft or hand drill and cut a bearing surface along the top edge of the inner sleeve. Take care to cut squarely into the sleeve. If the burr cuts off center, the stone will not set flush. Trial fit the stone and recut the bearing if needed. Wax or soap can be used to lubricate the setting burr.

6 The bottom portion of the setting can be shaped and finished as needed. Emery and polish the setting and solder it to the workpiece with easy solder.

7 Setting the stone is essentially the same as with any prong setting. The workpiece must be held securely and stabilized in some manner. Small pieces can be held in the ring clamp and braced against the bench

pin. Place the face of the stone pusher or prong-setting tool squarely against a prong and push in until the prong just touches the stone. Alternately push down opposite prongs. Check to see that the stone sets square to the setting and flush in the bearing. If not flush, push in a little harder on one side to level the stone. Go back and push each prong securely against the stone. Setting pliers with specially shaped jaws can be used for tightening the prongs. These are purchased from jewelry suppliers.

8 A safe-edge, flat-needle file is used to make final adjustments to the shape of the prongs. Finish the prongs with a small, hard-felt buff.

11–23 *Setting burr size relative to the stone.*
11–24 *Setting burrs.*

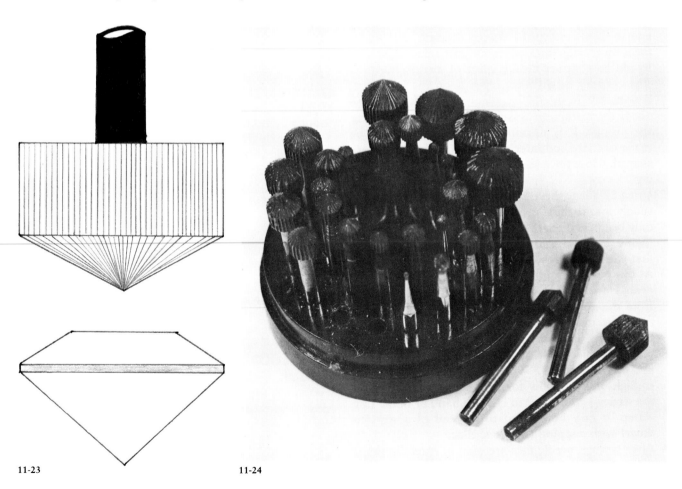

11-23   11-24

Crown Setting Variations

1 To set a cabochon, delete step 6. The inner sleeve or bearing surface need not be angled. A bevel can be filed around the outside edge of the inner sleeve to prevent the possibility of creating a solder fillet in this area as the sleeves are joined (figure 11–26).

2 A one-piece crown can be fabricated using relatively thick sheet metal. Dimensions of the cylinder should be such to allow the thickness of the wall to form both the bearing and prongs. The cylinder's inner diameter should be somewhat less than the diameter of the stone (figure 11–27). Construction is essentially as that discussed earlier. One further variation of the crown setting is a cone-shaped crown. The techniques of cone construction are covered in chapter 3.

11–25 Susan Noland. *Forged and constructed ring of 14-karat yellow gold with citrine. The artist constructed simple but elegant prongs to wrap over the bearing and to repeat the graceful curves of the forged shank. Courtesy of the artist. Photograph by Leslie Becker.*

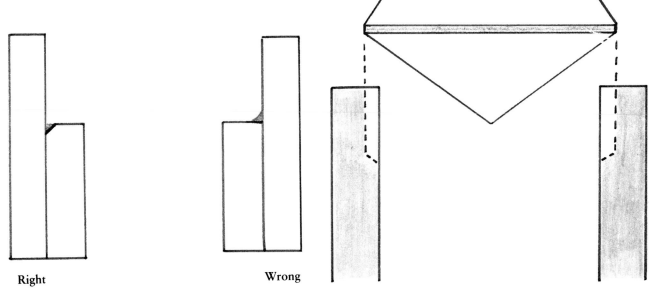

Right

Wrong

11–26 *Bevel filed around the bearing to prevent solder buildup.*

11–27 *Crown diameter relative to the stone's size.*

ADDITIONAL SETTINGS

Figures 11–28, 11–29, and 11–30 illustrate two additional types of open settings. The setting in figure 11–28 is composed of a cylinder with half-round or square wire soldered to its sides to create prongs. The top edge of the cylinder remains flat for cabochons and is beveled inward as a bearing for faceted stones.

Figure 11–29 shows a relatively simple channel setting. The stone is held by pressure exerted by tension within the metal. Grooves are cut with a needle file. The width of the channel is slightly narrower than the width of the stone. The stone should slide snugly into the groove. Some jewelers cut small tabs to push over the ends of the channels or bring over a small bead with a graver. Sections of the channel may be cut away for decorative effect or to allow more light under the stone (figure 11–30).

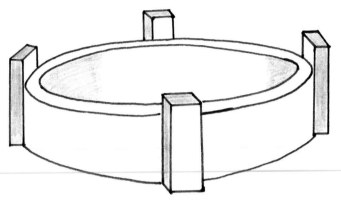

11–28 *Setting using square or half-round wire as prongs.*

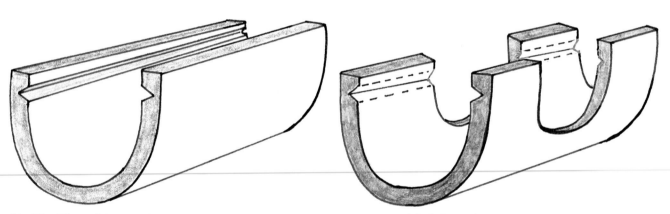

11–29 *Channel (pressure) setting.*

11–30 *Modified channel setting.*

11–31   Susan Noland. *Forged and constructed ring of 14-karat yellow gold with channel-set emerald-cut garnet. Courtesy of the artist. Photograph by Leslie Becker. Collection of Terry Hammer.*

11–32   Susan Noland. *Cast ring of 14-karat gold with channel-set diamond. Courtesy of the artist. Photograph by Leslie Becker.*

Weights, Measures and Proportions

WEIGHTS AND MEASURES

Precious Metals—Troy Weight

1 pennyweight—24 grains

1 ounce troy—20 pennyweights

1 pound troy—12 ounces

1 pound troy—5,760 grams

1 ounce troy—31.104 grams

1 pennyweight—1.555 grams

Carat Weight

1 carat—.20 grams

1 carat—3,086 grains troy

1 carat—.007 ounce avoirdupois

1 carat—100 points

¼ carat—25 points

RING SIZES

Size	Inner Diameter
3	.554 inch
3½	.570
4	.586
4½	.602
5	.618
5½	.634
6	.650
6½	.666
7	.682
7½	.698
8	.714
8½	.730
9	.746
9½	.762
10	.778
10½	.794
11	.810
11½	.826
12	.842
12½	.858
13	.874

FRACTIONAL AND DECIMAL INCHES TO MILLIMETERS

Fractions	Inches	MM
$1/64$	.0156	0.3969
$1/32$	.0313	0.7937
$3/64$	.0469	1.1906
$1/16$	.0625	1.5875
$5/64$	.0781	1.9843
$3/32$	.0937	2.3812
$7/64$	.1094	2.7781
$1/8$	.1250	3.1750
$9/64$	.1406	3.5718
$5/32$	.1562	3.9687
$11/64$	.1719	4.3656
$3/16$	.1875	4.7624
$13/64$	.2031	5.1593
$7/32$	.2187	5.5562
$15/64$	.2344	5.9530
$1/4$	.2500	6.3499
$17/64$	.2656	6.7468
$9/32$	.2812	7.1437
$19/64$	.2969	7.5405
$5/16$	.3125	7.9374
$21/64$	.3281	8.3343
$11/32$	.3438	8.7312
$23/64$	.3594	9.1280
$3/8$	.3750	9.5249
$25/64$	.3906	9.9217
$13/32$	.4062	10.3186
$27/64$	.4219	10.7155
$7/16$	.4375	11.1124
$29/64$	.4531	11.5092
$15/32$	.4687	11.9061
$31/64$	.4844	12.3030
$1/2$	.5000	12.6999

JEWELER'S TWIST DRILL CHART

Number	Decimal Inch	Number	Decimal Inch	Number	Decimal Inch	Number	Decimal Inch
1	.228	21	.159	41	.096	61	.039
2	.221	22	.157	42	.093	62	.038
3	.213	23	.154	43	.089	63	.037
4	.209	24	.152	44	.086	64	.036
5	.205	25	.149	45	.082	65	.035
6	.204	26	.147	46	.081	66	.033
7	.201	27	.144	47	.078	67	.032
8	.199	28	.140	48	.076	68	.031
9	.196	29	.136	49	.073	69	.029
10	.193	30	.128	50	.070	70	.028
11	.191	31	.120	51	.067	71	.026
12	.189	32	.116	52	.063	72	.025
13	.185	33	.113	53	.059	73	.024
14	.182	34	.111	54	.055	74	.022
15	.180	35	.110	55	.052	75	.021
16	.177	36	.106	56	.046	76	.020
17	.173	37	.104	57	.043	77	.018
18	.169	38	.101	58	.042	78	.016
19	.166	39	.099	59	.041	79	.014
20	.161	40	.098	60	.040	80	.013

GAUGE COMPARISON CHART

B&S Gauge Number	Decimal Inch	Decimal Millimeters
4	.204	5.18
5	.181	4.62
6	.162	4.11
7	.144	3.66
8	.128	3.26
9	.114	2.90
10	.101	2.58
11	.090	2.30
12	.080	2.05
13	.071	1.82
14	.064	1.62
15	.057	1.44
16	.050	1.29
17	.045	1.14
18	.040	1.02
19	.035	.91
20	.031	.81
21	.028	.72
22	.025	.64
23	.022	.57
24	.020	.51
25	.017	.45
26	.015	.40
27	.014	.36
28	.012	.32
29	.011	.28
30	.010	.25

ROUND WIRE
Weight in Pennyweights or Ounces per Foot in B&S Gauge

B&S Gauge	Inch Thickness (Ozs.)	Fine Silver (Ozs.)	Sterling (Dwts.)	Fine Gold (Dwts.)	18KY Gold (Dwts.)	14KY Gold (Dwts.)	10KY Gold (Dwts.)	Platinum (Ozs.)
4	.204	2.17	2.14	80.1	64.6	54.2	48.0	4.45
5	.181	1.72	1.70	63.5	51.2	43.0	38.0	3.53
6	.162	1.36	1.35	50.4	40.6	34.1	30.2	2.80
7	.144	1.09	1.07	39.9	32.2	27.0	23.9	2.22
8	.128	.859	.848	31.6	25.6	21.4	19.0	1.76
9	.114	.682	.673	25.2	20.3	17.0	15.1	1.39
10	.101	.541	.534	20.0	16.1	13.5	11.9	1.11
11	.090	.429	.423	15.8	12.7	10.7	9.46	.877
12	.080	.339	.335	12.6	10.1	8.47	7.50	.695
13	.071	.270	.266	9.9	8.01	6.72	5.95	.552
14	.064	.214	.211	7.8	6.36	5.33	4.72	.437
15	.057	.169	.167	6.2	5.04	4.23	3.74	.347
16	.050	.135	.132	4.9	4.0	3.35	2.97	.275
17	.045	.107	.105	3.9	3.17	2.66	2.35	.218
18	.040	.084	.083	3.1	2.51	2.11	1.87	.173
19	.035	.067	.066	2.4	1.99	1.67	1.48	.137
20	.031	.053	.052	1.9	1.58	1.33	1.17	.109
21	.028	.042	.041	1.5	1.25	1.05	.931	.086
22	.025	.0335	.033	1.2	.994	.833	.738	.068
23	.022	.0265	.026	.977	.789	.661	.585	.054
24	.020	.021	.020	.775	.625	.524	.464	.043
25	.017	.0167	.016	.615	.496	.416	.368	.034
26	.015	.0133	.013	.488	.393	.330	.292	.027
27	.014	.0105	.010	.386	.312	.261	.231	.021
28	.012	.0083	.008	.306	.247	.207	.184	.017
29	.011	.0065	.006	.243	.196	.164	.145	.013
30	.010	.0052	.005	.193	.155	.130	.115	.010

MELTING POINT AND SPECIFIC GRAVITY OF METALS

Metal or Alloy	Symbol	Melting Point °F	Specific Gravity
Aluminum	Al	1220	2.7
Copper	Cu	1981	8.94
Gold	Au	1945	19.36
18-karat yellow	Au, Ag, Cu	1700	15.58
18-karat white	Au, Pt, Pd	1730	14.64
14-karat yellow	Au, Ag, Cu	1615	13.07
14-karat white	Au, Pt, Pd	1825	12.61
10-karat yellow	Au, Ag, Cu	1665	11.57
10-karat white	Au, Pt, Pd	1975	11.07
Iron	Fe	2795	7.86
Lead	Pb	621	11.36
Magnesium	Mg	1204	1.74
Nickel	Ni	2645	8.85
Palladium	Pd	2831	12.0
Platinum	Pt	3224	21.45
Rhodium	Rh	3551	12.5
Silver	Ag	1761	10.53
Sterling silver	Ag, Cu	1640	10.40
Tin	Sn	450	7.3
Zinc	Zn	787	7.14

SHEET METAL
Weight per sq. in. by B & S gauge

B & S Gauge	Thickness Inches	Fine Silver Ozs.	Sterling Silver Ozs.	Fine Gold Dwts.	10K Yel Gold Dwts.	14K Yel Gold Dwts.	18K Yel Gold Dwts.	Platinum Ozs.
8	.128	.713	.714	26.2	15.7	17.7	21.1	1.45
10	.102	.565	.558	20.8	12.4	14.0	16.7	1.15
12	.080	.448	.443	16.5	9.85	11.1	13.3	.913
14	.064	.356	.351	13.1	7.81	8.82	10.5	.724
16	.050	.282	.278	10.4	6.21	7.00	8.35	.574
18	.040	.224	.221	8.22	4.91	5.55	6.62	.455
19	.036	.199	.196	7.32	4.38	4.94	5.89	.406
20	.032	.177	.175	6.52	3.90	4.40	5.25	.361
22	.025	.141	.139	5.17	3.09	3.49	4.16	.286
24	.020	.112	.110	4.10	2.45	2.77	3.30	.227
26	.016	.0884	.0873	3.25	1.94	2.19	2.62	.180
28	.013	.0701	.0689	2.58	1.54	1.74	2.08	.143
30	.010	.0556	.0549	2.04	1.22	1.38	1.65	.113

CHART FOR DETERMINING INVESTMENT AND WATER REQUIREMENTS FOR VARIOUS SIZE FLASKS TO BE USED WITH SATIN CAST 20, SUPERVEST 20 AND CRISTOBALITE INLAY INVESTMENTS

This chart provides a quick reference, showing at a glance the correct amounts of investment and water required for flasks of different dimensions. This chart was developed specifically for use with KERR SATIN CAST 20, KERR SUPERVEST 20 AND KERR CRISTOBALITE INLAY investments.

Top Figure — Investment
Lower Figure — Water

Height of Flask

Diameter of Flask	2″	2½″	3″	3½″	4″	5″	6″	7″
2″	5 oz. / 57 cc	6 oz. / 68 cc	7.5 oz. / 85 cc	9 oz. / 102 cc	10 oz. / 114 cc			
2½″	8 oz. / 91 cc	10 oz. / 114 cc	12 oz. / 136 cc	14 oz. / 160 cc	16 oz. / 182 cc	20 oz. / 228 cc		
3″	12 oz. / 136 cc	15 oz. / 170 cc	18 oz. / 205 cc	21 oz. / 240 cc	1½ lb. / 274 cc	30 oz. / 340 cc	32 oz. / 410 cc	2¾ lb. / 500 cc
3½″	1 lb. / 182 cc	1¼ lb. / 228 cc	1½ lb. / 274 cc	1¾ lb. / 320 cc	2 lb. / 364 cc	2½ lb. / 456 cc	3 lb. / 548 cc	3½ lb. / 640 cc
4″	18 oz. / 205 cc	23 oz. / 262 cc	27 oz. / 308 cc	2 lb. / 364 cc	2¼ lb. / 410 cc	3 lb. / 546 cc	3½ lb. / 637 cc	4 lb. / 728 cc
5″					3¾ lb. / 682 cc	4¾ lb. / 864 cc	5½ lb. / 1000 cc	6½ lb. / 1182 cc

WAX ELIMINATION
SUGGESTED BURN-OUT CYCLES

The following burn-out cycles are recommended:
Select proper burn-out cycle according to size of flasks.

5-Hour Cycle

For flasks up to 2½″ × 2½″ preheat furnace to 300°F/149°C

1 hour— 300°F/149°C
1 hour— 700°F/371°C
2 hour—1350°F/732°C
1 hour—See note

8-Hour Cycle

For flasks up to 3½″ × 4″ preheat furnace to 300°F/149°C

2 hour— 300°F/149°C
2 hour— 700°F/371°C
3 hour—1350°F/732°C
1 hour—See note

12-Hour Cycle

For flasks up to 4″ × 8″ preheat furnace to 300°F/149°C

2 hour— 300°F/149°C
2 hour— 600°F/315°C
2 hour— 900°F/482°C
4 hour—1350°F/732°C
2 hour—See note

Note: During last hour the temperature must be adjusted so that flasks are at correct temperature for casting.
Example: Mold temperature for ladies ring or items of lacey or intricate design should be 900°F to 1000°F (482°C to 538°C) Mold temperature for gents ring or items of relative heavier design should be 700°F to 900°F (371°C to 482°C)

CASTING TEMPERATURE CHART

Alloy	Casting Temperature (°F)	Casting Temperature (°C)	Ratio of Metal to Wax	Flask Casting Temp. (°F)	Flask Casting Temp. (°C)
Silver	1750-1775	954-968	9 — 1	800	427
Gold 10 KY	1850	1010	14 — 1	950	510
Gold 14 KY	1825	996	14 — 1	900	482
Gold 10 KW	2025	1107	14 — 1	1000	538
Gold 14 KW	1925	1052	14 — 1	950	510
Bronze	1950	1065	10 — 1	900	482
B. Cu.	1900	1038	10 — 1	800	427
Platinum	3000	649	21 — 1	1400	760
Aluminum	1400	760	2-½ — 1	400	204

Note: 1. Casting temperature will vary slightly depending upon particular alloy used.
2. Flask temperature will vary depending upon size of casting.
3. Pure Silver melts at 1762°F/961°C
4. Pure Gold melts at 1945°F/1063°C

RECOMMENDED PROPORTIONING CHART
FOR KERR INVESTMENTS

SATIN CAST 20/SUPERVEST 20
CRISTOBALITE INLAY

Wt. of Investment in Pounds	Recommended Proportioning for Heavy Casting 38/100			Recommended Proportioning for Regular Casting 40/100			Recommended Proportioning for Extra Fine Casting 42/100		
	WATER CC.	Oz.	Yields Approx. Cu. In.	WATER CC.	Oz.	Yields Approx. Cu. In.	WATER CC.	Oz.	Yields Approx. Cu. In.
1 lb.	173	6	21.3	182	6.4	21.9	191	6.72	22.5
5 lbs.	862	30.4	106	908	32	110	953	33.6	112
10 lbs.	1725	60.8	213	1816	64	219	1907	67.2	225
15 lbs.	2588	91.2	320	2724	96	328	2860	100.8	338
20 lbs.	3450	121.6	426	3632	128	438	3814	134.4	450
25 lbs.	4312	152	532	4540	160	548	4767	168	562

ALLOYS AND SOLDERS

For alloying small quantities of metal, a depression cut into a charcoal block can act as a crucible. A strand of binding wire around the block's sides will help avert leakage of metal in the event the block cracks while heating. A pinch of flux is sprinkled over the alloy components, heat is applied until the metals are molten, and they are stirred with a carbon rod. The resulting alloy can then be forged, rolled out, or cast as needed.

Not all of the following formulas add up to 100 percent. This is because the recipes are for basic components. Individual jewelers and refiners tailor their golds to create alloys which have specific, sought-after characteristics. Additional constituents might be various amounts of one or several metals: copper, zinc, nickel, etc.

Silver Alloys

Sterling—925 parts fine silver, 75 parts copper

820 reticulation stock—820 parts fine silver, 180 parts copper

Electrum—50 parts fine silver, 50 parts pure gold

Gold Alloys

Yellow 22K—91.6% pure gold, 4.2% fine silver, 4.2% copper

Yellow 18K—75% pure gold, 12.5% fine silver, 12.5% copper

Yellow 14K—58.3% pure gold, 20.8% fine silver, 20.8% copper

White 18K—75% pure gold, 25% palladium

Gold Solders (Shop Alloying)

While those routinely working with gold will have a range of solder at hand, some jewelers may have only occasional need and may not have

White 14K—48% pure gold, 41.7% palladium

Green 18K—75% pure gold, 25% fine silver

Green 14K—58.3% pure gold, 41.7% fine silver

Bluish 18K—75% pure gold, 25% iron

Silver Solders (Shop Alloying)

Easy—2 parts fine silver, 1 part yellow brass

Medium—3 parts fine silver, 1 part yellow brass

Hard—5 parts fine silver, 1 part yellow brass

I.T.—7 parts fine silver, 1 part yellow brass

the needed materials. The following formula will provide an adequate general repair solder.

Mix four parts of the gold alloy being used to one part fine silver. For example, to solder a 14 KY band, use four parts 14 KY and one part fine silver.

Flux (Hard Soldering)

50 grams—boric acid crystals
32 grams—sodium phosphate
34 grams—powdered borax
1 pint—distilled water
Mix and bring to a boil.

COPPER ALLOYS (JAPANESE)

The alloy formulas listed here are those commonly used in moKume-gane. In most instances there is considerable room for experimentation to develop the working characteristics and colors desired. Those who wish to study Japanese techniques and their alloying procedures are encouraged to refer to several of the publications listed in the bibliography.

Shakudo

Copper—94–96%
Gold—4–5%
Silver—1½% or less

Shibuichi

Copper—51–68%
Silver—32–49%
Gold—1–10% or less
This is one of many grades traditionally used.

Kuromi-do

Copper—99%
Metal arsenic—1%
Especially hazardous to alloy and should only be attempted under ideal safety conditions.

Mohs' Scale of Hardness	Hardness	Mohs' Scale of Hardness	Hardness
Agate	7	Labradorite	6 to 6.5
Amber	2 to 2.5	Lapis Lazuli	6
Apatite	5	Malachite	3.5 to 4
Azurite	3.5	Nephrite	5 to 6
Beryl	7.5 to 8	Obsidian	5 to 5.5
Calcite	3 (copper coin)	Olivine	6.5 to 7
Chrysoberyl	8.5	Opal	5 to 6
Chrysocolla	2 to 4	Quartz	7
Corundum	9	Rhodocrosite	4
Diamond	10	Rhodonite	5.5 to 6.5
Diopside	5 to 6	Sodalite	5.5 to 6
Feldspar	6 (knife blade)	Spinel	8
Fluorite	4	Talc	1
Fluorspar	4	Tektite	5.5 (window glass)
Garnets	6.5 to 7.5		
Gypsum	2	Topaz	8
	2.5 (fingernail)	Tourmaline	7 to 7.5
Hematite	6	Turquoise	5 to 6
Jadeite	6.5 to 7 (steel file)	Zircon	7 to 7.5

Formulas

GRANULATION FORMULAS

The following are formulas used by Henry Littledale in his research of granulation and eutectic bonding. As pointed out in the section on granulation, formulas are used in conjunction with varying amounts of glue, borax, and water. These formulas are intended for gold and silver work.

1. Copper hydrate—50%
   Zinc hydrate—30%
   Tin dioxide—20%

2. Silver oxide—66%
   Copper hydrate—22%
   Zinc hydrate—12%

3. Silver oxide—50%
   Copper hydrate—50%

4. Silver oxide—50%
   Antimony trioxide—50%

5. Silver oxide—80%
   Antimony trioxide—20%

COLORATION FORMULAS

The following formulas are provided as merely starting points. The resulting colors will depend upon how the mixture is applied: hot, cold, dipped, or brushed. In a few instances, the metals that tend to react best have been noted. As in any process involving acids, use proper ventilation, add acid to water, and wear protective glasses, gloves, and an apron. Mix and use all components in a heat-resistant ceramic or glass container.

1. 1 small chunk—liver of sulfur
   1 quart—cold tap water
   Mix to light yellow color.
   Works especially well on copper, bronze, NuGold, sterling.

2. 50 grams—sodium hyposulfite
   2 milliliters—nitric acid
   850 milliliters—tap water
   Add the nitric acid to the water and stir. Add the sodium hyposulfite.
   Works well on copper, bronze, Nu-Gold, and nickel silver.

3. 30 grams—cupric nitrate
   30 grams—ammonium chloride
   30 grams—calcium chloride
   750 milliliters—tap water
   Works well on copper, NuGold, nickel silver.

4. 6 grams—copper sulfate
   ½ teaspoon—table salt
   850 milliliters—water
   Used at boiling temperature for moKume-gane, various copper alloys.

NIELLO FORMULAS

History has passed along many niello formulas. This allows plenty of room to experiment with the material's color, hardness, and adhesive qualities.

1. Silver—1 part
   Lead—3 parts
   Copper—2 parts
   Sulfur—12 parts

2. Copper—1 part
   Lead—1 part
   Silver—8 parts
   Bismuth—1 part
   Sulfur—3 parts

3. Silver—1 part
   Lead—3 parts
   Copper—2 parts
   Sulfur—9 parts

4. Silver—1 part
   Copper—1 part
   Lead—2 parts
   Sulfur—6 parts

5. Silver—3 parts
   Copper—5 parts
   Lead—7 parts
   Sulfur—6 parts
   Ammonium Chloride—2 parts
   Borax—24 parts

6. Sterling Silver—12 parts
   Lead—4 parts
   Copper—4 parts
   Sulfur—24 parts

7. Sterling Silver—1 part
   Copper—2 parts
   Lead—3 parts
   Sulfur—6 parts

8. Silver—6 parts
   Copper—2 parts
   Lead—1 part
   Sulfur—1 part

9. Silver—2 parts
   Copper—4 parts
   Antimony—1 part
   Lead—1 part
   Sulfur—1 part

10. Silver—3 parts
    Copper—2.5 parts
    Lead—2 parts
    Borax—3 parts
    Sulfur—30 parts

Hardening and Tempering

HARDENING AND TEMPERING SMALL TOOLS

Jewelers may have an occasion to make or reshape small tools: gravers, chisels, punches, etc.

The following is the general procedure required to anneal, harden, and temper tool steel.

1 First anneal the steel to soften it for shaping or reshaping. Use a torch or forge to heat the steel to a bright cherry red and allow the piece to air cool slowly in a bed of dry sand or fine ash.

2 After the material has cooled and the tool has been reshaped, again heat it to cherry red and quickly submerge it in a pail of water. Use tongs to swirl the tool around in the water to ensure uniform cooling. This hardens the steel to its maximum hardness. Depending on the application and type of steel, it may be quenched in oil or brine.

3 Remove scale from one side of the tool with fine emery cloth. Assuming for a moment a small chisel is being heat treated, clean from midway to the tool's point. Abrading the surface down to clean metal will give an accurate view of the oxidation colors as tempering occurs. Once again apply heat to the tool. Use a small flame on the center portion of the punch and observe the surface colors as they travel toward the point. Just as the band of dark straw color reaches the end, quench the tool in a pail of water or oil. In this process greater heat is being applied to the shank, making it softer and leaving the tip

relatively hard. The process draws hardness and brittleness from the steel.

The following gives the temperatures and colors applicable to specific types of tools.

Temperature/Color Comparison for Tempering Steel

Temperature (°F)	Color	Applications
420°	Faint, faint yellow	
430°	Faint yellow	Razors
440°	Light straw	Engravers
450°	Straw	Scrapers
460°	Full straw	
470°	Dark straw	Wood-cutting tools, chisels
480°	Gold	
490°	Brown	Drills
510°	Brown purple	
530°	Purple	Punches, chasing tools, hammer faces
550°	Deep purple	Springs, saws
560°	Blue	
600°	Dark blue	Hot chisels
620°	Gray blue	

Suppliers

Jewelry Suppliers and Services

A—General supplies, tools, equipment, metal
B—Stones
C—Refiners
D—Blacksmith tools
E—Casting services
F—Casting supplies
G—Coal and coke

Billanti Casting Co. **E**
64 W. 48th St.
New York, NY 10036

Allcraft Tool and Supply
Co. **A, F**
100 Frank Rd.
Hicksville, NY 11801

Anchor Tool and Supply
Co. **A, F**
231 Main St.
Chatham, NJ 07928

William Dixon Co. **A, F**
750 Washington Ave.
Carlstadt, NJ 07072

Paul Gesswein & Co. **A, F**
255 Hancock Ave.
Bridgeport, CT 06605

T. B. Hagstoz and Son **A, F**
709 Sansom St.
Philadelphia, PA 19106

C. R. Hill Co. **A, F**
2734 W. 11 Mile Rd.
Berkley, MI 48072

Kerr Manufacturing Co. **F**
P.O. Box 455/28200 Wick Rd.
Romulus, MI 48174

Swest Inc. **A, B, C, F**
10803 Composite Dr.
Dallas, TX 75220

TSI, Inc. **A, F**
P.O. Box 9266
101 Nickerson St.
Seattle, WA 98109

G & G Miracle House **A, F**
5621 W. Hemlock St.
Milwaukee, WI 53223

Rio Grande Jewelers
Supply **A, C, F**
6901 Washington N.E.
Albuquerque, NM 87109

Kenneth F. Rose **B**
P.O. Box 84
Southfield, MI 48037

Raymond Gabrial **B**
1469 Rosena Ave.
Madison, OH 44057

The Thomas Co. **A, F**
742 N. Woodward Ave.
Birmingham, MI 48011

C. W. Somers and Co. **A, F**
387 Washington St.
Boston, MA 02108

ARE, Inc. **A, C, F**
Box 8, Rt. 16
Greensboro Bend, VT 05842

Myron Toback, Inc. **A, F**
23 W. 47th St.
New York, NY 10036

Hauser & Miller Co. **A, C, F**
4011 Forest Park Blvd.
St. Louis, MO 63108

Centaur Forge Ltd. **D, G**
117 N. Spring St.
Burlington, WI 53105

Schneider Fuel & Supply
Co. **G**
3438 W. Forest Home Ave.
Milwaukee, WI 53215

U.S. Lapidary & Jewelers
Supply, Inc. **A**
5523 Hemlock St.
P.O. Drawer 41526
Sacramento, CA 95841

Castex Casting Crafts **A, F**
P.O. Box 1954
Lancaster, CA 93539

California Crafts Supply **A, F**
1096 N. Main St.
Orange, CA 92667

Electroforming and Plating Suppliers

1. Anodes

Amax Copper
200 Park Ave.
New York, NY 10017

Paul H. Gesswein and Co.
255 Hancock Ave.
Bridgeport, CT 06605

2. Bus Bars

Central Steel and Wire Co.
3000 W. 51st St.
Chicago, IL 60626

3. Chemicals

Curtin Matheson
1850 Greenleaf Ave.
Elk Grove, IL 60007

J. T. Baker Chemical Co.
Phillipsburg, NJ 08865

Fisher Scientific Co.
Chemical Manufacturing
Division
Fair Lawn, NJ 07410

Sargent Welch Scientific
7300 N. Linder Ave.
Skokie, IL 60077
(Sells in small amounts to
schools, universities, and
companies only.)

Matheson, Coleman and Bell
Manufacturing Chemists
Norwood, OH 45212

4. Conductive Sprays and Paints

Burt Bricker Inc.
P.O. Box 171
Wilmington, DE 19898

Warner Electric Co.
1512 W. Jarvis St.
Chicago, IL 60626

5. Immersion Heaters

Cleveland Process Co.
5703 Brookpark Rd.
Parma, OH 44129

6. Metal Salts/Plating Baths

Paul H. Gesswein Co.
255 Hancock Ave.
Bridgeport, CT 06605

Technic, Inc.
P.O. Box 965
Providence, RI 02901

7. Pumps and Filters

Brucar Equipment and Supply
  Co.
55 Lamar St.
West Babylon, NY 11704

Serfilco
1234 Depot St.
Glenview, IL 60025

8. Rectifiers

Paul H. Gesswein Co.
255 Hancock Ave.
Bridgeport, CT 06605

Technic, Inc.
P.O. Box 965
Providence, RI 02901

9. Resists

Tolber Division, Pyramid
  Plastics
220–5th Ave.
Hope, AR 71801

SUPPLIERS OF PHOTOETCHING MATERIALS

The author recommends that those wishing to do photoetching first contact these firms requesting the technical data sheets pertaining to the process.

Eastman Kodak Co.
Kodak Park
Department 454
Rochester, NY 14650

KRP-3 Kodak Photo Resist
Kodak Ortho Resist Developer
Kodak Ortho Resist Thinner
KRP Dye

Dynachem Corp.
13000 E. Firestone Blvd.
Santa Fe Springs, CA 90670

Dynachem CMR-5000 Resist
Dynachem CMR-5000 Thinner
Dynachem CMR-5000
  Developer
Dynachem CMR-5000 Black
  Dye

SUPPLIERS OF MATERIALS USED IN THIN-SHELL CASTINGS

Local dental laboratory supply firms may also stock the needed materials.

**1. Lang's Jet Repair Acrylic
  (#125-1013)**

Henry Schein, Inc.
5 Harbor Park Drive
Port Washington, NY 11050

**2. Organa II No-Wash All
  Purpose Duplicating
  Hydrocolloid (#300-1A)**

Niranium Corporation
34–37 11th Street
Long Island City, NY 11106

TITANIUM SUPPLIERS

1. Titanium and Tantalum

Astro Metallurgical Corp.
3225 Lincoln Way, West
Wooster, OH 44691

Fansteel
#1 Tantalum Place
North Chicago, IL 60064

2. Niobium

Teledyne Wah Chang
P.O. Box 460
Albany, OR 97321

ANODIZED ALUMINUM DYES AND SEALERS SUPPLIERS

Sandoz Colors and Chemicals
Metals Department
East Hanover, NJ 07936

Lea Manufacturing Company
Chemical Finishes Division
49 Waters Ave.
Everett, MA 02149

Health Hazards and Shop Safety

It is not an exaggeration to say that almost all the materials and processes jewelers use are potential safety or health hazards. Many of the hazards have only recently been realized and I believe that as time passes we will discover a greater number. I cannot strongly enough impress upon the reader that it is vital to read all manufacturers' instructions and labels carefully, seek out health information relative to all unfamiliar or new materials, and in general stay abreast of new data regarding health hazards and safety in the jewelry field.

While every effort has been made to point out the dangers throughout this text, space does not allow a complete explanation of the medical implications or even detailed solutions to all potential hazards. In addition to staying abreast of the general topic of health and safety standards in our field, one's work attitude, in-shop practices and personal habits will play a major part in the jeweler's future safety and health. The written word alone is not sufficient.

Keep in mind that while harmful effects of some substances are instantaneous, the human body is slow to react to others, and with some the cumulative effect may take decades and be irreversible. Foreign substances can enter the body through the skin, by inhalation, or through the digestive system. In addition to this, the jeweler may be exposed to eye and ear hazards plus the various dangers associated with injuries inflicted by power tools, heat sources, chemicals, electrical shock, and explosive materials. Despite all these potential problems, a well designed shop, appropriate safety devices, and precautions and common sense will contribute significantly to the longevity of one's jewelry making career.

Measures which may be taken against the hazards of harmful substances can be classed in four basic categories: ventilation, barriers, filtration, and substitution. In many instances, a combination or all of these measures may be required.

VENTILATION

This is perhaps the single most important consideration in initial shop design. Properly installed, the system should exhaust all dust, fumes, vapors and a considerable amount of the heat generated by kilns, torches, electrical equipment, forges, etc. A proper vent system should be equipped to bring in fresh air as it removes contaminants. Those systems that bring in as much air as is removed from the space I refer to as *positive ventilation systems*.

Ducting and hoods should be constructed to provide air movement free of constrictions and should be situated to pull contaminants out of the worker's breathing space. Ideally, the suction inlet should be located behind and above the work point, thereby drawing contaminants directly back and upward, away from the worker. Placed elsewhere, exhaust may be drawn past and inhaled or ingested by the worker. In some shops it might be appropriate to vent several machines or operations beneath one hood while in other situations more than one hood may be required. For example, burnout kilns and casting machines might be located away from etching, pickling, enameling, and soldering. In designing the system, one must consider traffic flow, room size, equipment layout, and the processes to be carried out. While small window fans and vented stove hoods are often used, I recommend use of more sophisticated hoods and ducts. In most cases, small fans and stove hoods do not provide enough positive air movement and therefore do not adequately pull contaminants out of one's breathing space. The practice of merely placing a fan in a window and opening a door or another window to replenish exhausted air can exacerbate existing hazards by stirring up contaminants and dust. These may be drawn over the worker and into his or her eyes, nose, and mouth. System design should make adjustments for replenishing a heated or air conditioned environment. All exhausted air should be directed away from the outside fresh air inlets. If this is overlooked, contaminated air will be recycled through the work space.

For information regarding specific hood and duct design and construction, readers are encouraged to consult their state or federal office of Occupational Safety and Health Administration or the Occupational Safety Division of their State Labor Department. Regional offices of O.S.H.A. are listed in this appendix.

FILTRATION

While in most instances a proper ventilation system will remove a considerable amount of contaminants, there may be times when additional precautions should be taken. When the worker is not absolutely sure or when vents do not adequately exhaust fumes, vapors, dust, or mist, a respirator should be worn over the mouth and nose. Respirator filter cartridges and canisters are designed to filter specific types of contaminants and should only be used in the presence of those contaminants. The National Institute of Occupational Safety and Health has labeled respirators which have been tested and approved.

BARRIERS

Any device used to stop out, cover, or shield the worker might be considered in this category and again will most likely be used in addition to other measures. For example, jewelers generally take the precaution of working with acids placed beneath a vented hood as they wear a respirator, safety goggles or face shield, acid proof gloves, and apron. Goggles, face shields, aprons, gloves, ear plugs, ear muffs, safety shoes, buffing machine shields, casting machine tubs, and power tool guards all are barriers placed between the worker and the source of danger. These devices always should be in good working order and close at hand.

SUBSTITUTES

Of all health hazards, those easiest to eliminate are those for which a safe substitute can be used. With ever advancing research in technology, health, and the occupational safety fields, we might expect more, safer alternative products and materials to work with. Today we need not use certain fluxes (fluorides), hard solders (cadmium), asbestos (a carcinogen), and a number of solvents and cleaners. We have substitutes for all of these which are quite adequate. A detailed, objective study of our working environments would likely reveal potential hazards that easily could be eliminated. For example, lead blocks, a hazard, used for sheet metal forming can be replaced by wooden blocks, stakes, anvils, tree stumps, or sand filled leather bags. Wooden blocks may also at times be used in lieu of pitch to hold work for repoussé, chasing, inlay, and engraving. In electroplating, acid baths are sometimes less hazardous substitutes for extremely hazardous cyanide solutions. Where some hazardous liquids cannot be replaced, their danger can be diminished somewhat by diluting them with water.

GENERAL SAFETY CONSIDERATIONS AND PRECAUTIONS

1 Eating utensils, coffee pots, extra clothing, and breathing respirators should be stored away from work areas. People should not eat, drink, or smoke in the shop. Hands should be washed after working with hazardous materials and especially prior to eating meals, taking rest-breaks, and leaving the shop.

2 Daily general cleanups will help eliminate solid contaminants. Vacuum cleaners work best. Brooms spread existing dust.

3 Special work clothes should be kept and washed separate from other clothing. Change work clothes frequently to prevent exposure to substances clinging to the clothing material. Frequent changes and separate washing can prevent living areas and other people from being exposed to possible hazards. There is evidence that asbestos workers over many years have transported fatal levels of asbestos particles into their homes.

4 All substances should be stored in non-breakable, lidded, clearly labeled containers. Containers should always remain covered when not actually being used. Containers whose contents may react with each other should not be stored in the same area. Storage of large containers on high shelves may result in their falling and possibly breaking open. It may be necessary to store some materials separately in an approved cabinet as prescribed by local codes. Where storage information is not provided on the label, consult your state's Division of Health or Fire Safety.

5 An all purpose (class A, B, C) fire extinguisher should be within easy reach. A two and one half pound or larger extinguisher is recommended. Class A, B, C extinguishers are designed to extinguish chemical, electrical, and ash producing fires. All those who work in the shop should become familiar with the extinguisher's location and operation. Small extinguishers are relatively inexpensive. Several of them hanging in critical areas of the work space provide cheap insurance.

6 Have a well stocked first-aid kit readily available to treat minor injuries. All workers should be versed in emergency treatment for all situations that might arise. Professional medical assistance should be called immediately in the case of serious accidents.

7 When using torches or other heat producing equipment, always have hair tied back and loose clothing secured to prevent them from dangling near and possibly catching fire from the heat source. Clothing made of synthetic materials is especially susceptible to heat. Dark welding glasses or a dark face shield should be worn while using torches or welders which produce intense light. This will prevent flash burns to the eyes and possible visual impairment. In instances where the hands may be exposed to heat, heavy leather gloves can be worn. Positive, local ventilation should be used. Never use cigarette lighters to ignite torches. Butane lighters can explode if accidently overheated; resulting injuries reportedly have been fatal.

8 All electrical equipment should be properly wired and electrically grounded as directed by the manufacturer's instruction and local codes. Clean up all spills immediately and keep the work area dry. Caution must always be taken with electrical or electrically driven equipment to avoid injury and electrical shock.

9 Do not wear neckties, jewelry, or loose clothing that might become entangled in power tools. Hair should be tied back when using power equipment.

10 When mixing acid and water, always add the acid to the water. The reverse, adding water to acid, can produce violent and dangerous gassing and spattering of the mixture. Acid preparation and work always should be properly vented. An apron, protective gloves, and goggles should be worn. If not familiar with a specific acid and its reaction with materials being processed, consult the appropriate information sources to avoid possible hazards and to find the necessary precautions. Use diluted acids if possible. Avoid all skin contact, inhalation, or ingestion of acids. Clean up spills immediately. Rinse immediately with water if acids or acid solutions contact skin or clothing.

For additional information regarding safety and health hazards, refer to the sources listed in the bibliography. Current information and printed documents may be obtained from the Regional Offices of O.S.H.A. listed below:

18 Oliver St.
Boston, MA 02110
Telephone (617) 223-6712

Room 3445, 1 Astor Plaza
1515 Broadway
New York, NY 10036
Telephone (212) 971-5941

15220 Gateway Center
3535 Market St.
Philadelphia, PA 19104
Telephone (215) 596-1201

1375 Peachtree St. NE
Suite 587
Atlanta, GA 30309
Telephone (404) 526-3573

230 S. Dearborn St.
32nd Floor, Room 3259
Chicago, IL 60604
Telephone (312) 353-4716

555 Griffin Square
Room 602
Dallas, TX 75202
Telephone (214) 749-2477

911 Walnut St., Room 300
Kansas City, MO 64106
Telephone (916) 374-5861

Room 15010, Federal Building
1961 Stout St.
Denver, CO 80202
Telephone (303) 837-3883

Box 36017
450 Golden Gate Ave.
San Francisco, CA 94102
Telephone (415) 556-0586

Federal Office Building, Room 6048
909 1st Ave.
Seattle, WA 98174
Telephone (206) 442-5930

COMPOUND	EFFECTS	PRECAUTIONS
Acetone	High levels of the vapor can result in stupor and unconsciousness. Contact can cause slight skin irritation. Extremely flammable.	Positive, local ventilation and protective gloves. Do not use near open flame.
Acetylene	High concentrations of acetylene and carbon dioxide become asphyxiants by preventing a normal supply of oxygen to the lungs. Acetylene also contains toxic impurities. Highly flammable and explosive.	Positive, local ventilation. Cylinders, which are pressurized, must be stored upright and secured by a safety chain. Never use pressure in excess of 15 P.S.I. Regularly check for leaks and have them professionally repaired.
Alcohol, isoamyl	Absorbed through the skin, it can cause digestive and nervous system damage. Acute inhalation or ingestion can be fatal.	Positive, local ventilation and protective gloves.
Alcohol, methyl	Inhalation and skin absorption causes stupor and unconsciousness, nervous system damage and possibly liver and kidney damage. Ingestion can result in blindness or death.	Positive, local ventilation and protective gloves.
Alcohol, butyl	May be absorbed through the skin. Can cause throat, nose, and eye irritation, stupor and unconsciousness.	Positive, local ventilation and protective gloves.
Alcohol, ethyl	Ingestion causes intoxication. Chronic ingestion can result in liver damage. Denatured ethyl alcohol contains methyl alcohol, making it poisonous.	Positive, local ventilation.
Alcohol, benzyl	Eye, nose, and throat irritation. Mild narcotic.	Positive, local ventilation.

COMPOUND	EFFECTS	PRECAUTIONS
Ammonia	Ingestion is intensely painful and injurious to the mouth and esophagus and can be fatal. Inhalation of vapors can cause respiratory irritation and pulmonary edema. Vapors may also damage the eyes. Skin contact should be avoided.	Positive, local ventilation, eye protection and protective gloves. Do not use in concentrated form. Dilute with water.
Arsenic	Sometimes used as an alloy constituent and may be released in the fumes of some enamels. Can cause nerve disorders and skin and lung cancer. Ingestion may be fatal.	Positive, local ventilation. Eye protection and protective gloves. Use a substitute.
Asbestos	Human carcinogen. Inhalation can cause asbestosis, lung cancer, mesothelioma, intestinal and stomach cancer. Ingestion may also cause cancer.	Do not use in any form. Substitute: wet sand, pea pumice, leather gloves, fire brick, or charcoal blocks.
Asphaltum	Toxic by skin contact and may cause skin cancer. Avoid inhalation and ingestion.	Positive, local ventilation and protective gloves.
Benzene (benzol)	Skin contact, ingestion, and inhalation can result in cumulative poisoning. May destroy bone marrow causing anemia and leukemia. Highly flammable.	Do not use.
Beryllium	Chronic ulcers may result from skin contact. Berylliosis, a severe pneumonia-like disease, is caused by exposure to small amounts and can be fatal. Inhalation may cause bronchogenic cancer.	Do not use.
Brass	Skin contact may cause allergies in some people. Frequent inhalation of fumes can cause metal fume fever or lead or arsenic poisoning from some alloys.	Positive, local ventilation. Avoid skin contact.
Brittania Metal	Skin contact may cause lesions and ulcers. Inhalation can cause respiratory irritation, possible pneumonia, liver, and kidney damage and possible heart damage.	Positive, local ventilation. Avoid skin contact.
Bronze	Skin contact may cause allergies in some people. Inhalation causes metal fume fever. Alloys containing lead can cause lead poisoning.	Positive, local ventilation. Avoid skin contact.
Buffing, polishing and abrasive materials	Due to the many types in use, only general guidelines will be given here. Some materials contain free silica that may cause silicosis if inhaled. All are potential eye hazards and all abrade fine metal particles which may be toxic.	Eye protection and an approved dust respirator should be worn if using machines having inadequate enclosures. Use properly vented and filtered machines. Change clothing after work. The reader should make further studies regarding specific buffing materials used.

COMPOUND	EFFECTS	PRECAUTIONS
Cadmium	Constituent in some silver solder and brazing materials. Fumes can cause severe lung irritation and fatal pulmonary edema. Can also result in kidney damage, anemia, and damage to the teeth, bones, and liver. May also cause lung and prostrate cancer.	Use only with positive, local ventilation. Substitute if possible.
Casting investment	Manufacturers use a variety of fine particled materials, some of which may be hazardous. Some investment components deteriorate at high kiln temperatures to give off toxic fumes.	Positive, local ventilation. An approved particulate respirator should be worn while mixing investment. Kilns should be properly vented.
Coal	Dust is toxic if inhaled. Can cause black lung or a disease similar to silicosis. Toxic fumes or ash may be released upon burning.	Positive, local ventilation or an approved respirator. Some workers substitute coke or charcoal which are cleaner burning fuels.
Copper	Skin contact can cause allergies in some people. Inhalation of copper oxide fumes may cause irritation to the lungs and intestines.	Positive, local ventilation. If allergies develop, use protective gloves.
Copper sulfate	May cause irritation of the skin, eyes, nose, and throat. Ingestion can cause gastrointestinal irritation, vomiting, or anemia.	Positive, local ventilation, protective gloves, and eye protection.
Cyanides: sodium, ferro, cuprous, free	May cause skin rashes and be absorbed through the skin. Ingestion is often fatal, resulting from chemical asphyxia. Inhalation may also cause asphyxia. Acid added to cyanide creates extremely toxic hydrogen cyanide gas which can be quickly fatal if inhaled. Cyanide is a component in some plating solutions.	Do not use if possible. Use only with positive, local ventilation and have an antidote kit available to administer. Consult medical help immediately in the event of an accident. Time is critical for survival.
Enamels	Hazards throughout the enameling process are numerous. Preparation and cleaning of the base metal often involve the use of acids and abrasives. Many of the vitreous media contain hazardous oxides which can be inhaled in their raw form or in firing. The use of a kiln or torch is inherently hazardous.	Use positive, local ventilation during the preparation and firing of enamels. The kiln must be properly vented. Use protective gloves while handling powdered enamels and while working at the kiln.
Flux (fluorides)	Fluorides found in some fluxes produce hydrogen fluoride vapor which produces hydrofluoric acid in the lungs causing them to be burned. Flux should be labeled by the manufacturer or supplier.	Positive, local ventilation. Use non-fluoride flux.
Gold	Some people may be allergic to alloy components.	Use substitute alloy or pure gold.
Hydrochloric acid	An irritant to the respiratory system and corrosive to the skin.	Positive, local ventilation, protective gloves, and eye protection. Always add acid to water, never the reverse. Clean up spills

COMPOUND	EFFECTS	PRECAUTIONS
		immediately, using baking soda to neutralize the acid before washing the area.
Iron or mild steel	Acute inhalation may cause metal fume fever.	Positive, local ventilation.
Ketones	Found in paint and varnish removers and used as a solvent of lacquer or plastics. All ketones are skin, eye, nose, and throat irritants. Can cause stupor and unconsciousness. Ingestion results in vomiting, nausea, and abdominal pain. Chronic contact can cause nerve damage.	Positive, local ventilation, protective gloves and glasses.
Lead	Lead is a cumulative poison and is taken in through the skin and through inhalation or ingestion. Can cause damage to the nervous system, brain, blood cells, bone marrow, kidneys, and liver. May be found in some metal alloys and enamels. Lead blocks sometimes are used in metal forming.	Positive, local ventilation and protective gloves. Wooden blocks, anvils, or sandbags sometimes can be substituted for use in metal forming.
Liver of Sulfur (potassium sulphide)	Will create highly toxic fumes of oxides of sulfur when heated to decomposition. Can cause damage to the eyes and lungs.	Positive, local ventilation. Use only a small amount mixed with water, to obtain a light yellow color. Do not heat. Use protective gloves.
Mercury	Sometimes used to gild silver or used in the refining of gold and silver. Mercury is a cumulative poison affecting the nervous system, kidneys, and brain.	Positive, local ventilation and protective gloves. Electroplating may be substituted. Avoid use if possible.
Nickel	Fumes of nickel may cause skin allergies and eye irritation. Chronic inhalation of fumes may cause lung or nasal cancer or irritation of the upper respiratory tract. Oxyacetylene welding with nickel can result in the formation of toxic nickel carbonyl gas that might cause pulmonary edema. Nickel silver (German silver) and stainless steel contain nickel.	Positive, local ventilation. Use substitutes if possible.
Nitric acid	Fumes given off in metal cleaning and etching are highly toxic by inhalation and can cause bronchitis and emphysema. Contact can burn the skin. Ingestion may be fatal.	Use positive, local ventilation. Wear protective gloves, apron, and eye protection. Use diluted. Substitute if possible. Always add acid to water, not the reverse. Clean up spills immediately using baking soda to neutralize the acid before washing the area.
Pewter	Care must be taken when working with older pewter alloys as these may contain lead.	See Lead.

COMPOUND	EFFECTS	PRECAUTIONS
Pitch	The dark black pitch is a derivative of coal tar and can be a skin irritant that could lead to skin cancer if the metalsmith is exposed to pitch for many years. The brownish, pure vegetable pitch is less hazardous. Both kinds are fire hazards when overheated and may explode if air pockets are allowed to develop, as might be the case in removing pitch from a hollow form. For additional information refer to the text and illustration in the section Repoussé.	Positive, local ventilation. Wear protective gloves and eye protection while heating pitch. Gloves may also be worn to handle pitch. Do not overheat. Heat slowly. For some work, wooden blocks, anvils, or sandbags can be substituted.
Plastics	The subject of plastics is too extensive to cover in this brief space. It is safe to say that almost all plastics work and many of the components involved are hazardous. Hazards range from mild skin irritation to cancer. Toxins can enter the body through the skin, by inhalation, or by ingestion.	Before embarking on projects involving plastics and related components, I strongly recommend that the reader make a complete study of the related hazards and precautions. In general, use positive, local ventilation, eye protection, and protective gloves.
Platinum	Heated platinum can give off fumes that may cause lung and skin irritation.	Use positive, local ventilation.
Dust from shells, gemstones, and wood	Dust produced by cutting, grinding, or polishing these materials can always be a potential eye hazard. Free silica in some stones can cause silicosis. Some contain asbestos and toxic metallic oxides. Some wood dust can result in skin irritation, allergies, and, over long periods, nasal and nasal sinus cancer.	Positive, local ventilation. An approved filtered respirator may sometimes be needed for large scale work. I encourage the reader to further study specific materials, the related hazards, and the necessary precautions.
Silver	Silver in dust or vapor form can cause argyria, a blue black discoloration of the skin and eyes. Thus far this condition has no known ill effects.	Use positive, local ventilation and eye protection when heating or using mechanical abrasion devices.
Solder, soft	See "Lead"	
Solder, hard	See "Cadmium"	
Stainless steel	See "Nickel"	
Styrofoam	Sometimes used for casting models. Releases toxic gases when heated or burned.	Positive, local ventilation at the work point and in the kiln area.
Sulfuric acid	A highly toxic acid used to clean metal. It is corrosive to the skin, eyes, respiratory system and stomach. Ingestion may be fatal. The heated acid releases toxic sulfur oxide gases. Some craftspeople substitute Sparex, a commercial granular material which is less hazardous in the dry, stored state. Once mixed with water, Sparex fumes, too, are hazardous.	Positive, local ventilation. Wear eye protection and gloves when handling acid. Always pour acids into water, never the reverse. Always use diluted, at room temperature, if possible. Clean up spills immediately, using baking soda to neutralize the acid before washing the area.

COMPOUND	EFFECTS	PRECAUTIONS
Tin	Inorganic tin compounds can be fatal if ingested. Vapors and fumes are toxic.	Positive, local ventilation. Wear protective gloves.
Wax	Many types of waxes are in use for making casting models. Manufacturers add various compounds to wax to develop desirable modeling qualities. Some add plastics which give off harmful fumes when heated and give off dust when hand worked.	Positive, local ventilation in the work and kiln areas.
Zinc	Exposure to fumes often causes metal fume fever.	Positive, local ventilation.

Glossary

Abrasives. Natural and synthetic materials in fine granular form incorporated in buffing compounds and attached to cloth or paper. Abrasives are generally used in grades of coarse to fine and may be identified by a numerical system (paper- and cloth-backed abrasives). For example, number 400 is relatively fine and number 80 coarse. Not all abrasives are identified by number.

Alloy. The result of combining two or more metals, or a metal and a chemical element. For example, sterling silver is an alloy composed of pure silver and copper.

Ampere. A measurement of electrical current.

Annealing. A heat treatment of metal that realigns its crystalline structure to its natural, more malleable state. Annealing removes stresses created in manipulation during the work process (bending, raising, forging, rolling, etc.).

Annealing booth. An enclosed area designed to keep light off the workpiece during the annealing process. The metal's color or annealing point can be seen much sooner in a darkened area.

Annealing pan. A circular pan that supports the workpiece while annealing. Pans are usually filled with pea pumice and designed to be rotated as heat is applied.

Anode. The positive electrical conductor submerged in a plating bath. In some instances, the anode also serves to replenish the bath with metallic ions.

Anodizing. The electrochemical application of an oxide film over aluminum causing its surface to become harder, abrasion- and corrosion-resistant, and chemically color absorbent.

Anvil. Usually a heavy supporting surface over which metal is hammered. Anvils have a traditional form composed of a squarish base, flat face, and tapered horn. Anvils are made of an iron body and hardened steel face. They are also being cast in one piece of steel that is then heat treated.

Asbestos. A natural rock fiber that is flame-resistant. It is used to make insulation, protective gloves, solder pads, flask liners, etc. There is considerable evidence that asbestos causes some types of cancer and should no longer be used in jewelry work.

Bearing. A supporting ledge built into stone settings. The edge of the stone lies over the bearing.

Bezel. A metal collar fitting around a stone to secure it to the jewelry piece.

Binding wire. Soft iron wire used to hold joints and pieces of metal in the desired position while being soldered.

Buff. Usually a motor-driven, spindle-mounted wheel, disc, or cone-shaped form made of layered cotton, felt, muslin, wool, or leather. Buffs are charged with abrasive compounds and spun against metal surfaces to cut away and polish—to buff—the metal.

Burnishing. Smoothing and polishing metal by rubbing with a hardened steel or stone burnisher. The tool has a short wooden handle and a curved or straight fingerlike work face. The steel face is oval in cross section.

Burr. A small, rough, sharp projection found on a cut metal edge. A sharp-tipped projection raised by an engraving tool. A rotary steel cutting tool generally used in a flexible shaft machine.

Butt joint. A flush, edge-to-edge fit between two pieces of metal.

Cabochon. A cut of stone generally having a domed top and flat bottom.

Capillary attraction. The force that causes a liquid to be raised against a vertical surface.

Carat. A unit of measure used to determine the weight of gem stones; one carat equals 200 milligrams.

Casting. The pouring or introduction of a molten material into a mold.

Cathode. The negative electrical terminal submerged in a plating bath. The cathode is generally the workpiece onto which metallic ions are deposited.

Centrifugal casting. A casting technique whereby molten metal is thrust into a mold by centrifugal force. The most common method is by means of a spring-driven arm supporting a crucible and mold flask.

Charcoal block. A block of dense charcoal used to support work being soldered. It may also be used as a carving medium to develop simple casting molds.

Charging. To apply abrasive compounds to buffing wheels.

Chasing. A surface embellishment technique applied to the front of a form. Chasing punches are commonly used to refine or delineate the front of cast or repoussé decorated work.

Chatoyance. A fibrous, satin-like sheen appearing on the surface of some polished stones.

Coloring. Usually the natural, chemical, or heat patination of metal. Oxidation, plating, and torches are a few of the methods used.

Constructed. Assembled of one or more elements to make a finished piece. Generally indicates that the work involves hand tools and fitting as opposed to forms created entirely by forging, casting, or electroforming.

Cross peen. A wedgelike hammer face used to forge or raise metal. In practice, the blows of the cross peen cause the metal to move perpendicularly to the peen.

Crucible. A ceramic or graphite container in which metal is melted.

Cuttlebone. The chalky internal shell of a cuttlefish. Cuttlebone is used as a mold material for metal castings. The resulting casting has a wavy, striated surface. Powdered cuttlebone is used as a polishing compound.

Damascene. A metal inlay technique. Its name derives from the city of Damascus, where it was popularized.

Damascus steel. Pattern-welded, laminated steel originally popularized in Damascus. Today's process is a modification of the original technique.

Dapping punch. A punch with a spherical work tip. It is used to form domed pieces from discs of flat sheet metal. The metal is tapped into a steel dapping block that has hemispherical recesses.

Die. Any of several types of positive or negative moldlike forms into which sheet metal is forced and formed. Dies are generally made of a hard material that permits the creation of multiple pieces.

Drawplate. A plate of hardened steel with holes of graduated sizes through which wire is pulled to alter its cross section or dimension.

Drill bit. A helically grooved steel tool used to cut holes. Bits are generally used in a hand brace, lathe, press, or flexible shaft.

Drop hammer. A large hydraulically, electrically, or pneumatically powered hammer used in blacksmithing or to exert great force against dies to create specific shapes.

Ductility. A metal's capacity to be drawn into wire. A good indicator of a metal's ability to stretch.

Electrodeposition. The process of electroplating and electroforming. An electrochemical process whereby metal ions are deposited onto an object.

Embossing. Pressing or imprinting a pattern in relief.

Engraving. The use of gravers or burins to cut lines and texture into metal.

Epoxy. Any of various resins capable of forming tight, cross-linked polymer structures characterized by toughness, strong adhesion, and corrosion resistance. Commonly used as a two-part adhesive.

Etching. The process of dissolving or wearing away metal with acid. In order to develop surface texture or patterns, selected areas are covered with an acid-resistant material.

Eutectic. An alloy of two or more metals combined to achieve a melting point lower than the melting points of the parent metals. This process is used in granulation. In this case, the parts to be joined fuse together only at the contact points.

Fibula. A decorative fastener used by ancient cultures to secure clothing. A forerunner to the kilt pin and safety pin.

File. A hardened steel tool having ridged or toothlike surfaces for cutting away metal. Files are purchased in the length and cross section suited to a particular purpose. A few of the shapes are: flat, round, half-round, triangular, and knife.

Fillet. The bulge formed if excess solder is used to join two pieces of metal in an angle.

Findings. Commercial or handmade fittings or fastenings used to attach jewelry to the wearer: clasps, catches, earring posts, pin assemblies, etc.

Fire scale. An oxide of copper that is brought on by heating in an open atmosphere. Fire scale will develop on copper-bearing alloys.

Flask. Most often a steel cylinder used to encase a casting mold.

Flexible shaft machine. A machine with a small, high-speed motor, a flexible, enclosed drive shaft, and a hand piece. Generally used for small-scale grinding, polishing, and drilling.

Flux. A liquid, granular, or paste material used to cover metals during heating to form a protective coat against oxygen. Flux also dissolves oxides that might inhibit the flow of solder. Simply stated, flux helps maintain a clean solder joint. Borax-based flux is commonly used for jewelry work.

Foil. Extremely thin sheet metal.

Forging. A process using hammers and an anvil or steel stakes. From a given shape or mass of metal, the material is redistributed by controlled hammer blows to create the desired form.

Fusing. Molecular bonding of metals without the use of solder. Pieces are brought up to heat and allowed to alloy together. Joining is controlled by quickly removing the heat at the moment of fusion.

Gate. An opening or system of openings through which molten metal enters a mold.

Gauge plate. A metal disc having graduated slots to calculate the thickness of sheet metal and wire. The slot widths are calibrated in B and S (Brown and Sharpe) gauge sizes and decimal inches.

Granulation. The process of bonding small spheres or chips of metal to a parent metal. Bonding is traditionally accomplished by eutectic soldering.

Gravity pour. A direct pouring of molten metal into a mold.

Graver. A narrow steel cutting tool used to engrave. Gravers come in a variety of cross-section shapes.

Hardening. The hardening of steel is accomplished by heating the metal to cherry red and quickly quenching it in brine, water, or oil, depending on the alloy or application.

Heat treating. The application of heat to metal to anneal, harden, or temper.

Ingot. A block or convenient cast shape that will be further processed by extruding, rolling, or forging.

Inlay. A process in which grooves, recesses, or negative shapes are cut into a base material and are then inset with corresponding shapes. A means used to create contrasting textures and patterns.

Jig. A fixture preset to accurately assemble or duplicate the components of a workpiece. For example, a jig can be used to secure metal in bending to assure exact duplicates.

Karat. The measure used to express the purity of gold, 24 karat being the highest or purest. An alloy of one-half pure gold and one-half other metal would be expressed 12 karat.

Lamination. The bonding of several layers of metal.

Liver of sulfur. Potassium sulfide. Often dissolved in water as a solution for oxidizing or coloring metal.

Lost-wax casting. A wax model is embedded in a plasterlike casting investment. After the investment has hardened, heat is applied to melt away the wax leaving a cavity with a detailed form corresponding to that of the original wax model. Molten metal is then poured or injected into the cavity.

Malleability. A metal's capability to withstand the compression of being rolled or hammer formed.

Mandrel. A tapered steel form used to support metal as it is being formed.

Mohs' scale. A numerical scale (1 to 10) generally used to rate the relative hardness of minerals, diamond being 10, the hardest.

MoKume. The Japanese term for "woodgrain." The effect is created by laminating layers of contrasting metals, cutting away or bumping out the layers, and then cutting to expose the inner striations.

Mold. A cavity into which molden metal is poured.

Niello. An inlay technique in which a compound of silver, lead, copper, and sulfur are set and then fired. The niello material flows into the inlay recesses of the base metal and bonds. The resulting pattern is deep black in color.

Oxidizing flame. A flame that has a fuel mixture rich in oxygen.

Paillons. Small snippets of solder.

Patina. The aged or chemical color of a metal's surface.

Photoetching. A photochemical process of creating positive or negative photo images on a metal surface.

Pickle. A water and acid solution used as a dip to clean metal of scale, oxides, and flux. The workpiece is usually dipped after soldering or annealing.

Piercing. The penetration of metal by a saw blade, drill, or cutter to achieve a decorative effect or as a functional consideration.

Pitch. A black or darkly colored residue of tree sap or asphalt. Mixed with oil and a powderlike binder, it is used to hold sheet metal for repoussé or engraving work.

Planishing. Smoothing metal with the blows of a planishing hammer while supporting the metal over a steel stake or anvil. Planishing hammer faces are flat and the other end of the hammer head is slightly domed. The metal is generally worked in a systematic path of overlapping blows to create a structure of uniform thickness.

Plating. An electrochemical process of depositing metallic ions onto a surface.

Pumice. A volcanic element used in lump and powdered form as an abrasive or as a heat-reflective material supporting pieces being annealed or soldered. Fine pumice may also be used as a binder in pitch.

Punch. Steel rods with variously shaped faces for repoussé, dapping, cutting, or chasing work.

Pusher. A stone-setting tool with a polished flat or indented face; used to push over bezels or prongs.

Quenching. To suddenly submerge a piece of hot metal in a fluid as in cleaning or heat treating.

Raising. The process of hammering flat sheet metal into three-dimensional forms.

Reducing flame. A flame having a higher concentration of gas than oxygen.

Repoussé. The technique of creating a relief surface outward from the back of sheet metal using hammers and punches.

Reticulation. A surface texture over metal caused by heat. The texture develops just at the melting point. Cooling and the resulting shrinkage pulls the metal's surface into a wrinkled cross section.

Rheostat. A variable electrical resistor used to regulate current.

Rifflers. Files having specially shaped ends used where common files will not reach.

Ring clamp. A hand-held wooden clamp used to grasp objects too small to comfortably hold by hand. The clamp is usually braced against the bench pin.

Rivet. A small pin or tubelike fastener used to secure jewelry components. Rivets are generally used where solder cannot be applied.

Rolling mill. A machine having two horizontal steel rollers through which metal is passed to decrease its thickness.

Scribe. A narrow, pointed tool used to scratch or mark metal.

Sinking. A method of giving form to sheet metal. Forms are usually developed by hammering the sheet into a preformed recess.

Soldering. Joining of metal pieces with an alloy of a lower melting point than that of the pieces being joined.

Sprue. For jewelry casting: wax wires used to connect the wax model with the casting mold's opening. In heating, or burnout, the wax is eliminated to leave channels through which molten metal flows into the mold cavity.

Stake. Polished steel, plastic, or wood forms over which metal is formed. Stakes are manufactured in many sizes and configurations to give the worker a broad choice of form possibilities. Stakes may be secured in a vise, bench plate, or the anvil's hardie hole.

Stamping. Imprinting or impressing with a texture or pattern, or forming or cutting out with a mold or die.

Stretching. Generally used as a means of raising hollow forms from thick billets of metal. Forming hammers are used to thin the metal's center area, thus causing the mass to be redistributed and forced upward.

Stripping. The removal of metal oxides by acid dipping or by reversing the polarity of a plating bath (the work to be stripped becomes the anode).

Tang. The short, taillike end of a file or graver that is fitted with a handle.

Temper. A heat treatment usually applied to steel. After fully hardening, the piece is slowly reheated and quenched at the desired moment of hardness. In effect, the process softens the steel.

Torch texture. A texture developed as the result of heat applied by torch over a metal's surface.

Tree. A method used to sprue multiple pieces in one flask. Pieces are arranged in layers and that radiate from one large central vertical sprue.

Upsetting. A forging technique whereby a metal edge or rod's end is struck squarely with a hammer, causing it to spread or thicken.

Vents. Narrow passages cut into a mold to allow the release of entrapped air or gas as the molten casting material fills the mold.

Vise. A two-jawed tool used as a clamping device. Most vises have one fixed jaw and the second jaw mounted on a threaded shaft. Vises may be hand held or bench mounted.

Viscosity. The measure of a liquid's ability to flow.

Volatility. The quality or state of being readily evaporated at normal temperatures and pressures.

Work hardening. The hardening of metal by the molecular compression of bending, rolling, twisting, or hammering.

Bibliography

Armstrong, Roger. *Beginning Jewelry*. Palo Alto, CA: Star, 1979.

Anderson, B. W. *Gem Testing*. New York: Van Nostrand Reinhold, 1971.

Barazani, Gail Coningsby. *Safe Practices in the Arts and Crafts*. The College Art Association of America, 1978.

Bealer, Alex. *The Art of Blacksmithing*. New York: Funk and Wagnalls, 1969.

Bovin, Murray. *Jewelry Making for Schools, Tradesmen, Craftsmen*. Rev. ed. by Peter Bovin. Forest Hills, NY: Bovin Publishing, 1979.

Brace, A. W. and Sheasby, P. G. *The Technology of Anodizing Aluminum*. 2nd ed. Gloustershire, England: Technicopy Ltd.

Brijbhusan, Jamila. *Masterpieces of Indian Jewelery*. Bombay, India: D. B. Taraporevala Sons and Co. Private Ltd. 1979.

Carnow, Bertram W., M.D. *Health Hazards in the Arts and Crafts*. 5340 N. Magnolia Street, Chicago, IL 60640. This is a 41 page book based on the author's talk given to Artists of Chicago, April 19, 1974, at the Theatre-Field Museum.

Choate, Sharr. *Creative Casting*. New York: Crown, 1966.

Choate, Sharr. *Creative Gold—And Silversmithing*. New York: Crown, 1970.

DiPasquale, Dominic. *Jewelry Making: An Illustrated Guide to Technique*. Englewood Cliffs, NJ: Prentice-Hall, 1975.

Fisch, Arline M. *Textile Techniques in Metal*. New York: Van Nostrand Reinhold Company, 1975.

Foote, Theodore P. *Jewelry Making: A Guide for Beginners*. Worcester, MA: Davis Publications, Inc., 1981.

Franke, Lois. *Handwrought Jewelry*. Bloomington, IL: McKnight and McKnight, 1962.

Gentille, Thomas. *Step By Step Jewelry*. New York: Western, 1968.

Goodden, Robert and Popham, Philip. *Silversmithing*. London: Oxford University Press, 1971.

Held, Shirley E. *Weaving*. New York: Holt, Rinehart and Winston, Inc. 1978.

Hollander, Harry. *Plastics For Jewelry*. New York: Watson-Guptill, 1974.

Hubner and Schiltknecht. *The Practical Anodizing of Aluminum*. London: MacDonald and Evans, date U/K.

Maryon, Herbert. *Metalwork and Enamelling*. New York: Dover, 1971.

McCann, Michael, Ph.D. *Artist Beware*. New York: Watson-Guptill Publications, 1979.

McCreight, Tim. *The Complete Metalsmith*. Worcester, MA: Davis Publications, Inc. 1982.

———. *Metalworking For Jewelry*. New York: Van Nostrand Reinhold, 1979.

Meek, James. *The Art of Engraving*. Montezuma, IA: F. Brownell and Son, 1973.

Meilach, Dona. *Decorative and Sculptural Ironwork*. New York: Crown, 1977.

Metal Finishing. 48th Guidebook-Directory Issue 1982. Vol. 78, No. 1A. Metals and Plastics, Inc., NJ.

Morton, Philip. *Contemporary Jewelry*. Rev. ed. New York: Holt, Rinehart and Winston, 1976.

Newman, Lee S. and Newman, J. H. *Electroplating and Electroforming for Artists and Craftsmen*. New York: Crown, 1979.

Newman, Thelma R., and Newman, J. H. *The Container Book*. New York: Crown, 1977.

O'Connor, Harold. *New Directions in Goldsmithing*. P.O. Box 17324, Denver, CO 80217: Dunconor Books, 1975.

Seppä, Heikki. *Form Emphasis For Metalsmiths*. Kent, Ohio: Kent State University Press, 1978.

Sinkankas, John. *Gem Cutting*. Rev. ed. New York: Van Nostrand Reinhold, 1962.

Sprintzen, Alice. *Jewelry: Basic Techniques and Design*. Radnor, PA: Chilton, 1980.

Thomas, Richard. *Metalsmithing For The Artist-Craftsman*. Radnor, PA: Chilton, 1960.

Untract, Oppi. *Metal Techniques For Craftsmen*. New York: Doubleday, 1968.

VanHorn, Kent R., ed. *Fabrication and Finishing*. Aluminum, vol. 3. Metals Park, Ohio: The American Society of Metals.

Watson, Aldren. *The Village Blacksmith*. New York: Thomas Y. Crowell Co., 1968.

Webster, Robert. *Gemmologists' Compendium*. Rev. ed. by E. Allan Jobbins. New York: Van Nostrand Reinhold. 1979.

Wernick and Pinner. *The Surface Treatment and Finishing of Aluminum and its Alloys*. Teddington, England: R. Draper Ltd.

Weygers, Alexander. *The Modern Blacksmith*. New York: Van Nostrand Reinhold, 1974.

Willcox, Donald. *New Design In Jewelry*. New York: Van Nostrand Reinhold, 1970.

———. *Body Jewelry: International Perspectives*. Chicago: Henry Regnery Co., 1973.

TECHNICAL PAPERS AND BULLETINS

"Aluminum Dyes." Bulletin 4–110/78, Sandoz Colors and Chemicals, Metals Department, East Hanover, NJ 07936.

Ard, William. "Studio MoKume," *Metalsmith*. Vol. 1, no. 2 (Winter 1981). Published by The Society of North American Goldsmiths.

"The Coloring of Anodized Aluminum." Bulletin 4–131/82, Sandoz Colors and Chemicals, Metals Department, East Hanover, NJ 07936.

"Decoral" (Aluminum Coloring). Bulletin CFD-782, Lea Manufacturing Company, Chemical Finishes Division, 49 Waters Ave., Everett, MA 02149.

Eckhardt, R. E., and Hindin, R. "The Health Hazards of Plastics," *Journal of Occupational Medicine*. Vol. 15: 808–819 (1973).

Hall, Joseph F. "Properties and Uses of Titanium, Zirconium, Hfanium, Niobium (Columbium), and Tantalum for the Artist-Metalsmith," *Goldsmiths Journal*. Vol. 5, no. 3 (June 1979). Published by The Society of North American Goldsmiths.

Members of the Graduate Program, Department of Art, Southern Illinois University: Marvin Jensen, Phil Baldwih, Steve Brunst, Laurie van Houten, William Ard, Janice Nathen, Randy Jones, Professor L. Brent Kington, and Professor Richard Mawdsley. "Return to the Forge (Extended Research Into MoKume-Gane and Granulation)." Compiled and edited by William Ard. Technical paper 9 (February 1979). Published by The Society of North American Goldsmiths.

Myers, Paulette. "Nickel Silver Perforation," *Goldsmiths Journal*. Vol. 6, no. 2 (April/May 1980). Published by The Society of North American Goldsmiths.

Pijanowski, Hiroko and Pijanowski, Eugene. "Update: MoKume-Gane (Woodgrain-Metal)," *Goldsmiths Journal*. Vol. 5, no. 1 (February 1979). Published by The Society of North American Goldsmiths.

"Questions and Answers About Anodizing Aluminum." 10-page pamphlet, Reynolds Metals Company, Richmond, VA 23261.

"Sealing Salt As Powder For High Grade, Deposit-Free Sealing." Bulletin 4–218/77. Sandoz Colors and Chemicals, Metals Department, East Hanover, NJ 07936.

Verhoeven, John D. and Trivedi, Rohit K. "The Metallurgy of Reticulated Silver Sheet," *Goldsmiths Journal*, Vol. 4, no. 1 (February 1978). Published by The Society of North American Goldsmiths.

Ward, James Brent. "Titanium: Metal of Many Colors," *Craft Horizons*. Vol. 37, no. 4 (August 1977).

———. "The Colouring and Working of the Refractory Metals Titanium, Niobium and Tantalum for Jewelry and Allied Application," Report no. 34/1 (September 1978). London, The Worshipful Company of Goldsmiths.

Weiss, Linda. "Goldsmithing Health Hazards," *Goldsmiths Journal*. Vol. 4, no. 5 (October 1978). Published by The Society of North American Goldsmiths.

Index